"A Region of

Astonishing Beauty"

Meriwether Lewis

"A Region of Astonishing Beauty"

THE BOTANICAL EXPLORATION
OF THE ROCKY MOUNTAINS

ROGER L. WILLIAMS

ROBERTS
RINEHART

Published by Roberts Rinehart Publishers
A Member of the Rowman & Littlefield Publishing Group
4501 Forbes Boulevard, Suite 200
Lanham, MD 20706

Distributed by National Book Network

Library of Congress Cataloging-in-Publication Data
Williams, Roger Lawrence, 1923–
    "A region of astonishing beauty" : the botanical exploration of the Rocky Mountains /
Roger L. Williams.
    p. cm.
    Includes bibliographical references.
    ISBN 1-57098-397-6 (pbk. : alk. paper)
    1. Botanists—United States—Biography. 2. Explorers—United States—Biography.
    3. Botany—Rocky Mountains Region—History. I. Title.
    QK26 .W46 2003
    581.978—dc21
                                                                        2002153363

∞™ The paper used in this publication meets the minimum requirements of American National Standard for Information Sciences—Permanence of Paper for Printed Library Materials, ANSI/NISO Z39.48-1992.

Manufactured in the United States of America.

Contents

✑✑✕✑✑

Preface

CRXX55

*I*t seems appropriate at the outset to offer a few observations about the genesis of this book. Because I was trained primarily in European history, my occasional ventures into American or botanical topics have provoked queries about my apparent defection. I have deflected such questions by recalling my interest in natural history during a childhood in the Rocky Mountain region. That explanation was ingenuous, to be sure; the interest had always been there, but the response had had the further advantage of evading profounder explanation that could invite tedious debate, in this postmodern era in particular.

Both the conception and the organization of this book reflect my conviction that there is no valid separation between European and American history. A geographical separation is an apparent reality, but our ideas and institutions are of common origin. Botany, or the study of plants, was not an innovation of the New World. We owe it to the Greeks, just as we do its name: *botane,* the Greek word for plant, first used to describe the science of botany about the mid-seventeenth century.

Botanical exploration, the organized search for new genera and species, was initially a European phenomenon. No civilization ever gave birth to a more impassioned quest for knowledge about both nature and about people living elsewhere than that of our European ancestors, beginning at the end of the fifteenth century with the recovery of the ancient classics. Modern science emerged as a major component of the new Humanism. As a consequence, our civilization became the most innovative and the least ethnocentric that the world has known.

Such prefatory remarks are meant to call attention to the fact that the botanical exploration of the Rocky Mountains in the nineteenth century was hardly a parochial phenomenon or only worthy of the attention of those happy few captivated by alpine beauties. The explorers themselves, whether of European birth or of recent European origin, all exposed themselves to daily rigors and dangers in their search for new knowledge, generally fully aware that their European predecessors of the eighteenth century had endured even greater privations. The thrill of new knowledge, itself a fundamental motive, was an indulgence morally justified by a conviction that they labored for the benefit of mankind: they sought better nutrition, more reliable medications, forest products adaptable for regenerating terrain left waste by generations of rapacious timbering, and new vegetal ornaments for house and garden.

Take note of their observations, therefore, not simply as records of new genera and species they proposed, but, given their botanical sensibilities, as reliable commentary on the state of the ecology; they offer speculation about where agriculture could, or could not, be suitably undertaken; evidence of invasive plants already observed or their apparent absence from areas where they are a pest today; and indications of plant distribution that can contribute to our assessment of which species are truly native, endemic, and which are probably naturalized, if widely regarded as native.

This project, long postponed given my preoccupation with the history of botany in eighteenth-century France, was abetted by several old friends whose encouragement I must acknowledge here with thanks: notably to Robert Righter and Ronald Hartman, the veterans in the campaign; but also to John and Charlotte Reeder and Mark and Gretchen Harvey. A more recent visit with Andrea Wolfe, Daniel Crawford, and Ronald Stuckey at The Ohio State University persuaded me that I ought not postpone the work any longer. For many years, the fine resources of the Rocky Mountain Herbarium—Ronald Hartman, curator—have been available to me as an affiliate; without them this book would not have been conceivable. Dieter Wilken, Meredith Lane, and Robert Dorn, occasional researchers in the herbarium, always fielded my questions helpfully and in good humor, a characterization that applies equally to Burrell Nelson (that's Ernie), herbarium manager. I am also pleased to offer thanks for the gracious reception extended by Connie Wolf and her staff at the library of the Missouri Botanical Garden. I am under obligation to meet the expectations all of the above have expressed.

Introduction

*At the outset, it is proper to define the chronological limits used in this book to describe the botanical exploration of the Rocky Mountains, in the knowledge that other historians of botany have employed a broader scope. The assumption here is that the botanical exploration of the Rocky Mountains began with Meriwether Lewis in 1805 and lasted about one century. Spanish and French explorers certainly did cross portions of that region long before Lewis and Clark; but their occasional references to plants did not conform to what became the rules of plant description, making them useless to scientific botany.

The era of the great collections of Rocky Mountain plants ended shortly after the turn of the twentieth century. To be sure, botanists have continued to go into the field since then, but for what we would call research rather than exploration: they go to gather fresh material or to examine living specimens previously seen only in herbaria. New species continue to be found every year in the Rocky Mountain region. But the scope of such research has become primarily monographic or phytographic, not the quest for novelties.

The restricted context favored here becomes more intellectually defined if one puts the peculiarities of Rocky Mountain botanical exploration into the larger context of European overseas exploration in the eighteenth century. In the seventeenth century, botanical collections overseas were usually made by members of religious orders, who had missionary obligations, and who were often preoccupied with finding plants reputed to have medicinal virtues. *Jesuit powder,* a popular name for quinine in the seventeenth century, derived from its association with Jesuit missionaries in Peru, who had learned of the efficacy of the bark of cinchona in treating fevers.

That pattern changed in the eighteenth century, in particular after Linnaeus's publication of *Genera Plantarum* in 1737. Thereafter, botanists traveling abroad predominantly would be laymen, either indifferent or antagonistic to proselytizing. This remarkable shift in intellectual leadership was not an isolated event but quite emblematic of the general laicization of ascendancy in both science and letters by the eighteenth century. The transformation was not wrought by a sudden or designed revolution, but was rather the capstone of Humanism, the intellectual revival inspired by the renewed study of the Greek and Roman classics in the sixteenth century. Individual botanists might well retain personal religious beliefs by the eighteenth century, but they would no longer designate theology as the queen of the sciences.

The lay botanists traveling abroad in the eighteenth century, if far from being unconcerned with the utility of plants, were more concerned with finding new genera and species, and with their placement in a stable classification, universally applicable. It bears emphasizing, furthermore, that even though we may now remember them primarily as botanists, they were in fact *naturalists,* interested in all life forms, including human beings. That character, it would appear, derived not simply from the humanistic climate of their day, but from the fact that one obtained botanical knowledge in that era in the course of studying for a medical doctorate.

Such a format was entirely congenial to the essential character of the West European Enlightenment: that is, the voracious quest for the universal knowledge that would enable *all mankind* to reform its institutions in the light of burgeoning scientific knowledge and, thus, would emancipate mankind from ignorance and superstition. That was the *humanists'* vision of liberty, and that is what they meant by *useful* knowledge. The concept of the Enlightenment is a far cry from the advocacy of *utilitarianism* frequently applied by historians of the eighteenth century. That misconception conceals the era's guiding belief that the study of nature could yield progress, and that theological speculation had been meant to reconcile us to the *status quo.* One was useful, the other useless.

Such a cluster of beliefs and practices carried over into America in the early nineteenth century, when the botanical exploration of the Rocky Mountains began. Yet, that pattern gradually broke down over the course of the century. By the end of the century, botanists would no longer be naturalists, but mainly specialists without prior medical training. Whereas in the eighteenth century lengthy expeditions or field trips, commonly of two or more years, had been the graduate schools for botanists, after about 1890 one attended a formal graduate school; and graduate degrees became the licenses to practice. Everyone is aware of what has been gained through that transition. Probably very few are conscious of what has been lost.

Several other historical watersheds need to be remembered to put the Rocky Mountain region within the context of international botany. Linnaean artificial classification was still used in America when western exploration opened at the beginning of the nineteenth century, despite the publication of the Jussiaean natural system of classification in 1789. John Torrey adhered to the artificial sexual system until he was finally nudged by William J. Hooker and made to pay some attention to the superior system. Torrey's publication of Dr. Edwin James's plants, collected in the summer of 1820, was the first botanical paper in this country to follow Jussieu.[1] Torrey's American edition of John Lindley's *An Introduction to the Natural System of Botany* was the logical sequel in 1831. Thereafter, most American botanists adopted natural classification.

The second historical watershed was the publication of *The Origin of Species* by Darwin in 1859. Widespread resistance to the idea of evolution no doubt reflected a reluctance to abandon the traditional view of species permanently fixed at the moment of their creation. But there is also an instinctive resistance to new knowledge if it threatens to make the acquisition of truth more complicated. Had not the botanical community already accepted natural classification before 1859, with its network of analogies and affinities, with its focus on similarities as well as on distinctions, it remains probable that the resistance to the Darwinian system within the scientific community would have been more formidable.

In the century of western botanical exploration, various groups of contributors may be distinguished. Some plant collectors, especially during the first half of the nineteenth century, were not trained botanists, not qualified to describe their own collections. Even among the qualified, few undertook the chore of publication. As Susan McKelvey remarked, Thomas Nuttall stood virtually alone as a collector, describer, and publisher. The greatest names in descriptive botany (Dr. de Candolle, Sir William Hooker, Dr. Torrey, Dr. Gray, and Dr. Engelmann) were scholars who only rarely worked in the field. They worked mainly from material gathered by others, usually dried specimens, rarely having seen the living plants they described and published, which earned them the title *closet-botanists*.[2] It was meant both to ridicule and to discredit. The chasm between the Western field collectors and the closet-botanists accounts for many of the personal antagonisms and professional hostilities that are inescapable in the botanical correspondence of the period.

The usual assumption, both then and later, that the closet-botanists were closer than the field collectors to intellectual advances in the profession is not necessarily valid. Nuttall would have used the Jussiaean natural classification as early as 1818 were it not a fact that the artificial system of Linnaeus was still generally taught in the United States. Nuttall called the Jussiaean system "the last and most perfect of systems, perfect because the uncontaminated gift of Nature, is about to be conferred upon and confirmed by the Botanical world. The great plan of natural affinities, sublime and extensive, eludes the arrogance of solitary individuals, and requires the concert of every botanist and exploration of every country towards its completion."[3]

Nuttall's choice of words exposes his rejection of any classification system "contaminated" by any botanist's apriorism, such as Linnaeus's essentialism; and he stated quite clearly that, in the preparation of his own *Genera of North American Plants,* he had derived important assistance from Jussieu's *Genera Plantarum* in describing his own generic groups, especially their habits or life-forms. We do not know what John Torrey knew at that time about natural classification or Lamarck's system of dichotomous keys. His biographer charitably surmised that Torrey had adhered to the sexual system only to perpetuate the uniformity so recently attained in classification after centuries of confusion. It seems more probable that Torrey, in response to Hooker's prodding, came to a decision very reluctantly by 1826 to change his system, as the change complicated the preparation of the great North American flora then underway.[4] In any event, Nuttall was simply more advanced in his early recognition of the superiority of the natural system.

In the latter half of the nineteenth century, most of the preeminent field-workers in the Rocky Mountain West followed Nuttall's example, whether consciously or otherwise, seeking to describe and publish despite criticism from eastern scholars. The Easterners held that the scholarly resources of the West were too limited to permit descriptive scholarship. The Westerners, believing that their critics only knew the plants of the West secondhand, persisted in publication, increasingly convinced that the flora of the West was distinctive. As in most such controversies, right and wrong were on both sides.

By the end of the nineteenth century, new wrangles over taxonomic principle and acceptable nomenclature preoccupied American botanists and tended to obscure the more traditional conflict. But it remained alive and probably affected every botanist's approach to the newer, more fashionable disputes. The long memory of such quarrels greatly contributed to the traditional conviction that botanists are by nature an exceptionally quarrelsome lot; but anyone familiar with academia in particular knows that botanists enjoy no monopoly.

"A Region of
Astonishing Beauty"

1

Lewis and Clark in the Rocky Mountains (1805–1806)

*N*o exploratory expedition in American history ever surpassed that of Meriwether Lewis and William Clark in national importance; and, at least from traditional textbook accounts of it, every American child would retain into later years some general recollection of a heroic and hazardous venture sponsored by Jefferson to prepare the way for American westward expansion. In recent years, the approach of the excursion's bicentennial has provided the justification for a burst of publications by historians perhaps uneasy about pedagogical trends meant to erase historical memory. Some of the recent work has been superb, a faithful reflection of the grandeur of the topic. Some of it shows compromise with the political opportunism that has characterized historical work in the past few decades.

The original French claim to Louisiana dated from 6 April 1682, based on La Salle's exploration during the reign of Louis XIV. The region was defined only by natural frontiers: the Mississippi River on the east, the Sabine River across Texas on the south, and the Continental Divide within the Rocky Mountains on the west. The defeat of France by the end of the Seven Years' War, in 1763, caused France to cede Louisiana to Spain; this was to compensate Spain for the loss of the Floridas and Minorca. But, on 1 October 1800, France secretly obtained the retrocession of Louisiana from Spain, Napoleon Bonaparte's intent being to recover a major base in North America to offset the prior loss of Canada.

This arrangement—a weak power being replaced in the western frontier by a strong power—was a serious threat to American westward aspirations. But, when war resumed in Europe in 1803, Bonaparte recognized that Louisiana was indefensible, given British naval supremacy, and that it could be advantageous to sell the region to the Americans. The treaty of cession was signed on 30 April 1803 for a payment of twelve million dollars, the greatest real estate bargain in

American history. The province could not actually be transferred to the United States until December of 1803, as many of the Spanish had never been removed; but Jefferson had already begun to complete long-contemplated plans for the exploration of the new territory.

Because of this work's emphasis on the expedition's forays into natural history and ethnography, it is critical to emphasize that the expedition was not primarily a scientific venture. It was, rather, a new attempt to find a trade route by water to Asia, a continuation of the search for the Northwest Passage—a quest that went back nearly to the time of Columbus. That search had always provided the opportunity for research into natural history and the study of geography, as it would for Lewis and Clark. By the beginning of the nineteenth century, the Missouri River was thought to be the probable route to the Pacific if followed to, and into, the mountains. It was presumed that there would be a short crossing of the mountains into another major river basin.

The success of such an undertaking was quite dependent on the intelligence of its leadership and on the degree of discipline that leadership would enforce. Both Lewis and Clark had seen prior service in the militia, largely in wilderness country. Meriwether Lewis (1774–1809) had served in the Virginia militia, and was subsequently in the regular army, reaching the rank of captain in 1800. When Thomas Jefferson asked Lewis in 1801 to become his private secretary, it may be supposed that he already anticipated using Lewis's knowledge of wilderness and Indians in a transcontinental exploration.

As the personnel for such an expedition would be drawn from the military, it was critical to have the selection made by someone who was an experienced judge of military character. Jefferson wisely left that choice to Lewis, who chose William Clark (1770–1838) as engineer and geographer for the expedition. Lewis gave him equality in command, with Jefferson's approval; and the two would always work together in such harmony that Lewis never had cause to exert his actual authority.

Both men were highly intelligent, although Lewis had had the advantage of a better education. In preparation for the trip, Jefferson sent Lewis to Philadelphia for instruction in botany, zoology, and celestial navigation from faculty members of the University of Pennsylvania. To the criticism that Jefferson ought to have sent a professional botanist on the trip, it must be answered that no such creature existed in 1803, and Lewis's training as a naturalist served him very well. Clark, younger brother of George Roger Clark, had been reared on the frontier, had participated in several campaigns against Indians, and had reached the rank of lieutenant in the army. He would in no small part be responsible for the sympathetic and tactful treatment of Indians for which that expedition remains memorable.[1]

Their humane conduct, evident from their journals, while undeniably a reflection of the explorers' own character, was also an adherence to the letter and spirit of Jefferson's instructions, dated 20 June 1803. The continuing vitality of the Enlightenment is obvious in Jefferson's directive that "the soil & face of the country, its growth & vegetable productions," its animals, and "the remains and accounts of any which may be deemed rare or extinct," were all objects worthy of notice. The Enlightenment spirit is also evident in Jefferson's instructions to obtain detailed information about the various Indian tribes that would be encountered.

Jefferson regarded our westward expansion as not only inevitable but desirable:

> [C]onsidering the interest which every nation has in extending & strengthening the authority of reason & justice among the people around them, it will be useful to acquire what knolege [sic] you can of the state of morality, religion & information among [the Indians], as it may better enable those who endeavor to civilize & instruct them, to adapt their measures to the existing notions & practices of those on whom they are to operate.

These instructions reveal Jefferson's vision of an eventual integration or assimilation of the tribes as the humane resolution of the confrontation of two unequal cultures.

> In all your intercourse with the natives treat them in the most friendly & conciliatory manner which their own conduct will admit; allay all jealousies as to the object of your journey, satisfy them to it's innocence, make them acquainted with the position, extent, character, peaceable & commercial dispositions of the U.S., of our wish to be neighborly, friendly & useful to them, & of our dispositions to a commercial intercourse with them. . . . If any of them should wish to have some of their young people brought up with us, & taught such arts as may be useful to them, we will receive, instruct & take care of them.[2]

Although the Lewis and Clark expedition began its venture up the Missouri from the Saint Louis area in May 1804, this narrative, with its Rocky Mountain focus, overlooks the early months before Lewis and Clark's arrival at Fort Mandan (now North Dakota). Both men kept journals, noting the natural features seen; and Lewis in particular collected specimens diligently. When in what is now northern Nebraska and South Dakota, they became familiar with a local tobacco plant, height about three feet, which, for the Arikaras, had great ceremonial value and was an important trade item. What became the type species of this Indian or Great Plains tobacco, *Nicotiana quadrivalis* Pursh var. *quadrivalis,* was collected by Lewis on 14 October 1804 in either Campbell or Carson County, South Dakota.[3] Per Axel Rydberg would later recognize that species in Montana and even westward into Oregon and Washington. Not recognized today as native to that region, the plants must have come from seeds spread through trade.[4]

The expedition passed the winter of 1804–1805 at Fort Mandan, not departing until the last week in March. Lewis was preoccupied during that winter with obtaining information from local Indians, material he would keep separate from his journal to be sent back to Jefferson before the expedition left Fort Mandan. While residing among the Mandans, Lewis obtained his principal information about the country to the west, which no white man had yet visited, from the Miniari, also known as the Gros Ventre and today preferably called the Hidatsa Indians. They were Dakota Indians in the Siouan language group like their neighbors the Mandans;[5] but the Hidatsa ranged farther westward.

The expedition had acquired several interpreters. George Drouillard, consistently misspelled Drewyer in Lewis's journal, was a Canadian who had enlisted as a hunter and interpreter at the start of the trip. It is obvious from both journals that Drouillard, in those capacities, was of greater worth to the expedition than any other individual in the party. No significant biography of him exists, apparently for want of evidence.[6]

Toussaint Charbonneau, who joined the expedition at Mandan, was also Canadian and understood the difficult Hidatsa language. Sacagawea, a Shoshone, or Snake, Indian, was the younger of Charbonneau's two wives. It appears that she had been captured by the Minitari, who had then sold her to Charbonneau. When Paul Cutright published his study of the Lewis and Clark journals in 1976, he felt obligated to expose the literature responsible for perpetuating errors about the Lewis and Clark expedition, among them the myth "that Sacagawea guided Lewis and Clark to the Pacific and back." He noted that Sacagawea had evidently been a girl of rare courage and spirit, and found it a disservice to her that so many writers had overemphasized her role as a guide, which was negligible, but failed to stress her aid as an interpreter, which was considerable when the party was among the Shoshone.

Both Cutright and James Ronda, somewhat later, pointed in particular to the work of Grace Raymond Hebard (*Sacajawea, a Guide and Interpreter of the Lewis and Clark Expedition*, 1933) as creating a powerful mythology meant to portray Sacagawea as an American heroine. The narrative went far beyond what can be known from reputable historical sources. Hebard's argument that Sacagawea had lived to an advanced age, dying late in the nineteenth century in the Wind River country of Wyoming, was baseless. It is reasonably certain that Sacagawea died of putrid fever (typhus) along the Missouri in December of 1812, at about the age of twenty-five.[7] Hebard's work, in the guise of history, was a feminist tract; it has continued to serve as such in recent decades because of a ready market.

Lewis and Clark gathered ethnographic material in several traditional ways: by direct questioning of both whites and Indians; by the collection of Indian artifacts; by recording firsthand observations; and by occasionally participating with Indians in ceremonies, games, and hunting. However admirable their desire for accuracy may have been, the explorers did not bring to their task the passion for impartiality that is advertised as characteristic of modern professional anthropology.[8] Instead, they were confident of the superiority of the civilization they represented and shared the Jeffersonian assumption that the Indians in time would be kindly guided into the mainstream of Western Civilization as the United States expanded westward. For a man of the Enlightenment, the alternative would have been an *entente cordiale* with barbarism.

Lewis, for instance, by the time he was among the Mandan, had become aware of the nearly constant warfare between tribes and believed it to be his duty to advise the chiefs to work for a peaceful coexistence. On 16 January 1805, he was visited by a Gros Ventre chief who told him of his intention to go to war in the spring against the Snake (Shoshone) Indians. "We advised him to look back at the number of Nations who had been destroyed by War, and reflect upon what he was about to do, observing if he wished the happiness of his nation, he would be at peace with all." Lewis argued that the Indians could acquire needed goods, including horses, through peaceful trade. Beyond this, if the chief went to war against a defenseless people, he would displease his great father, Jefferson, "and he would not receive that protection & care from him as other nations who listened to his word."[9] The chief replied that he would not do anything displeasing "to us"; and in any case he had horses enough.

On 3 April 1805, specimens and artifacts were sent from Fort Mandan by Lewis to Jefferson, including plant specimens numbered from one to sixty, before the expedition moved westward toward Montana. The permanent party included twenty-seven enlisted men; Clark's servant, York; the two interpreters; and Sacagawea and child. During a halt for lunch on 9 April 1805, Sacagawea began to probe the ground and procured a good quantity of roots that resembled those of Jerusalem artichoke; the plant was also similar in both flavor and stalk. As specimens collected from that phase of the expedition (Mandan to Great Falls) did not survive, it was surmised that the species had been *Helianthus giganteus* L. It is now known that that species does not occur in the West, and that the roots most likely were those of the closely related *Helianthus nuttallii* T. & G.[10]

Near Great Falls (Montana) in mid-July, the expedition made a cache for specimens collected since leaving Fort Mandan, expecting to recover them on the return trip. Continuing upstream toward Three Forks, Lewis noted (15 July 1805) that the "prickly pear is now in full blume and forms one of the beauties as well as the greatest pests of the plains." He also found a blooming sunflower very abundant, most likely *Helianthus quinquenervis* (Hook.) Gray; and noted as very common the lambsquarter, probably *Chenopodium album* L.; the wild cucumber, *Echinocystis lobata* (Michx.) Torr. & Gray; and a narrow dock, possibly *Rumex maritimus* L. None of these species can be found in the Lewis and Clark Herbarium.

During the next two days, Clark indicated not only the expected cottonwoods and willows along the river, but also a box-elder, a viburnum, red dogwood, chokecherry, buffaloberry, "Sarvis berries," a species of "Shomake," and red and yellow currants.[11] Among these observed plants, only yellow currant, *Ribes aureum* Pursh, can be found in the herbarium (no. 149; *no.* when cited with a plant will refer to its number in the Lewis and Clark Herbarium) as collected at Three Forks of the Missouri (Gallatin County, Montana) on 29 July 1805. That situation raises several questions about Lewis's collecting that remain unresolved. In the first place, we have no reliable evidence of what his criteria were in deciding which plants merited collecting. All attempts to find a telltale pattern of collecting have fallen short. Secondly, could it be that a substantial amount of plant material collected was either lost or misplaced before it reached Philadelphia?

Several other examples illustrate the mystery. On 22 July 1805, still in Gallatin County, Lewis described collecting nearly a half-bushel of wild onions, crisp, white, and well flavored. The main motive, obviously, was to enliven camp cookery, but there is no record of that onion in the Lewis and Clark Herbarium. Another onion, *Allium textile* A. Nels & J. F. Macbr., collected along the Walla Walla River on the return trip in 1806, is included in the herbarium (no. 4).[12]

On 26 July 1805, Lewis mentioned a mature grass,

> the seeds of which are armed with a long twisted hard beard at the upper extremity while the lower point is a sharp subulate point beset at it's base with little stiff bristles standing with their points in a contrary direction to the subulate point to which they answer as a barb and serve also to pres it forward when onece entered a small distance. These barbed seeds penetrate our mockerson and leather leggings and give us great pain untill they are removed.[13]

Lewis has given us a clear description of needle-and-thread grass, *Stipa comata* Trin. & Rupr.; yet no collection number from that date or site survived. Even so, the plant does appear in the Lewis and Clark Herbarium as number 164, collected on 8 July 1806, on the return trip a year later, in either Lewis and Clark or Teton County, Montana. Complaint about the uncomfortable grass was more than matched in July of 1805 by repeated complaints about the masses of prickly-pear cacti encountered but understandably not collected. The cacti may well testify to widespread overgrazing.

At Three Forks on 28 July 1805, Lewis and Clark quite agreed that it would be improper for them to designate any one of the three major tributaries as the Missouri, deciding instead to name them after the president and his secretaries of state and the treasury, Madison and Gallatin. The more westward branch, which Lewis and Clark meant to ascend, they called the Jefferson. From Three Forks on, they hoped to encounter a band of Shoshones from whom they might acquire packhorses and guides. Once they got into the Bitterroot Range, Sacagawea was in home country and could tell Lewis where her people usually spent the summer. The party crossed the Continental Divide through Lemhi Pass on 12 August 1805 into what today would be Lemhi County, Idaho.

Four days later, having met a band of Shoshones, Lewis made some observations of them that were greatly similar in character to those made of aborigines in the Pacific by French botanists in the 1790s. That is, the observations were humanitarian and compassionate in spirit, but without any illusions about the nobility of savage existence. That illusion was of literary or philosophical invention in the seventeenth century, not shared by naturalists who visited aborigines; and its revival in new dress after the mid-twentieth century has not been an indulgence of natural scientists.

But even if Lewis had no inflated notions about Shoshone life, neither did he expect, especially in the favorable season, to find the degree of degradation the Shoshone revealed. He found them near starvation, totally without meat, barely surviving on cakes of dried serviceberries—pemmican.[14] Lewis met the situation by ordering his hunter-interpreter, Drouillard, to go out to kill game for the Indians. When word came back that Drouillard had shot a deer, Lewis and a few Indians went to the scene of the kill.

Described by Lewis (16 August 1805), the Indians:

> dismounted and ran in tumbling over each other like a parcel of famished dogs each seizing and tearing away a part of the intestens which had been previously thrown out by Drewyer who killed it; the seen was such when I arrived that had I not have had a pretty keen appetite myself I am confident I should not have taisted any part of the venison shortly. Each one had a piece of some discription and all eating most ravenously. Some were eating the kidnies the melt [spleen] and liver and the blood running from the corner of their mouths, others were in a similar situation with the paunch and guts but the exuding substance in this case from their lips was of a different discription. One of the last who attracted my attention in particularly had been fortunate in his allotment or rather active in the division, he had provided himself with about nine feet of the small guts one end of which he was chewing on while with his hands he was squezzing the contents out at the other. I really did not untill now think that human nature ever presented itself in a shape so nearly allyed to the brute creation. I viewed these poor starved divils with pity and compassion.[15]

Recent work in Indian history offers a possible commentary on what Lewis witnessed. The Shoshone Indians of central Wyoming and southern Idaho in the nineteenth century were descendants of a Ute-Aztecan migration from Asia. That is, the numerous languages in that group are all variations of a single parent tongue spreading from an apparent homeland in southern California and western Arizona. Those who spread southward reached the Valley of Mexico only about 350 years before the Spanish conquest, and were able to advance toward the more complex cultures that had preceded them in Mexico. Those groups that gradually spread through the Great Basin, beginning about two thousand years ago, into a less hospitable environment may have undergone a degenerative process.[16]

Two days later, perhaps still under the influence of what he had recently witnessed, Lewis gave himself to the reflection that all of us should have midway through this life we are bound upon.

> Sunday, 18 August 1805. This day I completed my thirty first year, and conceived that I had in all human probability now existed about half the period which I am to remain in this Sublunary world. I reflected that I had as yet done but little, very little, indeed, to further the happiness of the human race or to advance the information of the succeeding generation. I viewed with regret the many hours I have spent in indolence, and now soarly feel the want of that information which these hours would have given me had they been judiciously expended. But since they are past and cannot be recalled, I dash from me the gloomy thought, and resolved in future, to redouble my exertions and at least indeavor to promote those two primary objects of human existence, by giving them the aid of that portion of talents which nature and fortune have bestoed on me; or in future, to live for *mankind*, as I have heretofore lived for *myself*.[17]

Thereafter, the party headed northward until it reached the area west of modern Missoula in September; after this it turned westward, having to cross the Lola Trail. This proved to be the most difficult part of the trip because of the onset of bitter cold. Lewis related that the party met Nez Percé Indians on 20 September 1805 on what would now be the Weippe Prairie in Clearwater County. These friendly Indians belonged to the Shahaptian branch of the old Penutian language group that had come down the West Coast and up the Columbia River more than thirteen thousand years ago. Their traditional location was along the Snake River and its tributaries.[18]

These Indians provided the Lewis party with a flour made from the camas root, *Camassia quamash* (Pursh) Greene, a plant in the Lily family with an ovoid bulb and still believed to be edible. (Lewis would only collect it on the return trip, 23 June 1806, no. 33.) Thereafter, and into October, the party experienced severe intestinal upsets to which the sudden change in diet may have contributed. Clark noted on 5 October 1805: "Capt Lewis & myself eate a Supper of roots boiled, which Swelled us in Such a manner that we were Scerceley able to breath for Several hours."[19] As several species of *Zygadenus* grow in that area, and could have easily been mistaken for *Camassia* by a camp cook; and as another lily, *Veratrum californicum* Dur., would be collected in that neighborhood on the return trip, 25 June 1806 (no. 174 in the herbarium), the true villain remains unconvicted.

By October the expedition had passed the season for plant collecting in the Rocky Mountains. Building boats to take advantage of the rivers, the party proceeded later in October and November to the mouth of the Columbia and went into winter quarters at Fort Clatsop, Oregon.

By late January 1806, Lewis had had occasion to treat a member of his party for a venereal infection with mercury. The expedition carried no physician or surgeon on the staff, and Lewis, as the naturalist, was in charge of administering medications. As the male Indians in that region were sufficiently exposed to make observations easy, Lewis believed he had seen at least a few individuals with unmistakable signs of what he called Louis Veneri, his rendition of the French disease or pox. It appeared that the Indians did not employ any simples as a specific cure. Lewis knew that one of the plants used by eastern Indians in decoction for syphilis, *Rhus glabra* L., a sumac, was available on the western side of the Rocky Mountains; but it was not employed in the West.[20] As a specific for syphilis, to be sure, it would have been just as useless as mercury.

The eastward trek of the expedition began in late March of 1806, but the party did not arrive to begin collecting in Idaho until early May. On 4 May 1806, Lewis described purchasing an Indian bread made of cows, the Indian word being *cous,* now known as a biscuitroot. The plant of origin was not collected on that date; but *Lomatium cous* (Watson) Coult. & Rose had been collected on 29 April 1806 on the Walla Walla River and was more likely to be located on the Clearwater River than *Lomatium geyeri* (Wats.) Coult. & Rose, also a biscuitroot.[21] The collection of *Lomatium triternatum* (Pursh) Coult. & Rose two days later on the Clearwater (no. 97), with a root five to six inches long, eaten raw or boiled by the Indians, could imply its distinction from *cous.*[22]

On 18 May 1806, when the party was resting at Camp Choppunish, Idaho County, Idaho, Lewis reported that Sacagawea was gathering roots of the fennel the Shoshone Indians called Year-pah (now Yampa), *Perideridia bolanderi* (Gray) Nels. & MacBr., to be dried for food in the mountains. Lewis found the roots very palatable, whether fresh roasted, boiled, or dried, varying between the size of a quill and that of a man's finger, and about the length of the latter. No specimen of any *Perideridia* can be found in the herbarium.[23]

On 30 May 1806, still at Camp Choppunish, which had become a major collecting site, a member of the party brought in wild onions from the high plains that were a different species from those found in moister ground near the river. He described them as growing double: two bulbs connected by the same tissue of radicles, each bulb with two long, linear, flat, solid leaves. It was not yet in bloom. The description fits *Allium textile* Nels. & Macbr.; it had previously been collected on 30 April 1806 in southwestern Washington (no. 4). It is found in dry ground.[24]

Clark's notes for 10 June 1806 indicate that the party had resumed the return trip, beginning to gain elevation along the Lolo Trail into the Bitterroot Mountains. The country was well wooded, and he cited in the vernacular trees and shrubs he recognized, from which citations conjectural identifications may be made: Larch (*Larix occidentalis* Nuttall); black alder (*Alnus sinuate* [Regel] Rydb.); red root (*Ceanothus sanguineus* Pursh, no. 36); honeysuckle with white berry (*Symphoricarpos albus* [L.] Blake, no. 165); a pine up to twelve feet high that may not have been a pine, given the popular tendency to call every conifer a pine; seven bark—surely ninebark (*Physocarpas malvaceus* [Greene] Kuntze); and purple haw (*Crataegus columbiana* Howell).[25]

By 15 June 1806 the party was reaching the snowline on the Lolo Trail as the dog-tooth violet (*Erythranium grandiflorum* Pursh, no. 65) had just come into bloom. Clark remarked that at that elevation "the vegitation is proportionable backward," and that the honeysuckle, huckleberry, and a small maple (*Acer glabrum* Torr.) were putting forth leaves where clear of the snow. Almost immediately the heavy snowpack became an impassable barrier, and there could be no forage for horses. A halt was necessary, and the party was unable to cross the high Bitterroot Range over Lola Pass until 26 June 1806.[26]

This brought them to that campsite in Missoula County, Montana, that had been designated as Travelers' Rest. Lewis made several important collections there on 1 July 1806, the bitterroot (*Lewisia rediviva* Pursh [no. 87 in the herbarium]) among them. After many months in dried condition, it would be found that the roots, if planted, would resume growth—hence the name *rediviva*, meaning to live again. The roots were a staple food for Indians, who boiled them until the bitterness disappeared; and the bitterroot later became the state flower of Montana.

Travelers' Rest was also the point where the expedition split into two parties to make possible the exploration of two different routes back to the Missouri. Clark, turning southward, returned along the expedition's previous route to Three Forks, but then pushed eastward into the valley of the Yellowstone, descending it until the confluence with the Missouri. Lewis took a more northerly shortcut to the Missouri, and all the plant collections that July were made along his route. The divergent routes are well illustrated by the index maps in the splendid recent atlas of the expedition.[27]

From Missoula County, Lewis moved into Powell County to collect on 5 and 6 July 1806, from which we have *Purshia tridentata* (Pursh) DC. He next crossed the Continental Divide over Lewis and Clark Pass into Lewis and Clark County. *Gaillardia aristata* Pursh was collected on that pass, and *Zygadenus elegans* Pursh within the county. It is unclear whether the blue flax, *Linum lewisii* Pursh, was collected there or after Lewis reached Cascade County, 11–17 July 1806.[28] Additional plants collected included:

Mimulus guttatus DC., 4 July 1806, Missoula County
Iris missouriensis Nutt., 5 July 1806

Lonicera involucrate (Rich.) Banks ex Spreng., 7 July 1806
Stipa comata Trin. & Rupert., 8 July 1806

On 13 July 1806 Lewis reached the site of the cache made a year earlier below Great Falls. Clark's map indicates that the cache had been close to the
river,[29] and Lewis discovered that virtually everything had been destroyed by
high water, including all plant specimens collected between Fort Mandan and
that spot.[30] Within the following week, Lewis did ascend the valley of the Marias
River into Toole County, Montana, collecting a few plants; but his collecting in
the Rocky Mountain region ended on 20 July 1806.

The scientific results of the Lewis and Clark expedition remained little
known in the nineteenth century. Jefferson, desiring to reward Lewis for his
great success, appointed Lewis to be governor of the Territory of Louisiana early
in 1807. However well intentioned, the appointment was misguided. Lewis had
had no prior experience in administration; and, as a man of action, he had little taste for it. What was worse, his duties as governor deflected Lewis from his
intention to write a full account of the expedition. On his way to Washington
on 11 October 1809, both to give an accounting for his unpopular administration and to consult about the development of his history, he met a violent end—
whether a murder or a suicide has never been resolved.

At the time, Lewis had made little progress on the three projected volumes,
the third of which was to be devoted to natural history. This unanticipated death
forced Jefferson and Clark to find others for the task. They chose Nicolas Biddle, a Philadelphia attorney, to edit the narrative. As Biddle had no scientific
background, Dr. Benjamin Smith Barton of Philadelphia, physician and naturalist, accepted the honor of contributing the scientific text; but, in failing health,
he produced nothing. As a consequence, when Biddle published his edition of
the *Journals* in 1814, all the significant botanical and zoological material, and
most of the ethnological material, was omitted.[31]

As for the botanical material itself, the packages sent by Lewis to Jefferson
from Fort Mandan in 1805 included cuttings, roots, seeds, and the dried specimens numbered from one to sixty. Jefferson turned the material over to the
American Philosophical Society, of which he also was the president. The dried
plants were then confided to Dr. Barton for examination and a report.

Jefferson knew of a private botanical garden near Philadelphia called Wood-
lands, owned by William Hamilton, that featured both gardens and green-
houses. In 1805, Jefferson gave a packet of the seeds sent from Fort Mandan to
Hamilton for cultivation. It is within that context that we first hear of Frederick
Pursh (1774–1820). Born at Grassenhayn in Saxony and schooled in Dresden,
Pursh found his initial botanical employment in the Royal Botanical Gardens of
Dresden. He came to America in 1799 to take over the management of a botan-
ical garden near Baltimore, but then moved to Philadelphia, where he directed
Hamilton's Woodlands from 1802 to 1805.[32]

The second batch of dried plant specimens, seeds, and roots were brought back to Philadelphia by Lewis himself in 1806. By then, Pursh had left Woodlands and had accepted employment as a plant collector for Dr. Barton. In that circumstance Lewis met Pursh. Once Lewis saw the state of Dr. Barton's health, it appears that Lewis decided to turn over the dried specimens directly to Pursh for examination. Certainly the collection was not to be Pursh's property, but was meant to remain in Philadelphia along with the material previously shipped.[33] To be precise, the material was the property of the American Philosophical Society.

The seeds and roots that Lewis brought back were largely confided, at Jefferson's recommendation, to Hamilton at Woodlands and to Bernard McMahon (ca. 1775–1816), the preeminent nurseryman and seedsman in Philadelphia. McMahon had emigrated from Ireland in 1796 and had recently published one of the earliest American works on horticulture, *The American Gardener's Calendar* (1806). The Reverend Henry Muhlenberg, the Lutheran pastor in Lancaster, Pennsylvania, from 1779 to 1815, made repeated attempts to obtain seeds from the expedition, all of them apparently futile.[34]

Both Hamilton and McMahon received packets of seeds in March of 1807. McMahon found the seeds in a fine state of preservation, reporting to Lewis on April 5 that some of each had been planted at once, and seven species were up and growing.[35] Frederick Pursh, meanwhile, after leaving Hamilton's employment in 1805 for that of Dr. Barton, had by 1807 begun boarding at Bernard McMahon's house. In the same letter in which McMahon reported seven species up and growing, he characterized the young botanist then boarding at his house as, in his opinion, "better acquainted with plants, in general, than any man I ever conversed with on the subject." Noting that Pursh had been collecting and arranging specimens for Dr. Barton during the past year, McMahon concluded: "He is a very intelligent and practical Botanist and would be well inclined to render you any service in his power."[36] This tells us not only that Lewis had good reason to entrust his dried specimens to Pursh, rather than the indolent Barton, but that Pursh acquired his knowledge of Lewis's material from three different sources.

We can identify several of the Rocky Mountain species grown from seed or root by McMahon and Jefferson:

Lewisia rediviva Pursh, bitterroot; roots grown by McMahon
Ribes aureum Pursh, golden currant; grown by McMahon and Jefferson
Ribes viscossissimum Pursh, sticky currant, grown by McMahon
Linum lewisii Pursh, blue flax, grown by Jefferson
Symphoricarpos albus (L.) Blake, grown by McMahon; two plantings of it by Jefferson in 1812, the species especially pleasing him at Monticello
The roots of both *Camassia quamash* (Pursh) Greene, camas; and *Lomatium cous* (S. Wats.) Coult & Rose were preserved in the museum of Charles Willson Peale in Philadelphia.[37]

Once Pursh's commitments to Dr. Barton ended in 1807, he gave his full time to drawing and describing Lewis's plants. Soon finding that some of the specimens were sufficiently incomplete as to require consultation with Lewis, he inquired when Lewis planned to return to Philadelphia. Lewis, consumed by tiresome administrative duties in Saint Louis, postponed departure. By the time he did set out for Philadelphia, in the fall of 1809—only to suffer a mysterious death at Grinder's Tavern on the Natchez Trace in Tennessee—Pursh had already moved on to New York for employment in a private botanical garden belonging to Dr. David Hasack, leaving in April of 1809.

McMahon, once he had word of Lewis's untimely death, realized that Jefferson might have to take a direct part in having Lewis's botanical discoveries published. On 24 December 1809, he conveyed several critical messages to Jefferson. McMahon wanted to assure Jefferson that none of the plants raised from seed, nor any of the seeds produced from them, had ever left his hands. He had taken this measure out of fear that they would be acquired by a botanist who might want to rob Lewis of his right to first describe and name his own discoveries: especially as McMahon had reason to believe that such an opportunity was coveted by an individual he would not name. His discretion in not naming that individual allows us only to surmise that he meant Pursh, though he may have meant Henry Muhlenberg, who had been aggressively trying to see Lewis's material.

Secondly, McMahon reported that the original Lewis specimens on which Pursh had been working "are still in my hands; but Mr. Pursh has taken his drawings and descriptions with him, and will, no doubt, on the delivery of them expect a reasonable compensation for his trouble."[38] It may be that McMahon was unaware that Pursh had received payments earlier. In a settlement account signed by both Lewis and Clark on 21 August 1809, two entries are shown for Pursh. Lewis had paid Pursh thirty dollars on 10 May 1807 for assistance in arranging plants and making drawings; and, on 26 May, an advance of forty dollars for preparation of additional drawings.[39]

Accordingly, whether or not Pursh believed he had been inadequately compensated, he took material that did not belong to him and without any official authorization: not only drawings and descriptions, but at least some plant material, whether duplicate specimens or snippets from specimens. There appears to have been no official attempt to recover the stolen goods, perhaps because the original specimens were returned to the American Philosophical Society and put into storage; perhaps because no one in authority could envision the scientific implications of the theft.

As for Frederick Pursh, he began the composition of a North American flora after his relocation to New York in 1809. In the winter of 1811, he moved on to London to pursue his project under the patronage of A. B. Lambert, then vice president of the Linnean Society. Lambert had become known for his study of the genus *Cinchona* (1797) and, in 1803, had begun a lengthy study of the genus *Pinus*. Pursh would reward the patronage by honoring him with *Oxytropis lambertii* Pursh.

Pursh published his two-volume North American flora in 1814, ever since regarded as an admirable piece of work. Given the dubious aspects of his prior actions, it seems necessary to provide his explanation, given in his prefatory account:

> A small but highly interesting collection of dried plants was put into my hands by [Meriwether Lewis], in order to describe and figure those I thought new, for the purpose of inserting them in the account of his travels, which he was then engaged in preparing for the press. This valuable work, by the unfortunate untimely end of its author, has been interrupted in its publication.
>
> The collection of plants was made during the rapid return of the expedition from the Pacific Ocean toward the United States. A much more extensive one, made on their slow ascent towards the Rocky Mountains and the chains of the Northern Andes, has unfortunately been lost, by being deposited among other things at the foot of those mountains. The loss of this first collection is the more to be regretted, when I consider that the small collection communicated to me, consisting of about one hundred and fifty specimens, contained not above a dozen plants well known to me to be natives of North America, the rest being either entirely new or but little known, and among them at least six distinct and new genera. This may give an idea of the discerning eye of their collector, who had but little practical knowledge of the Flora of North America, as also of the richness of those extensive regions in new and interesting plants, and other natural productions.
>
> The descriptions of those plants, as far as the specimens were perfect, I have inserted in the present work in their respective places, distinguishing them by the words "v.s. in Herb. Lewis." Several of them I have had an opportunity of examining in their living state, some being cultivated from seeds procured by Mr. Lewis, and others since my arrival in England from seeds and plants introduced by Mr. Nuttall.[40]

As indicated, Pursh made a scrupulous acknowledgment of the 124 plants collected by Lewis and Clark. He honored the men by creating two new genera, *Lewisia* and *Clarkia;* and three new species were named to honor Lewis: *Linum lewisii* Pursh (wild blue flax), *Mimulus lewisii* Pursh (Lewis monkey-flower), and *Philadelphus lewisii* Pursh (Lewis mock-orange). Of the twenty-seven illustrations in the work, thirteen are drawings from the Lewis and Clark Herbarium. The flora was dedicated to Aylmer Bourke Lambert. There could not be, of course, any acknowledgment of an authorization to publish the Lewis material. Those plants ever after have been linked to Pursh's name; and a visitor to the

Rocky Mountains today has no inkling that many of the plants admired are linked to the Lewis and Clark expedition.[41]

Pursh died in 1820. He had neglected to send any specimens back to Philadelphia, and they became part of the Lambert herbarium. After Lambert's death, in 1842, his collection was put up for auction. The American botanist Edward Tuckerman was present and recognized not only the Lewis specimens, but some from Simon Fraser, John Bradbury, and Thomas Nuttall as well. Tuckerman bought them and ultimately presented them to the Academy of Sciences of Philadelphia in 1856.[42]

The reader knows that when Nicolas Biddle published his edition of the Lewis and Clark *Journals* in 1814, he had to omit the significant botanical and zoological material. This material did not get a proper restoration until the Reuben Gold Thwaites edition of 1904–1907. By the time he began work, Thwaites had learned of the discovery of Lewis's dried specimens in 1896 at the American Philosophical Society, where they had rested untouched in storage since being returned by the conscientious Bernard McMahon. Found and examined by the botanist Thomas Meehan, the specimens were next sent to the Gray Herbarium for review by Benjamin L. Robinson and Jesse M. Greenman. Their report included, in a parallel column, Pursh's treatment of the species in his flora. The specimens were then placed at the Academy of Natural Sciences in Philadelphia, which had superior facilities for preservation than those of the American Philosophical Society.[43]

This assembly of plant material at the Academy of Natural Sciences in Philadelphia came to be called generally the Lewis and Clark Herbarium. After so many years of neglect, full and unqualified answers about the Lewis material may never be possible. A major advance was made in 1966, when Paul Russell Cutright, with the assistance of Alfred E. Schuyler, undertook to locate and examine all the Lewis specimens in the academy's collection, including those in the Type Collection, bringing them together into one herbarium. Arranged alphabetically by genus, the Lewis specimens were assembled for the first time as a unit. A catalogue of the unit was published.[44] The final achievement has been the 1999 publication of the definitive illustrated *Herbarium of the Lewis & Clark Expedition* edited by Gary E. Moulton.

ROCKY MOUNTAIN TYPES PUBLISHED BY PURSH

Cascade County, Montana

Linum lewisii Pursh 1:210

Gallatin County, Montana

Ribes aureum Pursh 1:164

Lewis and Clark County, Montana

Buphthalnum sagittatum Pursh 2:563→*Potentilla floribunda* Pursh 1:355
Gallardia aristate Pursh 2:573
Lupinus argenteus Pursh 2:468
Zygadenus elegans Pursh 1:241

Missoula County, Montana

Lewisia rediviva Pursh 2:368
Barsia tenuifolia Pursh 2:439→*Orthocarpus tenuifolius* (Pursh) Benth
Philadelphus lewisii Pursh 1:329; also collected in Nez Perce County, Idaho
Sedum stenopetalum Pursh 1:324
Trifolium microcephalum Pursh 2:478

Powell County, Montana

Pedicularis elata Pursh 2:425 (*nom. illeg.*)→*Pedicularis cystopteridifolia* Rydb.
Pentaphylloidea floribunda (Pursh) A. Löve (1954)→*Pentaphylloides fruticosa*
    (L.) O. Schwartz (1949)
Tigares tridentata Pursh 1:313→*Purshia tridentata* (Pursh) DC.

Clearwater County, Idaho

Geum triflorum Pursh 2:736
Jussieua subacualis Pursh 1:304→*Camissonia subacaulis* (Pursh) Raven
Lupinus sericeus Pursh 2:468
Mimulus lewissii Pursh 2:427
Polygonum bistortoides Pursh 1:271
Phalagium quamash Pursh 1:226→*Camassia quamash* (Pursh) Greene
Swertia fastigiata Pursh 1:101→*Frasera fastigiata* (Pursh) Heller
Trillium peticolatum Pursh 1:244
Helonias tenax Pursh 1:243→*Xerophyllum tenax* (Pursh) Nutt.
Erigeron compositus Pursh 2:535
Santolia suaveolens Pursh 2:520 (*nom. illeg.*)→*Matricaria discoidea* DC.

Idaho County, Idaho

Actinella lanata Pursh 2:560→*Eriophyllum lanatum* (Pursh) Forbes
Aira brevifolia Pursh 1:76→*Poa secunda* J. Presl
Calochortus elegans Pursh 1:240
Cantua aggregata Pursh 1:147→*Ipomopsis aggregata* (Pursh) Grant ssp. *aggregata*
Caprifolium ciliosum Pursh 1:160→*Lonicera ciliosa* (Pursh) Poir. ex DC.
Ceanothus sanguineus Pursh 1:167
Clarkia pulchella Pursh 1:260
Claytonia lanceolata Pursh 1:175

Clematis hirsutissima Pursh 2:385
Festuca spicata Pursh 1:81→*Pseudo-roegneria spicata* (Pursh) A. Löve
Gerardia fructicosa Pursh 2:423→*Penstemon fructicosus* Pursh Greene
Ilex? myrsinites (Pursh) Rafinesque 1:119→*Pachistima myrsinites* (Pursh)
   Rafinesque
Phacelia heterophylla Pursh 1:140
Rhamnus alnifolius Pursh 1:266 (*nom. illeg.*)→*Frangula purshiana* (DC.) Cooper
Ribes viscossissimum Pursh 1:163
Santolina suaveolens Pursh 2:250 (*nom. illeg.*)→*Matricaria discoides* DC.
Scutellaria angustifolia Pursh 2:412
Spiraea discolor Pursh 1:342→*Holodiscus discolor* (Pursh) Maxim
Veronica reniformis Pursh 1:110 (*nom. illeg.*)→*Synthyris missurica* (Raf.) Pennell

Nez Perce County, Idaho

Erythronium grandiflorum Pursh 1:231
Lilium pudicum Pursh 1:228→*Fritillaria pudica* (Pursh) Spreng.
Sesile triternatum Pursh 1:197→*Lomatium triternatum* (Pursh) Coult. & Rose
Phlox speciosa Pursh 1:149

A list of type-specimens collected in the Rocky Mountain region cannot include type-specimens collected by Lewis east and west of the Rockies, also published by Pursh in 1814. While Lewis had to report to Jefferson that a practical commercial route to the Pacific did not exist, from which some may have inferred that the expedition failed in its mission, no botanist can be unaware of the foundation for Rocky Mountain botany that is Lewis's legacy. Given the rules of botanical nomenclature, the wrong done to him by the larcenous Pursh cannot be erased; but there should be no rules against preserving the memory of a man who matched our mountains.

2

Edwin James and the Long Expedition

*I*t would be quite unwarranted to assert that the botanical exploration of the Rocky Mountains was all downhill after the record of Lewis and Clark. Greater collections remained to be made. But undeniable is the fact that no other exploration in the nineteenth century left such an imprint on the national memory as that of Lewis and Clark. Most of those who followed, in fact, never loomed large on the national stage, often remaining obscure or long forgotten in the very states in which they worked. Even the name of an imposing mountain peak will fail to ring any bells; James Peak, at an elevation of 13,260 feet and intruding on three Colorado counties (Clear Creek, Gilpin, and Grand), has been dwarfed by the glory of the Eisenhower Memorial Tunnel. For, as Linnaeus might have put it, *natura non facit saltum.*

The Long expedition of 1819 to 1820, a mission of the United States government, was meant to be the successor to the Lewis and Clark expedition and initially was destined to visit the region of the upper Missouri River drainage. Known popularly as the Yellowstone expedition, it had been promoted to both President James Monroe and his secretary of war, John C. Calhoun, by Major Stephen H. Long, a topographer in the U.S. Army who had taught mathematics at West Point.

While in several respects the Long expedition was, in fact, the successor to the Lewis and Clark expedition, it is necessary to recall that the War of 1812 had intervened between the two expeditions. As a consequence, the Long expedition was undertaken not merely to explore and open up property acquired in the Louisiana Purchase—not merely as a sequel to the Lewis and Clark expedition—but in fear that the British had not yet abandoned hope of blocking the westward expansion of the United States. Because the British were also suspected of encouraging Indian tribes to obstruct that westward expansion, the American attitude toward Indians had undergone some alteration since Jefferson's days.

Stephen H. Long came from a New Hampshire farming family and graduated from Dartmouth. He began his professional life as a teacher in New Hampshire, but an opportunity to work as a school principal in Germantown, Pennsylvania, now a part of Philadelphia, enabled him to become acquainted with the American Philosophical Society. His pursuit of an interest in surveying brought him to the attention of the army's Corps of Topographical Engineers, in which he was commissioned in 1814. Thereafter, he had experience exploring the lower reaches of the Arkansas and Red Rivers. By 1819, at the age of thirty-five, he was suitably qualified to be assigned by Calhoun to the Yellowstone expedition. That enterprise was organized into two sections, one military, the other scientific, and command of the latter section was given to Long.

He chose a better professional staff than had been recruited by Jefferson. Thomas Say, a Philadelphian, had not had a formal education; but he was a descendent of John Bartram, the preeminent Philadelphia botanist during the colonial period (1699–1777), and had been an enthusiastic collector of natural history specimens from an early age. He became a virtual habitué of Charles Willson Peale's public museum and, in 1812, was a charter member of the Academy of Natural Sciences in Philadelphia. Long chose him, at thirty-three, to be the zoologist for the expedition; and with him, Titian R. Peale, twenty-one, to be an assistant naturalist. Son of the above-mentioned Charles Willson Peale, Titian, an artist, was prepared to serve as illustrator of natural objects. Samuel Seymour of Philadelphia was chosen to be the expedition's official artist, but he was primarily a landscape painter.[1]

Thomas Nuttall was the most qualified of the applicants for the appointment as botanist on the expedition. As a collector for Benjamin Smith Barton, Nuttall had taken his first trip into the interior as early as 1810. In 1818, he had published a *Genera of North American Plants* in Philadelphia and was ahead of his time in America in recognizing the superiority of Jussiaean natural classification. But Long wanted a botanist who could serve as physician for the expedition, and Nuttall did not have a medical degree. Consequently, the appointment went to Dr. William Baldwin of Philadelphia in 1819, despite Baldwin's record of poor health. The misjudgment was confirmed only some months after the expedition had been launched, when Baldwin died, at forty-one, in Franklin, Missouri. Edwin James, M.D., twenty-three (1797–1861), from Vermont, was then engaged to join the expedition as botanist, geologist, and surgeon; by this time the party's destination had been altered. James was a graduate of Middlebury College, where he had studied botany under Amos Eaton and John Torrey.[2]

It is evident that Calhoun had examined Jefferson's instructions to Lewis before preparing his own instructions for Major Long. Long was ordered to record "everything interesting in relation to soil, face of the country, water course and productions, whether animal, vegetable, or mineral." The Indians were not only to be conciliated, but studied as to the number and character of the various tribes, "with the extent of country, claimed by each." A copy of Jefferson's instructions to Lewis was actually appended by Calhoun.[3]

But Jefferson, as a man of the Enlightenment, seems to have assumed that when two civilizations unequal in scientific advancement collided, both sides would recognize the advantages of assimilation into the more advanced civilization. In the aftermath of the War of 1812, Calhoun faced the possibility that the Indian tribes might be encouraged to resist assimilation for reasons that had nothing to do with their welfare, which could thwart his nationalist ambitions. Although that insight did not alter his instructions to Major Long, he would later create the Bureau of Indian Affairs, in 1824; and he conceived the idea of removing Indians who failed to assimilate to the west of the Arkansas Territory and the state of Missouri.[4]

The Yellowstone expedition, as it was first known, with Colonel Henry Atkinson commanding the military section, departed from Pittsburgh in May of 1819. By late September the expedition had established winter quarters near what is today Council Bluffs on the Missouri. Because of financial miscalculations, the Yellowstone venture would be cut short at that point. The very substantial effort was reduced to a rump expedition with Major Long in charge, but final instructions and necessary funds did not reach the reduced party until early June in 1820.

The revised itinerary eliminated any farther travel up the Missouri. Instead, the party was to go by land to find the source of the Platte River, returning by way of the Arkansas and Red Rivers to the Mississippi. Unable to set off in May, the party was forced to cross the plains of Nebraska in June, the memory of which lingered. The instructions originally prepared for William Baldwin now applied to Edwin James:

> A description of all the products of vegetation, common or peculiar
> to the countries we may traverse, will be required of him, also the dis-
> eases prevailing among the inhabitants, whether civilized or savages,
> and their probable causes, will be subjects for his investigation; any
> variety in the anatomy of the human frame, or any other phenomena
> observable in our species, will be particularly noted by him. Dr. Bald-
> win will also officiate as physician and surgeon for the expedition.[5]

The party reached the Platte on 14 June 1820, proceeding upstream to reach the confluence of the north and south branches by 22 June. The following day they crossed to the south side of the South Platte, heading into Colorado. "On the 30th we left the encampment at our accustomed early hour, and at 8 o'clock were cheered by a distant view of the Rocky Mountains [near the site of Fort Morgan, Morgan County]. We soon remarked a particular part of the range divided into three conic summits, each apparently of nearly equal altitude. This we concluded to be the point designed by Pike as the Highest Peak."[6] It is now known by the name Longs Peak, flanked by Mount Meeker and Mount Lady Washington.

On 1 July 1820, and into Weld County, James remarked in his diary that the common purslane, *Portulaca oleracea* L., was very evident "in depressed and saline soils," particularly in places disturbed by bison or other animals, along the base of the Rocky Mountains. As the plant, often cultivated as vegetable, has generally been thought to have been introduced and likely to be found around dwellings, Goodman and Lawson suspect that James must have collected a different species.[7] The plant is believed to be of West Asian origin and has long been cultivated in Europe. In Colorado today, the species is widespread, both in cultivated and waste areas, from forty-five hundred to eighty-five hundred feet. Since James mentioned the plant again a month later in what would now be New Mexico, the possibility of Spanish introduction cannot be ruled out, as in the case of *Erodium cicutarum* (L.) L'Hér. ex Aiton. Curiously enough, the species is reported in northeastern Siberia, quite far from southwestern Russia, where it is common; yet it has not been reported from Alaska. James thought the plant to be indigenous to the West, and John Torrey published it as such.[8]

On 4 and 5 July 1820, the party was in Adams County. James made several gratifying collections: "a large suffruticose species of Lupine" that became *Lupinus decumbens* Torr., now a synonym of *Lupinus argenteus* Pursh var. *argenteus;* and several species of what John Sims had called *Bartonia,* namely *Mentzelia nuda* (Pursh) T. & G., and *Mentzelia decapetala* (Pursh ex Sims) Urban & Gilg. ex Gilg. Camped on the South Platte at a spot appearing to them to be about five miles from the mountains, James and two companions left camp to walk to the base of the mountains along Clear Creek. After walking about eight miles "without finding the apparent distance to the base of the mountain had very considerably diminished," they had to return to camp.[9]

Moving southward along the river on 6 July 1820 into what is now northern Douglas County, James admired the high sandstone formations at the base of the Rocky Mountains. "About the sandstone ledges we collected a geranium intermediate between the crane's bill and herb Robert." James was probably referring to *Geranium robertianum* L., which he would have known from the East. Consequently, his initial publication of the species would be *Geranium intermedium* James (1823).

The plant later appeared as *Geranium caespitosum* James in Torr. (1827). The latter name is still used, despite the evident priority of *intermedium,* because it is now presumed that the proper date for the publications was 1823. The type specimen, although collected, never reached Torrey for reasons unknown. A century later, George Osterhout of Windsor, Colorado, revisited the site, finding only *Geranium parryi* (Engelm.) Heller. In effect, that discovery reduced *G. parryi* to a synonym of *G. caespitosum.*[10] Subsequently, it has become conventional to regard the nonglandular *Geranium fremontii* Torr. ex A. Gray as a variety of *G. caespitosum* James. James also collected a beautiful calochortus at that site, which could only have been *Calochortus gunnisonii* Wats.

The South Platte emerges from the mountains near where the party was camped (they called it the Chasm of the Platte), and Calhoun's instructions directed them to seek the river's source. The Platte, as of 6 July, was still much too swollen to permit a passage up the canyon. An attempt was made, therefore, to penetrate the mountains by climbing over them, an effort that was abandoned on 7 July after several miles because of rough terrain. A descent to the proximity of the river seemed to be the more feasible of two uncomfortable routes. In the canyon that day, James noted *Humulus lupulus* L., hops; *Acer negundo* L., boxelder; and both *Aralia nudicaulis* L. and *Aralia racemosa* L., both known as wild ginseng.[11]

One can only deduce that the severity of the terrain discouraged any further ideas of pursuing the South Platte to its origins. Moreover, many in the party had begun to experience a violent and debilitating illness that James attributed to their having eaten "hard and juiceless currents . . . and large and delicious raspberries of a species approaching the flowering raspberry." As no collections were apparently made, one is left to wonder whether the former was *Ribes cereum* Dougl. The latter was more likely *Rubus idaeus* L. than the badly misnamed *Rubus deliciosus* Torr., which could have been named only by a closet-botanist. In any case, James did recognize that the party was not used to fresh fruit after so many months without it.

Beginning 9 July 1820, the party turned southward, traveling parallel to the Front Range. On the 11th, they crossed the small ridge dividing the tributaries of the South Platte from those of the Arkansas, now known as the Palmer Divide. There, James collected a large species of columbine that he thought might as yet be unknown in the United States. "If it should appear not to have been described," he noted, "it may receive the name of *Aquilegia caerulea*."[12] It would become the state flower of Colorado. Somewhere along the Front Range, the exact location not recorded, James collected waxflower, the plant later becoming the type for a new genus: *Jamesia americana* Torr. & Gray (1840), a shrub in the Hydrangeaceae and still abundant along the east side of the Front Range today.[13]

After crossing the Palmer Divide into El Paso County, the Long expedition had its grandest botanical moment. James, accompanied by two members of the party, Joseph Verplank and Zachariah Wilson, began the ascent of the great mountain Lieutenant Zebulon Pike had seen from a distance in 1806, but, the season being unfavorable, had failed to climb. The James ascent began on 13 July 1820, and the men were above timberline by two o'clock on the 14th, nearly exhausted. Even so, they pushed on to the summit, reaching it by four o'clock, remaining only a few minutes given the need to get back at least to timberline by sunset, which they did.

During the ascent on the 14th, James noted an undescribed white-flowered species of *Caltha,* the familiar marsh marigold that, in fact, had been published by Candolle in 1818. He also noted the shrubby cinquefoil now known as *Pentaphylloides fruticosa* (L.) O. Schwarz. But the great surprise came above timberline, an elevation never before botanized in the Rocky Mountains. James called it:

> a region of astonishing beauty, and of great interest on account of its productions; the intervals of soil are sometimes extensive, and are covered with a carpet of low but brilliantly flowering alpine plants. Most of these have either matted procumbent stems, or such as inclining the flower, rarely rise more than an inch in height. In many of them, the flower is the most conspicuous and the largest part of the plant, and in all, the coloring is astonishingly brilliant.
>
> We met, as we proceeded, such numbers of unknown and interesting plants, as to occasion much delay in collecting, and were under the disagreeable necessity of passing by numbers which we saw in situations of access. As we approached the summit, these became less frequent and at length ceased entirely.[14]

In retrospect, a century later, George Osterhout would call these hours above timberline the most notable moments for botany during the Long expedition: the Western introduction to the true alpine flora of the central Rocky Mountains.[15]

At a somewhat lower elevation, James observed a pine he thought had been hitherto unnoticed. He described it as having:

> five leaves in a fascicle; the leaves are short and rather rigid, the sheathes which surrounded their bases, short and lacerated; the strobiles erect, composed of large unarmed scales, being somewhat smaller than those of *P. rigida* [Miller], but similar in shape, and exuding a great quantity of resin. The branches which are covered with leaves chiefly at the ends, are numerous and recurved, inclining to form a dense and large top: they are also remarkably flexile, feeling in the hand somewhat like those of the *Dirca palustris* [L.]. From this circumstance, the specific name *flexilis,* has been proposed for this tree. . . . The fruit of the *Pinus flexilis* [limber pine] is eaten by the Indians and French hunters about the Rocky Mountains.[16]

This ascent was the first of any of Colorado's fourteen-thousand-footers, and Major Long quite appropriately proposed to name the peak for Edwin James. Popular usage, however, always favored Pike's Peak in honor of the explorer who had first seen and described it, and Long's designation did not stand. A second ascent of Pike's Peak by a botanist would not be made until 1 July 1862, by

Dr. Charles Parry. A lesser peak would, in time, be named for James, appropriately within a cluster of peaks bearing other botanical names: Grays, Torreys, Engelmann, and Parry.[17]

James's Rocky Mountain collecting came virtually to an end after the descent from Pike's Peak on 15 July 1820. With three companions, he did begin an exploration of the Arkansas valley into the mountains on 17 July. Hampered by timber and rough, uncongenial terrain, the party held to the north rim of the canyon going up; and they reached the eastern end of the Royal Gorge. They did not penetrate the great canyon any farther before turning back downstream, meaning that the expedition never got close to discovering the source of the Arkansas. Complaints about the lack of decent food suggest the principal motive for turning back. James's chronicle for that period mentions mostly fauna rather than plants.[18]

By 21 July 1820, the expedition had moved down the Arkansas to a campsite near the present town of Rocky Ford. There they met an isolated Kaskaskia Indian and his squaw, learning from him that a number of tribes were encamped a few days' journey down the river on a war expedition against the Spanish on the Red River. If he could be believed, the encampment included Kaskaskias, Cheyennes, Arapahoes, Kiowas, Kansas, and some Shoshones. This seemed to account for the fact that the expedition had not encountered Indians since leaving the Pawnees in Nebraska. Expecting to find tribes around both the upper South Platte and Arkansas, they had met none.

During the pause near Rocky Ford, preparations were made to split the expedition into two parties. Major Long would lead a party southward in search of the headwaters of the Red River; Captain John Bell would direct the second group down the Arkansas to Fort Smith. Edwin James's account of the meeting between Bell's group and the large encampment of Indians downstream around 26 July 1820 had to have been derived from notes provided by the zoologist Thomas Say, as James himself had accompanied Long's party southward toward New Mexico.[19]

James had learned a limited Kaskaskia vocabulary from Calf, the isolated Kaskaskia previously encountered near Rocky Ford, and had recorded it. Long's party ran into a much larger band of Kaskaskias on 10 August 1820 in Potter County of the Texas panhandle. Camping in the proximity of the Indians, James hoped to make more extensive study of their language and situation, but the Indians appeared to be suspicious. Given the uncertainty about the Indians' intentions, the Long party would not remain long enough to make as many observations as desired.

James depicted the younger females as still handsome, but added that the women appeared to lose all feminine charm early in life due to childbearing and the drudgeries of married life. Their breasts became so flaccid and pendulous that some could give suck to their children while both mother and child were standing erect on the ground. Weaning was evidently considerably delayed. James noted that these Indians, in common with other tribes he had witnessed, had a tolerance for filth and vermin, the women in particular seeking and eating lice with avidity. It seemed apparent, given their ulcers and abscesses discharging matter, that these Indians were subject to numerous rheumatic and scrofulous diseases, either untreated or treated fruitlessly with traditional remedies.

"Though we saw much to admire among this people," James summarized,

> we cannot but think them among the most degraded and miserable of the uncivilized Indians on this side of the Rocky Mountains. Their wandering and precarious manner of life, as well as the inhospitable character of the country they inhabit, precludes the possibility of advancement from the profoundest barbarism. As is common among other western tribes, they were persevering in offering us their women, but this appeared to be done from mere beastliness and in the hope of reward rather than any motive of hospitality.[20]

The Long party pushed on from that campsite on the morning of 12 August, grateful for not having been attacked by Indians far from friendly, and from whom nothing more of the Kaskaskia had been learned. Meanwhile, the experience of Bell's party on the Arkansas was much more rewarding. Not only were the Indians immediately friendly, but the party had the service of two French Canadians who had been enlisted when the expedition left Council Bluffs in June: Joseph Bijeau as a guide and interpreter; Abraam Ledoux as a hunter and farrier. The two had taken up residence with the Pawnees as hunters and trappers, and both had become familiar with several Indian languages. James would make extensive use of the notes Thomas Say made of his observations, which have been reliably useful for Indian historians ever since, especially as they encompass the half-dozen tribes Calf had indicated would be met. A Kiowa chief proved to be memorable, patiently helping with the pronunciation of Kiowa words so that they could be directly transcribed to paper. Much of what was learned about the Pawnee language came directly from Abraam Ledoux. The party did not break camp until 30 July 1820, moving on toward a reunion with the Long party at Fort Smith.[21]

For Edwin James, while the Rocky Mountain exploration may have been behind him, there remained the disposition of his plant collections. Since James was a former student of John Torrey, it was an easy matter to turn to Torrey for assistance in publication; but the species deemed to be new were not published in one place as a group or at one time, offering the possibility for some confusion. The initial publication was James's *Account of an Expedition from Pittsburg to the Rocky Mountains, Performed in the Years 1819 and '20.*[22] Therein were three species, two of which are already known to the reader from the text:

Aquilegia caerulea James 2:15. 1823. Palmer Divide, El Paso County, Colorado
Pinus flexilis James 2:27, 34–35. 1823. Pike's Peak, El Paso County, Colorado
Rudbeckia tagetes James 2:68. 1823. Otero County, Colorado→*Ratibida tagetes*
  (James) Barnh.

James next published his own "Catalogue of Plants Collected During a
Journey to and from the Rocky Mountains, during the summer of 1820."[23]
But this list was incomplete, meant to include only plants already established
as belonging to the flora of North America. Even so, one new species did appear:

Veronia plantaginea James 2:273. 1825. Foothill, El Paso County, Colorado→
  Besseya plantaginea (James) Rydb.

The new plants withheld from this catalogue were those published by John
Torrey in 1824 and 1826–1827: "Descriptions of Some New or Rare Plants from
the Rocky Mountains, collected in July 1820, by Dr. Edwin James."[24] These
were new species collected on Pike's Peak, 14 July 1820:

Androsace carinata Torr. 1:30. 1824. Alpine.→*Androsace chamaejasme* Wulfon
  ssp. *carinata* (Torr.) Hultén
Primula angustifolia Torr. 1:34. 1824. Alpine or lower
Trifolium nanum Torr. 1:35. 1824. Alpine
Penstemon alpinus Torr. 1:35. 1824. Not a true alpine→*Penstemon glaber*
  Pursh var. *alpinus* (Torr.) Gray

James was uncertain about another plant collected that day, an alpine, that resembled a penstemon. Torrey was uncertain about it, too, and it would be published only later as the basis for a new genus: *Chionophilia jamesii* Benth. in DC.
(1846).[25]

The following plants were published in Torrey's "Some Account of a Collection of Plants Made During a Journey to and from the Rocky Mountains in
the Summer of 1820, by Dr. Edwin P. [sic] James, M.D., Assistant Surgeon
U.S. Army":[26]

Stellaria jamesiana Torr. 2:169. 1827. Along the Front Range
Arenaria obtuse Torr. 2:170. 1827. Pike's Peak. Subalpine-alpine. *Nom. illeg.*→
  Arenaria obtusiloba (Rydb.) Fernald.
Acer glabrum Torr. 2. 172. 1827. Palmer Divide
Rubus deliciosus Torr. 2:196. 1827. South Platte Canyon
Saxifraga jamesii Torr. 2:204. 1827. Pike's Peak→*Telesonix jamesii* (Torr.) Raf.
Tiarella ? bracteata Torr. 2:204–205. 1827. South Platte Canyon→*Heuchera*
  bracteata (Torr.) Ser. in DC.

Sedum lanceolatum Torr. 2: 205–206. 1827. Along Front Range
Pulmonaria ciliata James ex Torr. 2:224. 1827. West of Denver→*Mertensia ciliata* (James ex Torr.) G. Don
Castilleja occidentalis Torr. 2:230. 1827. Pike's Peak. Alpine

The Long Expedition has been subject to frequent criticism for having failed in its mission to find the headwaters of the South Platte, the Arkansas, and the Red Rivers. However, the makeshift character of the expedition, forced to proceed from Council Bluffs on an itinerary that bore little relation to the time allotted, made such goals unrealistic. The positive scientific results of the expedition, not only the collections of Edwin James and Thomas Say, but the valuable maps that were the responsibility of Major Long, results that were known long before those of Lewis and Clark, should have elevated the reputation of the expedition more than was the case.

It would appear that those positive scientific results were immediately overshadowed by the description both Long and James gave to the land east of the Rocky Mountains, calling it the "Great American Desert." The negative implications were quite unwelcome to those espousing westward expansion, including the sponsors of the expedition. Long characterized the area as a region unfit for cultivation, a verdict emphasized by Edwin James:

> We have little apprehension of giving too unfavourable an account of
> this portion of the country. The lack of water and timber make the
> land an unfit residence for any but a nomade population. The trav-
> eler who shall at any time have traversed its desolate sands, will, we
> think, join us in the wish that this region may for ever remain the
> unmolested haunt of the native hunter, the bison, and the jackall.[27]

We must understand this as the reaction of New Englanders who had labored across that untouched, arid terrain under the summer sun. Their designation opened a debate over the use, misuse, or abuse of arid country that has continued ever since. Its irresolution after so many decades reflects the spectrum of irreconcilable interests at stake, whether political, economic, or ethnic; not to speak of the fact that a knowledge of the plant sciences seems never to have been regarded as a prerequisite for participation.[28]

As for Edwin James himself in the aftermath of the expedition, not much detail on his later years has been available. To some degree he fitted the classic pattern of the French botanical explorers of the eighteenth century who had enjoyed many months in pristine country, greatly dependent upon self-reliance and a sturdy independence; but who, upon returning to the life known before going into the field, never satisfactorily accomodated themselves to life in settlements.

Individual cases always differed in detail, of course; and in James's case, his preoccupation with the probable fate of the Indians he had observed seems to have been a moral dilemma for which no happy ending could be contrived. Assimilation might be the most humane solution imaginable; but, to have seen aboriginal conditions as they actually were was to have sensed that the gulf between the nomadic and the urbane was too vast to be bridged in the brief time that the westward expansion would permit. The alternative, the Indian removable policy hatched by Calhoun and first inaugurated during the Jackson administration, turned out to be a disaster for the Indians.

After the conclusion of the Long expedition, James asked Calhoun to reassign him to the Medical Department of the army. He subsequently served on posts in Wisconsin and northern Michigan. He resumed his study of Indian languages, and we may surmise that his translation of the New Testament into the Ojibwa language was both a measure of growing preoccupation with religion and an indication that he could see no secular solution to the Indian dilemma.

James resigned from the army in 1834, then only thirty-seven, and settled on a farm in Iowa where he would live until his death, in 1861. His philanthropic energy soon embraced Indian welfare, the temperance movement, and abolitionism. The obvious merit of such causes has never protected them from being attractive to cranks; and James's admission to John Torrey in 1854 that he had become immersed in "the chill and foggy domains of theology," having lost all hope of going forth again "to gather weeds and stones and rubbish," rings sadly of the gifted naturalist's ending as eccentric and mystic.[29] As for why he failed to build an eminent career in science, given the promise he displayed on the Long expedition, there are few reliable clues.

3

Thomas Drummond in the Northern Rocky Mountains

*T*homas Drummond (1780–1835) may be counted among that substantial group of energetic naturalists in the nineteenth century who would be forgotten today were their names not preserved in the nomenclature of numerous species. Like his contemporary David Douglas (1799–1834), Drummond was born in Scotland; but biographical detail for his life remains obscure. He comes to our attention only after his appointment to be assistant naturalist to Dr. John Richardson on the second Arctic expedition of Captain John Franklin, owing his appointment to the influence of William J. Hooker.

Richardson's name also remains familiar to us in biotic nomenclature, although his publications indicate a greater interest in zoology than botany. He had obtained a medical degree at Edinburgh, becoming a naval surgeon in 1807. He served as surgeon-naturalist on Franklin's first Arctic expedition (1819–1822), and again on the second (1825–1826). The scientific results in Franklin's *Narrative* were written by Richardson. He was knighted in 1846, and a biography of him was published by John MacIlraith in 1868. Hooker was the beneficiary of his plant collections, as he was of those from the Pacific Northwest made by David Douglas and from the Canadian Rockies made by Thomas Drummond. For, in fact, Drummond had been detached from the main Franklin expedition at Cumberland House, the Hudson's Bay Company fort on the Saskatchewan River. He was left alone on 28 June 1825 to explore westward while the main party veered to the north.

More than a word needs to be added about William Jackson Hooker (1785–1865), as he was a major link between European and American botany. Yet, with the significant exception of Asa Gray, few American botanists were acquainted with him. Hooker was doubly fortunate in his birth: he was born to a prominent and affluent family, which meant inherited wealth for life; and in

Norwich, where Sir James Edward Smith was his eminent townsman. None of that would have mattered had Hooker not evinced a passion for natural science at an early age. Once he had completed high school, he had the means to travel in his study of natural history. It is said that he sought the advice of Smith about a moss and received the additional advice that he specialize in botany.

Hooker's earliest trips into the field were to the wildest parts of Scotland, the Hebrides, and the Orkneys. He undertook a more major field trip to Iceland in the summer of 1809. Although his collections were destroyed by a fire at sea during the voyage home—an incident that nearly cost him his life—the trip reinforced his early interest in mosses. He went to London in the aftermath, becoming acquainted with Sir Joseph Banks, Jonas Dryander, Daniel Solander, and Robert Brown, all the right people as the saying goes. Botanizing on the continent in 1814—in Switzerland, Italy, and France— Hooker sought out the major botanists of the day. Such acquaintances led to a wide correspondence in later years and account for Hooker's valuable service as a link between European and American botany. They also enabled him to build a private herbarium unrivaled in its day.

After imprudent investments by Hooker greatly reduced his income, Joseph Banks sponsored him in 1820 for the Regius Professorship of Botany at the University of Glasgow, where he would remain for the next twenty years. During this period Hooker became known for his efforts to have botanists appointed to accompany governmental expeditions; from these botanists he would receive valuable contributions from western North America for his herbarium. Also during this period, Hooker founded several expensive publications, dependent on his income, as they could not be remunerative; and he brought out his most important contribution to North American botany, *Flora Boreali-Americana,* in two volumes (1833, 1840). In 1836, Hooker was made a Knight of the Hanoverian Order by William IV, the last British monarch who could bestow the title.

In 1841, Hooker moved back to England to take the directorship of the Royal Gardens at Kew, until then a private garden of the crown, but thereafter to be recast as a national scientific establishment. Hooker's greatest energy thenceforth went into rebuilding an establishment that had seriously deteriorated under his aged predecessor, W. T. Aiton, and the growth would be prodigious. During Hooker's twenty-five-year tenure, Kew Gardens expanded from eleven to seventy-five acres, with many new greenhouses and an arboretum of 270 acres. But the appointment marked the end of Hooker's patronage of Rocky Mountain botany.[1]

The best available account of Thomas Drummond's lonely journey was written several years after the event. He had not kept a journal while in the field, so his brief sketch, as he called it, amounted to recollections. Collection dates and locations, as a consequence, were unreliable; and those who later published his plants frequently could only cite a regional location. More certain is the evident fact that he suffered great hardship over many months, especially from the cold during the winter of 1825–1826.

Drummond departed from Cumberland House on 28 June 1825 and consumed much of the summer on the prairie of southern Canada. He did not reach the mountains until the autumn of 1825; he stated in his sketch that Jasper's Lake, in southwestern Alberta, should be considered his entrance to the Rocky Mountains. Following the Athabasca River, he claimed, he observed plants as late as October, mentioning *Arbutus alpina* L.→*Arctostaphylos alpina* (L.) Spreng., *Dryas drummondii* Richards. ex. Hook., and *Dryas tenella* Pursh. Evidently meaning to cross the Rockies despite the approach of winter, he persisted up the river until the extreme cold forced him to descend to Jasper's House.

In that vicinity, he found the first spring plants on 7 May 1826, noting species we know as *Anemone nuttaliana* DC.; *Pulsatilla patens* (L.) P. Mill.; *Anemone drummondii* Wats.; *Saxifraga oppositifolia* L.; *Lesquerella arenosa* (Richards.), which he believed to be an *Alyssum;* and *Alyssum arcticum* Wormsk. ex Hornem, which has since been transferred to *Lesqurella*. Because the country was late in opening up, he remained near Jasper's House until 15 June 1826.

Thereafter, in the summer of 1826, Drummond pushed northwestward on the eastern side of the Continental Divide. He camped at Lac-la-Pierre, now more usually known as Rock Lake; and then traveled about thirty miles west to what he recalled as Wolf Plain. Collections there were *Claytonia lanceolata* Pursh., again *Pulsatilla patens* (L.) P. Mill., and *Lupinus perennis* L. Drummond's next major collecting region was the drainage of the Smoky River, where he worked into late September, estimating that he reached an area about two hundred miles beyond Jasper's House. From that area he recorded *Rhododendron lapponicum* (L.) Wahlenb., which proved to be *Rhododendrum albiflorum* Hook. (1834); a cordate-leaved *Mitella* known now to us as *Mitella petandra* Hook. (1829); and a fern he thought might be a new *Woodsia,* possibly the same fern collected by Richardson—*Woodsia glabella* R. Br. ex Richards. (1823). With the onset of winter, he retreated to the security of Edmonton House, in central Alberta.

Drummond's sketch of his botanizing during the following summer, 1827, was even more truncated than his sketches of the two prior years. He traveled westward from Edmonton House with a brigade belonging to the Hudson's Bay Company, whose members were more interested in speed than in plants, hampering his collections. The party seems to have crossed the Continental Divide over Athabaska Pass, then followed the Wood River down to the upper Columbia River. Drummond separated from the brigade at that point and would return across the Divide alone.

By then he seems to have begun concentrating on observing the fauna, but also, knowing of Hooker's interest, on collecting mosses, a number of which were later published. Drummond also collected seeds whenever possible to facilitate later examination of species observed. In the later summer he turned homeward. He had the good fortune to meet David Douglas for a day and showed him his collection. Douglas had crossed the continent from Fort Vancouver that summer, also crossing the Athabaska Pass with a guide from the Hudson's Bay Company. The meeting took place at Carlton House, in eastern Ontario.[2]

Drummond's account of his travels and collections has frustrated researchers who seek to work on his material ever since. But Susan McKelvey recognized correctly that Hooker had made the matter worse, when preparing his great two-volume work, *Flora Boreali-Americana,* by rarely identifying plant collectors. Although a considerable number of Rocky Mountain type-specimens are attributable to Drummond's efforts, some of his specimens must have become waifs adopted by others.

Familiar Rocky Mountain Plants Honoring Drummond Collections

Salix drummondiana Barratt ex Hook. (1838)
Arabis drummondii A. Gray (1866) from seeds collected by Drummond
Silene drummondii Hook. (1830) collected by both Richardson and Drummond
Astragalus drummondii Dougl. ex Hook. (1831)
Potentilla drummondii Lehm. (1830)
Geranium albiflorum Hook. (1831) (*nom. illeg.*)→*Geranium richardsonii* Fisch. & Trautv. (1837)
Juncus drummondii E. Meyer (1853)

Further indication of Hooker's reliance on Drummond's collections may be found in the number of composites alone published by Hooker in *Flora Boreali-Americana* without dedication to the collector:

Troximon aurantiacum Hook. 1:300 (1833)→*Agoseris aurantiaca* (Hook.) Greene (1891)
Antennaria carpathica Wahl. var. *lanata* Hook. 1:329 (1834)→*Antennaria lanata* (Hook.) Greene (1898)
Antennaria carpathica Wahl. var. *pulcherrima* Hook. 1:329 (1834)→*Antennaria pulcherrima* (Hook.) Greene (1897)
Antennaria racemosa Hook. 1:330 (1834)
Arnica cordifolia Hook. 1:331 (1834)
Arnica mollis Hook. 1:331 (1834)
Aster modestus Lindl. in Hook. 2:8 (1834)
Erigeron grandiflorus Hook. 2:18 (1834)
Erigeron lochophyllus Hook. 2:18 (1834)
Erigeron lanatus Hook. 2:17 (1834)
Erigeron radicatus Hook. 2:17 (1834)
Hieracium albiflorum Hook. 1:298 (1834)
Hieracium gracile Hook. 1:298 (1834)
Donia lanceolata Hook. 2:25 (1834)→*Pyrrocoma lanceolota* (Hook.) Greene (1894)

Donia uniflora Hook. 2:25 (1834)→*Pyrrocoma uniflora* (Hook.) Greene (1894)
Senecio canus Hook. 1:333 (1834)
Senecio triangularis Hook. 1:332 (1834)

In passing, the reader may have noted the attention Edward Lee Greene later paid to Hooker's nomenclature, as well as Greene's readiness to contest the authority of botanists who published without having seen the plant material in the field. Some of Hooker's determinations, it is true, were based on plants grown from seed collected by Drummond. A notable example was *Mitella pentandra* Hook. (1829). The species stood despite Candolle's effort to honor Drummond by transferring it to a new genus, *Drummondia mitelloides* DC. (1830), a genus that did not survive.

Hooker's seeming casualness about identifying his plant collections was no fair measure of his regard for them. After Drummond returned to England in the fall of 1827, he became curator of the Botanical Garden in Belfast; and he owed that appointment to the influence of Hooker. Well placed though he was, Drummond proved to be no stay-at-home. He made a second trip to North America between 1831 and 1835, not to Canada but to the American Southwest, Texas in particular: he was active, in other words, to the end of his life.

4

The Ascendancy of Thomas Nuttall
(1786–1859)

*A*lthough Thomas Nuttall was English in both birth and death, his scientific work and publication was almost entirely American, taking place between 1808 and 1842. Born in Yorkshire, Nuttall became a journeyman printer, the vocation he expected to pursue when he came to America in 1808. Nothing in that beginning hinted that, on the basis of scientific qualifications, a knowledge of living plants based on field experience, and the publication of personal discoveries, Nuttall would be unequalled as a botanist in the first half of the nineteenth century.[1]

That judgment, certainly tenable, was rendered several years before the publication of Hunter Dupree's monumental biography of Asa Gray. No study of Nuttall can sidestep his eventual conflict with Gray, which did not make "a pretty chapter" in the history of American botany.[2] Any interested reader of the Gray biography ought to consider whether Dupree's moderate judgment, which favored Gray, reflected sympathy for the scholar who aspired to be the administrator of botany in America. Nuttall had no such ambition. Consequently, he could not command either the authority or the loyalty that Gray's control of patronage assured. The conflict between the two unquestionably knowledgeable botanists became merely the first in a series of comparable squabbles that would enliven botanical research in the second half of the century.

Soon after his arrival in America, Nuttall was induced to undertake the study of plants by Benjamin Smith Barton, becoming Frederick Pursh's successor as an employee of Barton. Although both Pursh and Nuttall were ostensibly employed to work in Barton's herbarium and to make collecting trips for him, there is good reason to suspect that the indolent Barton's tacit intention was to provide himself with an assistant who could do the botanical work on the Lewis and Clark material that Barton had agreed to contribute to Nicolas Biddle's narrative.

Pursh's peculiar performance of his duties has already been laid bare, but a word about Barton: He held the professorship of Natural History and Botany on the medical faculty of the University of Pennsylvania, being prominent also in the American Philosophical Society and in the local Linnaean Society. Such connections have evidently obscured the fact that his scholarship was never distinguished. His eminence rested on two textbooks that had no competition in the Philadelphia of his day: *Materia medica of the United States* (1798–1804); and *Elements of Botany: Or Outlines of the Natural History of Vegetables* (1803), the latter being the first textbook on botany written in the United States. In the academic world such a record testified to a supremely ambitious man rather than to one dedicated to scholarly research. What is more, given his employment of botanical assistants, it appears Barton meant to advance himself on the work of others—another revelation of his character.

Jefferson's favorable opinion of Barton was possibly influenced by the creation of a new genus, *Jeffersonia* Bart., in the Barberry family. Barton had noticed that the classification *Podophyllum diphyllum* L. had not been based on a knowledge of the plant's flowers, so he created the new genus to accommodate them. Jefferson was secretary of state at the time; but later, after his retirement from the presidency, he had it planted at Monticello. The species was *Jeffersonia diphylla* (L.) Pers., twinleaf.[3]

It would appear that Nuttall's first trip into the interior of the United States was made at Barton's suggestion. Barton prepared a contract, which both men signed. Nuttall was to receive a salary of eight dollars a month plus expenses; he was to keep a daily journal for *Barton's exclusive use;* and he was to collect not only plants, but animals, minerals, and Indian artifacts, all of which would be Barton's property.

Nuttall left Philadelphia on 12 April 1810 and reached Michilimackinac four months later, in mid-August. He learned there that British authorities would not allow him to proceed into Canada, so he backtracked to Saint Louis. By fortunate coincidence, the expedition led by Wilson Price Hunt—which meant to follow the Lewis and Clark route to the mouth of the Columbia, there to establish a fur-trading post for the John Jacob Astor interests—had reached Saint Louis in September to wait out the winter months. (The party has always been known as the Astorians.)

The nearly forgotten English naturalist John Bradbury (1768–1823) also arrived in Saint Louis that autumn, commissioned to collect plants by the Liverpool Botanic Garden. He accepted an invitation to join the Astorians, and Nuttall also found it convenient to join the party. The group resumed the trip up the Missouri in March of 1811. Unlike Lewis and Clark, who became great friends during their exploration, Bradbury and Nuttall seem never to have become very congenial. Bradbury, the elder and more experienced, must have been of help to Nuttall; but, as would be the case for much of his life, Nuttall was so exclusively occupied by plants that he gave little time to companions. The observation of Henry M. Brackenridge, with Manuel Lisa and the Missouri Fur Company, that Nuttall "appears singularly devoted, and which seems to engross every thought, to the total disregard of his own personal safety, and sometimes to the inconvenience of the party he accompanies," has been frequently cited. "To the ignorant [French] Canadian boatmen, who are unable to appreciate the science, he affords a subject of merriment; *le fou* is the name by which he is commonly known."[4]

From such evidence would be drawn the conclusion that Nuttall had no capacity for sociability. It bears remembering, therefore, that anyone with intense professional preoccupations will likely be remembered as unfriendly by those infrequently absorbed by anything. The later record will show that Nuttall did have close friends, William J. Hooker among them; and he would offer considerable friendly assistance to William Gambel.

Bradbury left the company of the Astorians and Nuttall in the vicinity of the Arikara villages in South Dakota, wandering northward to the Mandan villages in North Dakota. In the fall, he returned to Saint Louis, then proceeded to New Orleans. From there, he shipped his plant collections to Liverpool, but remained in the United States until the end of the War of 1812. Frederick Pursh, still preparing his *Flora Americae Septentrionalis,* took advantage of Bradbury's absence. Visiting Liverpool, he was given access to the Bradbury collection and, apparently without a qualm, published what he thought to be the most important of the plants. Bradbury only discovered what had happened after his return to England following the war. The incident may explain why he never resumed professional plant collecting. He did publish a journal, *Travels in the Interior of America in the Years 1809, 1810, 1811* (1817) that has been of interest to historians of the Louisiana Territory, but in which references to Nuttall are few.[5]

Nuttall, meanwhile, had remained with the Astorians until they reached the Mandan post of the Missouri Fur Company. He spent the summer of 1811 botanizing, sometimes walking alone many miles from the post; but there is no evidence he explored as far west as Montana. In the fall, he returned to Saint Louis, from where, according to the terms of his contract with Barton, he was required to return by land to Philadelphia. Instead, he took his baggage by water to New Orleans. From there he shipped his herbarium specimens, seeds, and the notes of his journey as required, evidently convinced that he had fulfilled his contractual obligations. Then, as war seemed imminent between Britain and the United States, he took advantage of a British ship in New Orleans about to sail for Liverpool and returned to Britain.[6]

Barton was furious that Nuttall had not returned overland, revealing inadvertently his anticipated dependence on Nuttall to describe and name the plants. His irritation would no doubt have been even greater had he known that Nuttall had taken a large duplicate collection with him to England, including seeds, a possibility obviously not anticipated at the time the contract had been designed and, thus, not a technical violation of it.

Francis W. Pennell, who was curator of the herbarium of the Academy of Natural Sciences in Philadelphia from 1921 to 1952, and who made repeated visits to the Rocky Mountain region, had a pronounced interest in Thomas Nuttall because of those connections. Pennell suspected that Nuttall's reason for not returning to Barton's employment was more complicated than the one given—that a sense of the approaching war recommended a return to Britain. By concentrating so heavily on plant collection, Nuttall had deviated from Barton's instructions and might anticipate recrimination as a consequence.[7]

The very fact that Nuttall, once on his own and in the field, dedicated his energy to the flora suggests an impending declaration of independence—a growing confidence that his powers of observation greatly surpassed those of his employer, and that a return to Philadelphia to labor for the greater glory of Benjamin Smith Barton made no sense. Nuttall could argue that he had fulfilled his contractual obligations by sending the plant material and journal to Barton; and, in order to keep faith with that contract, Nuttall refrained from publishing anything in England based on the duplicates. To be sure, much of what he had collected for Barton soon appeared in Pursh's flora (1814), albeit derived from other sources. Nuttall had given some duplicates to A. B. Lambert, quite unaware that Pursh would see them. Nuttall ultimately recognized that Pursh had seen, and published as his own, some of the plants given to Lambert. One was *Viola nuttallii* Pursh 1:174, a plant that had not been in Lewis's collection.[8] As Nuttall had learned in Philadelphia of Pursh's tactics, he had avoided Pursh in England and was angered that his precaution had been circumvented.

The war with Britain ended indecisively at the end of 1814, offering Nuttall the opportunity to return to the United States in 1815, the exact date being unclear. The death of Benjamin Smith Barton in December of 1815 opened the way for Nuttall to publish, as Barton had accomplished nothing with the material sent to him. In the preface to his two-volume *Genera of North American Plants,* published in Philadelphia in 1818, Nuttall remarked that the work was the result of *personal collections and observations.* The remark reflected not only his annoyance at the theft of some of his plants, but drew for the first time the line separating the field collector from the closet-botanist; he would return to this distinction later, in the matter of his Rocky Mountain collections. Nuttall took to the field again in 1819 and 1820, exploring up the Arkansas River, but no farther west than eastern Oklahoma, gathering material for a flora of the Territory of Arkansas. Such activities led to his appointment to Harvard in 1823.[9]

William Dandridge Peck, who had held the Harvard professorship in natural history without notable distinction, died in 1822. The administrators of Harvard, faced with a declining budget for the maintenance of the botanic garden, met the crisis by leaving Peck's chair vacant and appointing Nuttall simply as curator of the garden at a small salary. This gave the college a man of outstanding experience in botany (and considerable knowledge of ornithology) for the mediocre income of about five hundred dollars a year.

Several years after his appointment, Nuttall offered to provide some instruction in natural history as a mere instructor, to be recompensed only by the tuition paid by students seeking instruction in natural history. This gave Harvard a distinguished scholar performing a professor's duties at a bargain rate of little more than seven hundred dollars a year.[10] As that teaching situation occupied very limited time, Nuttall was free to make frequent trips into the field, which contributed to his failure to become active in the Cambridge community. Such an ardent emphasis on research will inevitably provoke criticism from those who engage in more trivial pursuits to escape the rigors of teaching and scholarship; it also may well be that Nuttall, after long periods of self-reliance in the field, had come to feel ill at ease to some degree in settlements.

Despite his alleged unsociability, Nuttall had become a friend of Nathaniel J. Wyeth (1802–1856), a young Cambridge businessman of ability and ambition who had shown no interest in going to college. In 1831, Wyeth began to organize a trading company meant to exploit the salmon and fur trade in the Oregon Territory. Nuttall, who saw Wyeth as a potential plant collector in the West, apparently encouraged the project.

Wyeth's initial westward trip, in 1832, was the first expedition to go from the lower Missouri to the lower Columbia by the route that came to be known as the Oregon Trail. He reached Fort Vancouver on 29 October 1832. Plant collecting was limited to the return trip, which began on 3 February 1833. Wyeth proceeded initially toward Spokane House and Fort Coville in eastern Washington, and by mid-April he was on Clark Fork. The latter receives water from both the Flathead and the Bitterroot Rivers in Montana, and Wyeth—and later Nuttall—would always refer to all three streams as the Flathead, thus confusing not only collection sites but dates as well.

We may assume that Wyeth's collecting for Nuttall began on Clark Fork in late April 1833, and that the first collection made across the Continental Divide in the Missouri system occurred on 27 May 1833. Wyeth then turned southward toward the Snake Valley and was on Henry's Fork on 7 July 1833. From there he crossed the mountains into the valley of the Green River in Wyoming. Although he next went over South Pass, he did not proceed to the Sweetwater River route, but instead turned northward along the base of the Wind River Range to reach the Big Horn River, following it downstream to reach the Yellowstone and ultimately the Missouri.

Nuttall was delighted to find Wyeth's collection well preserved, including 112 species, of which he thought about fifty would be new. The commercial aspects of Wyeth's venture had not been successful, leaving him determined to make a second trip; and, as Nuttall worked up his plants for a paper to be presented before the Academy of Natural Sciences early in 1834 in Philadelphia, his passion to accompany Wyeth on a second trip intensified.[11]

Since John Torrey had published an American edition of John Lindley's *Introduction to the Natural System* in 1831, Nuttall was free to use the natural system, which he had not been in 1818. Among the twenty-six new species he published in 1834 was the type-species for a new genus to honor the collector, *Wyethia*. Because of imprecision in the citation of collection dates and sites, the lists below reflect only the probable watershed:[12]

Sources of the Columbia

Delphinium bicolor Nutt. 7:6
Nasturtium linifolium Nutt. 7:12→*Schoencrambe linifolia* (Nutt.) Greene
Streptanthus sagittatus Nutt. 7:12→*Thelypodium sagittatus* (Nutt.) Endl. in Walpers
Eulophus ambiguous Nutt. 7:27→*Lomatium ambiguum* (Nutt.) Coult. & Rose
Cymopteris glaucus Nutt. 7:28
Crepsis occidentalis Nutt. 7:29
Chrysopsis acaulis Nutt. 7:33→*Stenotus acaulis* (Nutt.) Nutt. 1841
Achillea lanulosa Nutt. 7:36→*Achillea millefolium* L. var. *lanulosa* (Nutt.) Piper
Helianthus uniflorus Nutt. 7:37→*Helianthella uniflora* (Nutt.) T & G.
Espeletia amplexicaulis Nutt. 7:38→*Wyethia amplexicaulis* (Nutt.) Nutt. 1840
Wyethia helianthoides Nutt. 7:40. Type species.
Phlox caespitosa Nutt. 7:41
Pulmonaria oblongifolia Nutt. 7:43→*Mertensia oblongifolia* (Nutt.) G. Don
Rachelia patens Nutt. 7:44→*Hackelia patens* (Nutt.) Johnst.
Penstemon pumilus Nutt. 7:46
Euchroma angustifolia Nutt. 7:46→*Castilleja angustifolia* (Nutt.) G. Don
Rumex paucifolius Nutt. 7:49
Eriogonum caespitosum Nutt. 7:50
Fritellaria atropurpurea Nutt. 7:54
Helonias paniculata Nutt. 7:57→*Zigadenus paniculatus* (Nutt.) S. Wats.

Sources of the Missouri

Oxytropis lagopus Nutt. 7:17
Astragalus mortoni Nutt. 7:19→*Astragalus canadensis* L. var. *mortoni* (Nutt.) S. Wats.
Solidago missouriensis Nutt. 7:32
Phlox muscoides Nutt. 7:42
Eriogonum heracleoides Nutt. 7:49
Eriogonum ovalifolium Nutt. 7:50

When Nuttall published Wyeth's new species in 1834, he was forty-eight and had had twenty-four years of field experience in North America. John Torrey of Columbia, ten years Nuttall's junior, had had the advantage of medical training, but nothing comparable to Nuttall's field experience. Asa Gray, only twenty-four at that point, also had a medical degree and was without doubt intellectually gifted. None of the three had had, in short, the specialized professional training that we would today consider a prerequisite for a career in botany, or that could be cited as a claim to authority. Torrey, recognizing Gray's promise, and having just begun work toward an immense flora of North America, recruited Gray as a partner in the project; and Gray lived for a time in Torrey's home in New York, becoming virtually a member of the family.

Gray's character clearly emerges in Dupree's biography: he was ambitious, self-confident, and insensitive to the achievements of others, at least in his early years. At the age of twenty-five, he wrote to a friend, "If I . . . pursue Botany un-divided for a little time I shall (entre nous) be soon the best botanist in the coun-try."[13] Torrey's criticism of Nuttall, in letters to William Hooker, began only af-ter the publication of Wyeth's plants, the letters evidently a reflection of Gray's aggressive personality. Gray and Torrey could hardly have been indifferent to the emergence of a publishing botanist whose firsthand experience with the flora of North America clearly surpassed their own. The news that Nuttall would ac-company Wyeth on a second trip beginning in 1834 amounted to a challenge to Gray's pretensions, about which Nuttall was entirely unaware.

All accounts of the Nuttall-Wyeth trip have relied heavily, if not wholly, on the journal kept during the trip by John Kirk Townsend (1809–1851), and later published. Townsend, an ornithologist of Philadelphia, was only twenty-four at the time Nuttall invited him to join the Wyeth expedition. He had been elected to the Academy of Natural Sciences the year before, and both the academy and the American Philosophical Society contributed a hundred dollars to his trip in anticipation of the collections he would make for them, one specimen of each object collected.[14] The journal has been valuable primarily for its geographical information, not as a record of Nuttall's collections. The second volume of Townsend's journal was lost on 19 July 1834 when he crossed the Green River in western Wyoming in unexpectedly deep water. It contained material begin-ning with the party's arrival at the Black Hills (the Laramie Mountains today) in early June. Townsend indicated that he was indebted to the kindness of his companion and friend, Professor Nuttall, for supplying, in great measure, the deficiency occasioned by the loss. Nuttall, of course, was keeping records through his collections, but he never published a journal.[15]

In preparation for the trip, Nuttall had believed he must offer his resignation from Harvard, but hinted he would accept a two-year leave of absence. The res-ignation was accepted with an alacrity suggesting little comprehension of the treasure Nuttall was. That lack of appreciation may explain why he never sought academic employment again, but the matter is unclear.

Nuttall and Townsend joined Wyeth in Saint Louis, from there taking a steamboat to Independence, which had become the point of departure for both the Santa Fe and Oregon Trails. As in the previous year, Wyeth's destination was Fort Vancouver. The party was approaching Wyoming along the North Platte near the present site of Scottsbluff on 28 May 1834. Townsend made the following note:

> The road was very uneven and difficult, winding from amongst in-numerable mounds six to eight feet in height, . . . and in the narrow passages, flowers of every hue were growing. It was a most enchant-ing sight; even the men noticed it, and more than one of our matter-of-fact people exclaimed, *beautiful, beautiful!* Mr. N. was here in his glory. He rode on ahead of the company, and cleared the passages with a trembling and eager hand, looking anxiously back at the ap-proaching party, as though he feared it would come ere he had fin-ished, and tread his lovely prizes under foot.[16]

On 31 May 1834, as the party approached the mouth of the Laramie River along the North Platte, Townsend added the observation: "None but a natural-ist can appreciate a naturalist's feeling—his delight amounting to ecstasy—when a specimen he has never before seen, meets his eye, and the sorrow and grief which he feels when he is compelled to tear himself from a spot abounding with all that he has anxiously and unremittingly sought for."[17]

During the first week of June, the party crossed the Laramie Mountains and headed for Red Buttes, just north of the present Alcova on the North Platte. Both *Polemonium viscosum* Nutt. 1848 and *Sphaeromeria capitata* Nutt. 1841→*Tanace-tum capitatum* (Nutt.) T. & G. 1843 were collected in that area on 7 June 1834. Two days later, the party camped on the Sweetwater by Independence Rock. From there, it traveled westward up the valley of the Sweetwater, across South Pass toward the Sandy River, reaching the Green River on 19 June 1834. Townsend crossed the river somewhat below where the remainder of the party had forded easily, and his horse slipped into deep water. His coat, loose on the back of his saddle, was swept away. It contained his pocket compass and the second volume of his journal—field notes beginning at the Laramie Mountains of great importance to him.[18]

On 22 June 1834, the party made camp on the Green adjacent to the tenth rendezvous of the fur trade. This rendezvous was a motley assembly of Indians (Nez Percé, Bannock, and Shoshone), French Canadians, and half-breeds, as well as parties led by such mountain men as William Lewis Sublette and Thomas Fitzpatrick. Debilitated after his accident in the river, and a Pennsylva-nia Quaker to boot, Townsend was ill disposed toward the assembled company:

> [T]hese people, with their obstreperous mirth, their whooping, and howling, and quarrelling, added to the mounted Indians, who are constantly dashing into and through our camp, yelling like fiends,

the barking and baying of savage wolf-dogs, and the incessant crack-
ing of rifles and carbines, render our camp a perfect bedlam. . . . I am
confined closely to the tent with illness, and am compelled all day to
listen to the hiccoughing jargon of drunken traders, the *sacré* and
foutre of Frenchmen run wild, and the swearing and screaming of our
own men, who are scarcely less savage than the rest, being heated by
the detestable liquor which circulated freely among them.[19]

The concept of noble savagery has rarely been better deflated. Not until 30
June was Townsend able to remove himself from such company and wander
into the lovely country beyond the campsite to appreciate the great number of
large trout, and some grayling and whitefish, that inhabited the Green River.
They were easily taken on a hook, as the fish were not shy. Complete emanci-
pation came only on 2 July 1834, when the Wyeth party decamped; they spent
two days ascending Ham's Fork. They then turned northwestward until they
reached a branch of the Bear River. Although they were close to Utah, they did
not enter that state, but rather continued into Bear Lake County, Idaho, bound
for the Snake River.[20]

Between 8 and 10 July 1834, the men camped at Soda Springs, which they
called Beer Springs, and where Nuttall collected *Salix branchycarpa* Nutt. 1842.
The horses refreshed, on 15 July 1834 the party moved on to the Snake River,
near which Wyeth selected a site for a trading post, Fort Hall. The party remained there until 6 August, when the fort was completed. *Salix melanopsis*
Nutt. 1843 was collected at that location. Some have pronounced this to be a
subspecies of *Salix exigua* Nutt. 1843, which Nuttall later collected in Oregon;
but Robert Dorn regards it as a good species.

West of Fort Hall, the terrain became exceedingly difficult, especially the passage through the Salmon River Mountains. Two of Nuttall's species came from
near Hyndman Peak: *Aster integrifolius* Nutt. 1840 and *Ledum glandulosum* Nutt.
1843. From Hyndman Peak the party descended to the Camas Prairie,[21] "so
called," Townsend noted:

> from a vast abundance of this esculent root which it produces [*Camas-
> sia quamash* (Pursh) Greene]. We encamped here . . . and all hands took
> their kettles and scattered over the prairie to dig a mess of kamas. We
> were, of course, eminently successful, and were furnished thereby with
> an excellent and wholesome meal. . . . There are several other kinds of
> bulbous and tuburous [*sic*] roots, growing in these plains, which are
> eaten by the Indians, after undergoing a certain process of fermentation
> or baking. Among these, that which is most esteemed, is the white or
> biscuit root, the *Racine blanc* of the Canadians, *Eulophus ambiguous* of
> Nuttall.[→*Lomatium ambiguum* (Nutt.) Coult. & Rose]."[22]

Once the Wyeth party had reached the main streams of the Columbia valley, they were in territory already crossed by Lewis and Clark, and by Wyeth the previous year; but Nuttall was the first collector to cross the width of Wyoming and Idaho. Far more notable was the extreme energy he put into exploration and collection. Townsend was aware of its exceptionality and was moved to preserve an illustration of it.

On 12 September 1834, several days before the expedition reached Fort Vancouver, the party hired canoes to pass the Dalles on the Columbia River. They encountered a gale that whipped up waves, soaking their baggage and forcing a return to shore. Townsend wrote:

> Mr. N's large and beautiful collection of new and rare plants was considerably injured by the wetting it received; he has been constantly engaged since we landed yesterday, in opening and drying them. In this task he exhibits a degree of patience and perseverance which is truly astonishing; sitting on the ground, and steaming over the enormous fire, for hours together, drying the papers, and re-arranging the whole collection, specimen by specimen, while the great drops of perspiration roll unheeded from his brow.
>
> Throughout the whole of our long journey, I have had constantly to admire the ardor and perfect indefatigability with which he has devoted himself to the grand object of his tour. No difficulty, no danger, no fatigue has ever daunted him, and he finds his rich reward in the addition of nearly a thousand new species of American plants, which he has been enabled to make to the already teeming flora of our vast continent.[23]

The observation may account for the field collectors' viewing of the closet-botanists as pampered, second-class colleagues.

The Wyeth party reached Fort Vancouver on 16 September 1834. It was not Nuttall's intention to return over land with Wyeth; his Rocky Mountain exploration had been completed. While he remained in the Oregon area for some months, long enough to learn that Wyeth's enterprise was in trouble, he seized the opportunity to sail to the Hawaiian Islands early in 1835. From there, he extended his tour to California, finally taking ship from San Diego to Boston via Cape Horn. He reached Boston Harbor on 20 September 1836, his destination being the Academy of Natural Sciences in Philadelphia.

Townsend, meanwhile, having accompanied Nuttall to the Hawaiian Islands, returned to Fort Vancouver and went into the field again in the spring and summer of 1836. Townsend had, by then, become a friend of Dr. William Fraser Tolmie, a naturalist who was serving as a company surgeon for the Hudson's Bay Company. In fact, Townsend even briefly took charge of Tolmie's hospital (as he was a doctor of science) during Tolmie's absence. This association in Fort Vancouver explains why Townsend, when he reached Fort Walla Walla at the end of August in 1836, anticipated meeting John McLeod there.

McLeod (1788–1849), primarily a fur trader for the Hudson's Bay Company, had been stationed in the Columbia River area at least since 1831 and was a friend of Dr. Tolmie. McLeod and Townsend met at Walla Walla and returned to Fort Vancouver in six days by boat. Dr. Tolmie was eager to use McLeod as a plant collector, and it is probable that Townsend gave McLeod some instruction during the winter of 1836–1837 to enable him to collect for Tolmie, though this has to be inferred from McLeod's subsequent collections.[24]

When Asa Gray visited William J. Hooker at the end of 1838, he saw specimens that had been collected by McLeod. They had been beautifully preserved by a collector who was obviously knowledgeable, yet McLeod was an obscure figure. The specimens in question had been collected during the summer of 1837 when McLeod traveled from Fort Vancouver to reach the thirteenth annual rendezvous of the fur trade, held on the Green River twelve miles south of Horse Creek in central Sublette County, Wyoming.

McLeod's precise route remains unclear; but it is known that he went up the Columbia from Fort Vancouver to Fort Walla Walla; then southeast across northeastern Oregon to reach Fort Boisé. He must then have ascended the Snake River for some distance before turning southeast again to cross the southeastern corner of Idaho. His plant records showed that he had gone up the Bear River, then passed between Henry's Fork and Smith's Fork, thus crossing Lincoln County in Wyoming to reach the Green River. The plants came from four general locations: the Blue Mountains of northeastern Oregon, the Snake River Valley, southwestern Idaho, and the Wind River Mountains of western Wyoming.[25]

After McLeod's specimens—seventy-seven of them—were delivered to Dr. Tolmie, they were forwarded to William Hooker and George Arnott Walker-Arnott at Kew. When the new species among them were published, they were attributed to Tolmie:[26]

Chaenactis stevioides Hook. & Arn. 353. 1839. Snake Country
Tetradymia spinosa Hook. & Arn. 360. 1839. Snake Country
Lobelia carnosula Hook. & Arn. 379. 1839→Porterella carnosula (H. & A.)
  Torr. 1872. Blackfoot River (Fort Hall)
Orthocarpus tolmiei Hook. & Arn. 379. 1839. Between Henry's and Smith's Rivers
Grayia polycaloides Hook. & Arn. 388. 1839. Snake Country. New
  genus→Grayia spinosa (Hook.) Maq. In DC. (In 1838, Gray had been uncertain as to whether this species was a Chenopodium.)

Allium tolmiei Baker ex. Wats. (1879) had originally been published by Hooker, Fl. Bor. Am. 2:185. 1839, simply as variety Beta of Allium douglasii Hook. from the Snake River country. It is known today in Idaho County, Idaho. John Gilbert

Baker was contemporary with George Bentham and Joseph Dalton Hooker in the Kew community of English botanists.

Having brought back to Philadelphia not only plants, but shells and fauna specimens as well, Nuttall had much to occupy his time. When he learned that Torrey had recently read a paper in New York on the Cyperaceae,[27] it made sense for Nuttall to turn over all the specimens in that family he had brought back. He notified Torrey that he would send them as soon as he could sort them out, and that he would be more than happy to accept any names Torrey might choose for new species among them. The gesture was generous, and he would be poorly repaid for it.

In the summer of 1837, Nuttall paid a visit to New York, where he learned firsthand of the planned collaboration of Torrey and Gray on a flora of North America, which they would undertake despite not having specimens from a vast part of the continent. Given Nuttall's extensive collections from substantial regions considerably west of the Hudson and the Charles, it once again made sense for him to arrange for the publication of his many new species within the new flora of North America. They were to be described by him and published under his own name.

As Jeannette Graustein observed some years ago, that arrangement was curious, which is to say, quite inconsistent with Torrey's recently expressed opinion that Nuttall had become too *rusty* in botany to work up his material to current standards in the field, and that the library facilities in Philadelphia were deficient in recent botanical works. Philadelphia had been unquestionably preeminent earlier in the century, but the facilities in both New York and Cambridge had much improved.[28]

There is good reason to believe that Asa Gray, aggressive, ambitious, and confident, if originally the junior partner in the collaboration with Torrey, quickly became the dominant personality, with Torrey reflecting Gray's views. Gray increasingly assumed the responsibility for recruiting American botanists to make plant contributions for the *Flora*. Gray's visit to Europe in 1838, inaugurating a friendship with Sir William Hooker and George Bentham, opened a source of taxonomic advice of the first rank. Gray was also able to borrow large numbers of North American specimens from Hooker's herbarium. Hunter Dupree would calculate that, by 1840, seventy-eight Americans had sent plants to Gray from their particular regions, virtually all of them having studied botany as amateurs, and usually sending along useful notes and observations. Plants from the Rocky Mountain region were sent by only two of those seventy-eight—Edwin James and Nuttall.[29]

Only someone with Gray's immense capacity for work could have coped with such an avalanche; this capacity would bring him the leading position in American botany. But any reader of Dupree's biography of Gray will come to sense that, beyond his taxonomic authority, Gray meant to be the administrator of American botany, with all others being respectfully subservient. The reemergence of Nuttall, with a record of prior publication and an impressive collection of plants from the West, had to be a threat to all of Gray's pretensions. Probably both Torrey and Gray were apprehensive about Nuttall's genuine ability, and the result was the beginning of a derogatory campaign carried on especially by Gray, becoming a habit of which he was perhaps not fully conscious.[30]

When Nuttall began to work up his plants after his return in 1836, he found himself handicapped by the fact that he had passed through the Rocky Mountains only once. His specimens frequently showed only one stage of development; flower and fruit were not always both evident. Specimens taken from one area could differ from specimens taken from another area, raising questions about splitting and varieties. As a consequence, Nuttall withheld a good number of his species, not submitting them to Torrey and Gray for publication until more conclusive study could be undertaken, a further hint that Nuttall was interested in advancing science rather than himself.

The first volume of the *Flora of North America* was published in 1838 and 1840. Only when the second section appeared in June of 1840 did Nuttall discover, to his great annoyance, that his conclusions had sometimes been modified by Torrey and Gray.[31] The treatment of his plants fell into three separate categories:

1. His own name and description were preserved and quoted; a treatment henceforth referred to as *in T. & G.* Examples:

> *Astragalus argophyllus* Nutt. in T. & G. 1:331. 1838
> *Astragalus plattensis* Nutt. in T. & G. 1:332. 1838
> *Epilobium suffruticosum* Nutt. in T. & G. 1:488. 1840
> *Oxytropis multiceps* Nutt. in T. & G. 1:341. 1838
> *Oxytropis sericea* Nutt. in T. & G. 1:339. 1838

2. His own name was retained, but the description revised; a treatment henceforth referred to as *ex T. & G.* Examples:

> *Epilobium paniculatum* Nutt. ex T. & G. 1:490. 1838
> *Heuchera parvifolia* Nutt. ex T. & G. 1:442. 1840

3. His own description was preserved, but the name changed, as in *Phellopterus montanus* Nutt., published as *Cymopterus montana* (Nutt.) T. & G. 1:624. 1840.

This transfer is cited in particular because, in its small way, it illustrates what would become a widening gulf separating the Eastern establishment from the Western botanical pioneers. *Phellopterus* happened to be one of Nuttall's own genera. Its principal segregating feature was the presence of a pseudoscape. Plants with otherwise similar characters, but no pseudoscape, were placed in *Cymopterus,* a genus published by Samuel Constantine Rafinesque.

Even though that basis for segregation is no longer recognized, we can understand that the character could have been the basis for a legitimate segregation. Indeed, despite Torrey and Gray, we find that both P. A. Rydberg and Aven Nelson still recognized that segregation after the turn of the twentieth century. Asa Gray's decision could be seen not only as arbitrary, but as disrespecting Nuttall's botanical judgment and reliability, especially as it was made without any prior consultation with Nuttall. In the larger context, the decision could be seen as evidence of Gray's belief that Western field-workers must ultimately subject their findings to the definitive authority of Asa Gray.

The upshot was that Nuttall declined to submit any further plants for publication by Torrey and Gray. He finished working up his own species in the Compositae in 1840 and read his paper on them in two parts to the American Philosophical Society on 2 October and 18 December 1840. They were then published in 1840–1841. Among the sixty-four new genera in the Compositae proposed, only those prominent in the Rocky Mountains are cited below.[32]

To begin with, Nuttall published six species whose new genus Asa Gray would not challenge:

Balsamoriza incana Nutt. 7:350. 1840
Chrysothamnus visidiflorus Nutt. 7:324. 1840
Lagophylla ramosissima Nutt. 7:391. 1841
Stephanomeria runcinata Nutt. 7:428. 1841
Psilocarphus brevissimus Nutt. 7:340. 1840
Wyethia amplexicaulus Nutt. 7:352. 1840

Secondly, Nuttall published some species whose new genus would be challenged by Gray or, later, by others. The current status of each species is starred for comparative reference:

1. *Ericameria resinosa* Nutt. 7:319. 1841
   Haplopappus resinosus (Nutt.) Gray. 1876
2. *Eriocarpum grindelioides* Nutt. 7:321. 1841
   Haplopappus nuttallii T. & G. 1842
   Machaeranthera grindelioides (Nutt.) Shinners. 1950
3. *Eucephalus glaucus* Nutt. 7:299. 1841
   Aster glaucus T. & G. 1841
   Aster glaucodes S. F. Blake. 1922
4. *Macronema suffruticosa* Nutt. 7:322. 1841
   Haplopappus suffruticosus (Nutt.) Gray. 1865
   Ericameria suffruticosa (Nutt.) G. Nesom. 1990
5. *Homopappas inuloides* Nutt. 7:333. 1841
   Haplopappus uniflorus (Hook.) T. & G. 1842
   Pyrrocoma uniflora (Hook.) E. L. Greene. 1894

6. *Euthamia occidentalis* Nutt. 7:326. 1841
   Solidago occidentalis T. & G. 1842
7. *Picrothamnus desertorum* Nutt. 7:417. 1841
   Artemisia spinescens Eat. 1871
8. *Stenotus acaulis* Nutt. 7:334. 1841
   Haplopappus acaulis (Nutt.) A. Gray. 1868
9. *Xylorhiza glabriuscula* Nutt. 7:297. 1841
   Aster glabriusculus (Nutt.) T. & G. 1841
   Machaeranthera glabriuscula (Nutt.) Cronq. & D. D. Keck. 1957

The current status, as starred above, will not accord with those who continue to claim the validity of the lumpy genus, *Haplopappus* Cass. For the rest, the disputes between Gray and Nuttall, especially regarding the Compositae, have been increasingly resolved in Nuttall's favor. Even *Picrothamnus* Nutt. has boasted die-hard adherents into the twentieth century: P. A. Rydberg and W. A. Weber.

In fairness to Gray, it must not be forgotten that, at the time he was working on the Compositae in preparation for the *Flora of North America,* he doubtless knew that bibliography better than Nuttall. But, as for Western plants, he had seen only those submitted to Torrey by Edwin James, plus specimens he had seen in Europe. Not only were Nuttall's collections far more important; but, as Pennell pointed out in 1936, Nuttall, as a result of his fieldwork, had grasped the remarkable degree of endemism in western North America, something that Gray had not recognized.

Nuttall, no doubt, made errors, and it seems evident that he failed to acknowledge formally some corrections he made at Gray's suggestion, most likely during Gray's visit to Philadelphia in November of 1840. The omission was highly irritating to Gray. But it is even more probable that Nuttall failed to accept numerous other suggestions for correction, encouraging Gray to suspect Nuttall's competence. It would not be the last time that an innovative explorer of the Rocky Mountains would run afoul of Gray's insistence on being regarded the definitive authority.[33]

Before leaving the matter of the Compositae, here is a brief list of familiar Rocky Mountain composites that were also published in the *Transactions* of the American Philosophical Society:

Antennaria parvifolia Nutt. 7:406. 1841
Artemisia tridentata Nutt. 7:398. 1841
Aster campestris Nutt. 7:293. 1840
Circium canescens Nutt. 7:410. 1841
Crepis acuminata Nutt. 7:437. 1841
Erigeron caespitosus Nutt. 7:307. 1840
Helianthus pumilus Nutt. 7:366. 1841

Rudbeckia occidentalis Nutt. 7:355. 1840
Senecio plattensis Nutt. 7:413. 1841
Solidago nana Nutt. 7:327. 1840
Townsendia incana Nutt. 7:305. 1840

It might be supposed that Nuttall's decision to return to England in late 1841 was a response to irritation resulting from Asa Gray's sniping. In fact, he had been conscious for some time that he was dissipating his private means for the advancement of science, never having attracted the patronage that scholarship usually requires. The latter complaint, made to Gray, enabled Gray to depict Nuttall as a man motivated by an *amor pecuniae*.[34] When Nuttall became the beneficiary of an inheritance, which he could only receive if he returned to live primarily in England, he concluded he had no alternative but to return to his native land; but he did so with the greatest reluctance.[35]

A year later, 29 October 1842, Nuttall told Hooker that he had not heard from either Torrey or Gray since his arrival in England; but that he could not imagine that they had been able to go much farther with their great project. Their *Flora of North America,* in fact, did not go beyond the second volume (1843), concluding with the Compositae, perhaps a tacit admission that the project had been premature. It would not be resumed until 1878, when Gray began publication of his *Synoptical Flora of North America.*

Meanwhile, when plants were brought back by the Wilkes expedition in 1842, Hooker remarked to Gray that, now that Nuttall had returned to England, there was no one left in America but Torrey and Gray to publish the plants. Gray let it be known that he thought Nuttall "extremely unfit for such an undertaking" (he would take it on himself), and he began to worry that Nuttall just might reappear to apply for the task. Gray seems never to have recognized that Sir William had maintained a high opinion of Nuttall, or that no one else but Gray had a low opinion of Nuttall's work. Therein lies the danger of either speaking or publishing *ex cathedra.* Gray would never cease trying to destroy Nuttall's reputation; but it remains possible today to regard Nuttall as having been more on the taxonomic frontier than Gray—like Hooker himself and Candolle.[36]

Despite Nuttall's removal to England, he retained a little-known link with American fieldwork in the person of William Gambel (1821–1849). The original spelling of the name had been Gamble. Left fatherless in 1832, the boy had altered the spelling of his name, evidently sensitive about its implications. Philadelphia-born, Gambel early showed an interest in the study of the natural sciences. Nuttall seems to have begun tutoring him around 1838 and allowed him to go along on field trips. It may be deduced that Nuttall was preparing Gambel to be a collaborator; in March 1841, Gambel, in his twenty-first year, started for the West as a collector for Nuttall.

At Independence, Missouri, Gambel joined a caravan of Santa Fe traders, which enabled him to reach the Rio Grande valley for collecting that July and

August. In September, he joined another party leaving northern New Mexico for California, where he began collecting in November. That was the moment of Nuttall's obligatory return to England, and he never received a substantial shipment of plants sent from New Mexico. Gambel's actual itinerary remains obscure, as even the place names for surviving collections are imprecise and uncertain.

In the summer of 1845, Gambel notified Nuttall that he was in Boston expecting to study for a medical doctorate, and that his main collection of plants would be sent to England. Nuttall received them sometime after March of 1846. He still had some unpublished western specimens of his own to be studied in comparison to the nearly 350 Gambel had sent to him. The upshot was that about 20 percent of the nearly one hundred species included in the resulting article were probably Nuttall's own, despite the title attributing all of them to Gambel.[37]

Many of the plants published, whether Gambel's or Nuttall's, were from California. Only seven of them were collected within the Rocky Mountain region. Those from northern New Mexico were clearly Gambel's, the remaining three evidently Nuttall's. Such figures suggest the magnitude of the loss when the first shipment went astray.

> *Phlox bryoides* Nutt. 1:153. 1848. Continental Divide, RM→*Phlox muscoides* Nutt. 1834
> *Phlox nana* Nutt. 1:153. 1848. Near Santa Fe
> *Polemonium viscosum* Nutt. 1:154. 1848. Sources of the Platte, RM
> *Gilia pumila* Nutt. 1:156. 1848. Near mountains on the Platte, RM→*Ipomopsis pumila* (Nutt.) V. Grant
> *Quercus gambelii* Nutt. 1:179. 1848. Along the Rio Grande
> *Orobanche multiflora* Nutt. 1:179. 1848. Along the Rio Grande→*Orobanche ludoviciana* Nutt. ssp. *multiflora* (Nutt.) Collins
> *Monarda pectinata* Nutt. 1:182. 1848. Near Santa Fe

To the extent that Gambel's name is remembered at all today, it is more likely to be associated with birds; for Nuttall's own secondary interest in ornithology had been reborn in Gambel. Our most beautiful quail, *Callipepla gambelii*, was among the specimens brought back to the Academy of Natural Sciences of Philadelphia from Gambel's western trip, as was the familiar mountain chickadee, *Parus gambelii*.[38]

After completing his medical degree in 1849, Gambel departed for a second time, meaning to establish a permanent residence in California for the practice of medicine. The party he accompanied was guided across the Humboldt Desert in Nevada with disastrous consequences, after which the survivors struggled across the Sierra Nevada in early winter. West of the mountains, the party encountered some placer miners in the Feather River suffering from typhoid fever.

Despite his own debilitated condition, Gambel attempted to treat them. He was easily infected and died on 13 November 1849 at the age of twenty-eight.[39]

Nuttall outlived his young friend by ten years. His plant specimens were left in three major locations: the Academy of Natural Sciences of Philadelphia, the Botanic Gardens at Kew, and the British Museum.[40] Stories of Nuttall's aloofness have also remained: he is portrayed as a man shy, unsociable, and eccentric because of his failure to become part of the Cambridge community during his early years at Harvard. The pittance paid to him by Harvard, to be sure, was hardly a welcoming gesture. It seems more likely that his early, lengthy field trips produced a self-reliance that equipped him poorly to cope with people uninterested in the natural sciences, for whom he became the reserved Englishman. His readiness to take on the young William Gambel as a student, and his later warm friendships within the British botanical and horticultural communities, suggest a highly selective sociability, not a lack thereof. Some of the negative impressions were undoubtedly sown through the efforts of Asa Gray over many years.[41]

Robert Dorn, in the first edition of his *Vascular Plants of Wyoming* (1977), dedicated the work to Thomas Nuttall, "first botanist in Wyoming, whose botanical perception and expertise were unmatched by any other American taxonomist of the nineteenth century." That verdict remains tenable.

5

George Engelmann

A LINK BETWEEN EAST AND WEST

George Engelmann (1809–1884) was born in Frankfurt-on-Main, Hesse-Nassau, the eldest of thirteen children. Biographical detail is surprisingly slim for him considering his eventual eminence. Bent on a medical degree, he enrolled at Heidelberg in 1827. His two principal companions and fellow-students were Karl Schimper and Alexander Braun. Schimper, from a botanically inclined family and evidently very gifted, would lay the foundation for the field of phyllotaxis—the study of the arrangement of leaves, or other lateral plant parts, on an axis or stem to define the geometrical principles of such arrangements. For reasons unknown, he prematurely abandoned his promising botanical career. Braun would become a notable cryptogamist, and Engelmann would maintain a correspondence with him until Braun's death in 1877. Louis Agassiz was a member of their circle, further evidence that Engelmann was immersed early in natural science.[1]

It is well known that the German universities became centers of the liberal-nationalist movement after the 1815 settlement disappointed hopes that Prussia would take the lead in bringing liberal-constitutional government to the German world. While it is unclear what active part Engelmann took in the liberal societies organized by students, the Burschenshaften, he was at least sympathetic to their goals. It has been presumed with good reason that the several transfers he made before obtaining his degree, from Heidelberg to Berlin, and then to Würzburg, where he completed his medical degree in 1831, were motivated by political necessity or expedience. His dissertation, published in Frankfurt in 1832, was a morphological study of vegetal monstrosities, a safer topic than political monstrosities.[2]

During the spring and summer of 1832, and again in the company of Braun and Agassiz, Engelmann was in Paris for additional medical and scientific study.

Paris was not only politically liberal, on account of the July Revolution of 1830, but intellectually liberal: the actual home of Georges Cuvier and the spiritual home of Alexander von Humboldt, close friend of Louis-Philippe I. In addition to such attractions, an even greater one came to Engelmann's attention that year.

Engelmann had relatives who had settled in Illinois not far from Saint Louis. Several of his other German uncles were eager to investigate investment opportunities in the Mississippi valley. They proposed to engage Georges as their agent to find suitable investments. If the details of the arrangement remain obscure, it may be supposed that Engelmann responded favorably to the opportunity to visit not only a great haven for liberals, but what for him was a vast botanical frontier; and he did sail for Baltimore in the fall of 1832. Engelmann would never claim that his subsequent searches uncovered suitable properties for investment, but they did yield a substantial collection of plant specimens.

He had found his home, and in 1835 he opened a medical practice in Saint Louis that would support his intellectual interests for the remainder of his life. He was always first and foremost a practicing physician, ultimately with a large clientele, carrying on scientific work during residual hours that otherwise could have been used for rest or recreation. Only in later years was Engelmann free to make exploratory trips to North Carolina, Tennessee, the region of Lake Superior, and into the Rocky Mountains. By 1840, he had become sufficiently prosperous to return to Germany to fulfill a promise of marriage to his cousin. On the return trip, he met Asa Gray, beginning their long friendship and scientific association.[3] Gray's appointment to Harvard in 1842 provided Engelmann a direct link with the resources of Harvard; and, in 1856, he awarded himself a sabbatical year for study in Cambridge.

It is chiefly through his correspondence with Asa Gray that we have a record of Engelmann's campaign to induce Henry Shaw to establish a botanical garden in Saint Louis. Shaw (1800–1889) was a wealthy, bachelor Englishman who retained a fond memory of Kew, but who was not easily parted from money. The foundation of Mr. Shaw's Garden, as it was originally known—now the splendid Missouri Botanical Garden—owed much to Engelmann's persistence, Shaw would also endow a botanical school for Washington University in Saint Louis, with the affiliate library based on Engelmann's personal library.[4]

Although Engelmann was not primarily an explorer, his name became linked to those of the leading explorers of his day. He became a veritable crossroads between East and West, an intermediary between the field and the closet-botanists—a distinguished scholar quietly building a major personal herbarium and library. Asa Gray and Charles Parry were his greatest friends, but his acquaintance with those going west through Saint Louis was unmatched. By sending out explorers to collect, as did Torrey and Gray, Engelmann directed the course of western botanical exploration to a remarkable degree. As a result, he received quantities of plants from collectors. Frémont was really the first to stop in Saint Louis for a visit with Engelmann as part of his preparation for his explorations.[5]

Engelmann's personal collections in the Rocky Mountains were not extensive, and he worked primarily on specimens collected by others. He did visit the Clear Creek country in Colorado in the summer of 1874, by then well-explored Parry country, but did so primarily to study the regional conifers. In 1880, he made a brief stop in Salt Lake City, meeting Marcus E. Jones, and taking the mandatory swim in the Great Salt Lake despite being unable to swim. Engelmann, who was by then markedly obese, waded out too far into the buoyant water, lost his footing, and floated helplessly facedown. He was rescued, and the incident became a treasured part of botanical folklore.[6]

Any reviewer of Engelmann's projects and publications will likely conclude that he was almost exclusively drawn to difficult groups, whether genera or families; and any given interest would be pursued intermittently, of necessity, over a number of years. The parasitic genus *Cuscuta,* largely submontane, was an early interest, studied at least by 1842 and only concluded in 1859, when he had prepared a systematic arrangement of seventy-seven species. (Nearly 170 species are recognized today.) A monograph in English was published in the *Transactions of the St. Louis Academy* in 1860, and a Latin translation in Berlin the same year.

The Cactaceae of the United States was another of Engelmann's sustained interests from the 1840s onward. He had not completed his study at the time of his death in 1884, despite preliminary publications.[7] Some cacti well known in the Rocky Mountain region bear his name:

Echinocactus simpsonii Engelm., *Trans. St. Louis Acad.* 2:197. 1863 → *Pediocactus simpsonii* (Engelm.) Britton & Rose
Echinocactus whipplei Engelm. & Bigelow in Engelm., *Proc. Am. Acad. Arts & Sciences* 3:271. 1856→*Schlerocactus whipplei* (Engelm. & Bigel.) Britt. & Rose
Echinocereus [new genus] *viridiflorus* Engelm. in Wislinzenus, *Mem. Tour. North. Mex.* 91. 1848
Echinocereus coccineus Engelm. in Wislinzenus, *Ibid.* 94. 1848
Echinocereus fendleri Engelm. in Gray, *Pl. fendl.* 50. 1849
Opuntia davisii Engelm. & Bigel. in Engelm., *Ibid.* 3:305. 1856→*Opuntia tunicata* (Lehm.) Link & Otto var., *davisii* (Engelm. & Bigel.) L. Benson
Opuntia phaeacantha Engelm. in Gray., *Mem. Amer. Acad.* ser. 2, 4:52. 1849
Opuntia camanchica Engelm. & Bigel., *Proc. Amer. Acad.* 3:293. 1856→*Opuntia phaeacanthe* (Engelm. in Gray) var. *camanchica* (Engelm. & Bigel.) L. Benson

Even though buffalo grass inhabits the plains and prairies rather than the mountains, found between three and six thousand feet, it is adjacent to the Rocky Mountains along their eastern flank and of regional interest. Engelmann took a special interest in it. Nuttall had recognized buffalo grass and put it in *Sesleria* in 1818. Engelmann transferred it to a new genus of his creation, *Buchloe dactyloides* (Nutt.) Engelm. *Trans. Acad. St. Louis* 1:432. 1859, which still stands as a genus with a single species.

After that novelty, Engelmann gave considerable attention to the Rush family, and his publications of new species were all made within a comparatively short time in the *Transactions of the Academy of St. Louis*. The following plants, known within the Rocky Mountains, comprise less than half the new taxa Engelmann launched within two papers:

Juncus balticus Willd. var. *montanus* Engelm. 2:442. 1866
Juncus parryi Engelm. 2:446. 1866
Juncus hallii Engelm. 2:446. 1866
Juncus vaseyi Engelm. 2:448. 1866
Juncus tenuis Willd. var. *congestus* Engelm. 2:450. 1866
Juncus xiphioides E. Mey. var. *montanus* Engelm. 2:481. 1868→*Juncus ensifolius*
    Wikstr. var. *montanus* (Engelm.) C. L. Hitchc.
Juncus kelloggii Engelm. 2:494. 1868

Engelmann's attraction to difficult oddities made the study of *Agave* and *Yucca* almost inevitable for him. The century plant, *Agave utahensis* Engelm. (1871) is owed to him; as is the Joshua tree, *Yucca brevifolia* Engelm. (1871). Of greater interest were his observations about the pollination of the yuccas. In a paper entitled "Notes on the Genus *Yucca:* Fecundation" (1873), Engelmann proposed that pollination can only take place where the nocturnal moth, *Pronuba yuccasella* Riley, is available. Other insects may visit the flowers without affecting pollination. Thus, many yucca plants remain sterile, notably if they are introduced into Europe.[8]

The conifers were another of Engelmann's continuing interests, and their classification would provoke a rare dispute with Asa Gray, discussed below. A good number of our most familiar Rocky Mountain species were published by Engelmann over a period of more than twenty years.

Picea engelmannii Parry ex Engelm., *Trans. Acad. St. Louis* 2:212. 1863. Engelmann spruce
Picea pungens Engelm., *Gard. Chron.* n.s. 11:334. 1879. Colorado blue spruce
Pinus albicaulus Engelm., *Trans. Acad. St. Louis* 2:2090. 1863. Whitebark pine
Pinus contorta Dougl. ex Laudon var. *latifolia* Engelm. in S. Wats., *Botany*
    (*Fortieth Parallel*) 331. 1871. Lodgepole pine
Pinus aristata Engelm. in Parry & Engelm., *Amer. J. Sci. Arts*, ser. 2, 34:331.
    1862. Colorado bristlecone pine
Pinus edulis. Engelm. in Wislizenus, *Mem Tour N. Mexico* 88. 1848. Pinyon pine

Pinus ponderosa Dougl. ex P. & C. Lawson var. *scopulorum* Engelm. in S. Wats.,
  Bot. California 2:126. 1880. Rocky Mountain ponderosa pine
Pinus strobiformis. Engelm. in Wislizenus, *Mem. Tour N. Mexico* 102. 1848.
  Southwestern white pine
Juniperus occidentalis Hook. var. *monosperma* Engelm., *Trans. Acad. St. Louis* 3:590.
  1878→*Juniperus monosperma* (Engelm.) Sargent (1896). One-seed juniper

From the time of the introduction and acceptance of natural classification in
the later eighteenth century, the gymnosperms (conifers) had been regarded as
a group within the dicots. After the mid-nineteenth century, thanks to new fossil evidence and acceptance of the new concept of phylogeny, it became possible to propose that the gymnosperms were a more primitive group than the
flowering plants and merited an independent position between the cryptogams
and the angiosperms.

Sir William Hooker would have none of it, representing the view that the
conifers, either monoecious or dioecious woody plants, reproduced by seeds.
The newer concept held that the ripening ovules in the conifers, borne on
scales, were largely uncovered, and that both an ovary and stigma were lacking.
Engelmann represented the latter view at a moment when he was regarded as
the great American authority on conifers. Asa Gray, while recognizing that authority, continued to temporize on the issue, anxious to maintain his valuable
ties to Hooker. Even after Hooker's death, Gray would write to Engelmann in
1877 about the dispute: "I should wish, of course, to follow Hooker." Even in
light of the fact that the phylogenetic position of the gymnosperms is more complicated than either side in the dispute could know in the 1870s, the incident,
as Hunter Dupree remarked, was not Gray's finest hour.[9]

The debate over the classification of the gymnosperms, and Gray's belated adherence to Engelmann's position, can be found in a review of a paper by the
Czech botanist L. J. Celakovsky (1834–1902) that both men authored in *Flora*
of June 1879, "The Gymnospermy of Coniferae." Engelmann's position that the
gymnospermy had been established, and that the gymnosperms should constitute a separate order, was clearly stated.[10]

Engelmann's major contribution to the wine-growing industry seems to be
little remembered. In the course of his studies on the American species of *Vitis*, begun about 1860, Engelmann discovered the immunity of the American
wildgrapes to *Phylloxera*, the root louse that attacked most varieties of cultivated grapevines. French vineyards, in particular, had been under attack for
some years, and the *Phylloxera* had been identified and described by Jules-
Emile Planchon (1823–1888), who held the chair of botany at Montpellier and
directed the medical school. After identification of the *Phylloxera* in 1868, dras-
tic measures of pest control were undertaken under Planchon's direction, but
to no avail. The destruction of French vines became immense, harvests reduced

by at least one-half. Taking advantage of Engelmann's finding, Planchon came to the United States in 1875 to collect the disease-free roots of American wild-grapes. In the end, French growers preserved their vines primarily by grafting them onto American stock, giving them substantial immunity. Planchon became a popular figure in France, while Engelmann's role in preserving French civilization went virtually unmentioned.[11] In passing, he did name a new western wildgrape—*Vitis arizonica* Engelm. *American Naturalist* 2:231. 1868, the canyon grape.

Because Engelmann received substantial quantities of specimens from western plant collectors, whom he either sponsored or advised over a period of forty-five years, he was among the earliest to notice changes in the local flora caused by the introduction of foreign plants. Some of the natives had apparently disappeared; weeds had vastly increased because of pasturing and the cultivation of the soil. Engelmann presumed that many of the immigrants were merely adventitious and hoped they would be temporary intruders. He recognized most of them to have entered through Atlantic and Gulf of Mexico ports, but attributed several notable naturalized successes introduced by the Spanish to California—*Avena fatua* L., wild oats; and *Erodium cicutarium* (L.) l'Hér. ex Ait., crane's bill, both becoming so common as to be assumed to be indigenous.[12]

As early as 1841, Asa Gray had named a new genus in Engelmann's honor—*Engelmannia* Gray ex Nutt. in the Compositae. The only species in the genus, *E. pinnatifida,* the Engelmann daisy, is not a Rocky Mountain plant, but is found mainly on plains and low hills from Arkansas to New Mexico. *Picea engelmanii* Parry ex Engelm. was a more appropriate memorial, as Asa Gray quite recognized: "The splendid Spruce, the fairest of them all, which bears the name of Engelmann, will still, it is to be hoped, cover with noble forests the highest slopes of the Rocky Mountains, recalling to men, as long as the study of trees occupies their thoughts, the memory of a pure, upright, and laborious life."[13]

6

John Charles Frémont (1813–1890)

AN UNRESOLVED ENIGMA

The modern pronunciation of Frémont's name, as given to towns, counties, mountains, and passes, would have displeased the man. Perhaps he would have found some solace in the comparable fate of such locations as Boisé in Idaho or Dubois in Wyoming, where modern renditions have obscured the intent of the original namers.

Frémont was born in Savannah, Georgia, on 21 January 1813, the illegitimate son of Jean-Claude Fremon and Anne Beverley Whiting Pryor, whose aged husband was still living. Her earlier attempt at divorce had been unsuccessful. Despite the irregular birth, the boy received a classical education in Charleston, where he was noted for a talent for mathematics. At about the age of twenty-five, he added the terminal t to his surname, and somewhat later added the acute accent to the e: his way of calling attention to his French origin and indicating the French pronunciation of his surname. Later, as the leader of several exploratory expeditions to the West, he would recruit Creoles and French-Canadian voyageurs for his parties more exclusively than other leaders had on previous expeditions. The Creoles and French Canadians had previous experience with primitive conditions, to be sure. But Frémont's ability to speak to them without interpreters enhanced comradery and contributed to discipline.

Unlike any of our other botanical collectors or explorers of the Rocky Mountains, Frémont would have a long public career. He remains a well-known figure in the military and political accounts of the nineteenth century, accounts that, by and large, pay little attention to his botanical record. What is more, Frémont was commissioned in the army as a topographical engineer; and the principal focus of his western expeditions was topographical, for which he had been prepared by accompanying Joseph-Nicolas Nicollet on his surveys between the Mississippi and Missouri Rivers. Therefore, the scientific consequences of Frémont's expeditions were inevitably touted as topographical. The unresolved aspect of that success is the degree to which those consequences should be attributed to Charles Preuss, the accomplished topographer who accompanied Frémont, rather than to Frémont himself.

The particulars of Frémont's marriage contribute to the uncertainty about Frémont's motives and talents. His marriage in 1841 to Jessie Benton, daughter of Senator Thomas Hart Benton of Missouri, had to be secret because the Benton family disapproved of the match. She was seventeen, he was twenty-eight, an army officer without any indication of a brilliant future. Yet, the senator soon saw his son-in-law as a useful instrument in furthering Benton's campaign to extend the United States to the Pacific. This helps to account not only for Frémont's expeditions, but for his surprising performance in California during the second expedition. The consequent notoriety generated Frémont's emergence as a glamorous public figure, which he would exploit to become the Republican candidate for the presidency in 1856. Even though the nation was not yet ready for a campaign waged against slavery and Mormonism (for its polygamy) as relics of barbarism, Frémont received a very respectable popular vote in losing.

Yet, the motives behind his political aspirations have remained clouded. Were the ambitions his own or those of his father-in-law, Senator Benton? It is remarkable that those who have examined his career, including the author of the most recent, fine study of Frémont's botanical record,[1] have revealed mixed opinions about his character. That Frémont was courageous and audacious, there has been no doubt. But those who have examined his western expeditions in detail have reason to suspect that, beneath the bold, handsome façade, lay an immense egotism and an equally great, if generally unrecognized, incapacity.

Both Frémont and Preuss published accounts of their experiences in the field. In his *Report*,[2] Lieutenant Frémont did not dwell on the contributions of others. To what degree his success in the field depended on what must have been the invaluable services of Christopher (Kit) Carson as a guide remains unknowable. As commander, he took full credit for the collections. Yet, it is known that Charles Preuss not only mapped the topography, but collected plant and mineral specimens as well.

Preuss, known now as Charles, was named George Carl Ludwig following his birth in Höhscheid in the principality of Waldeck in 1803. (Waldeck was an enclave within western Prussia.) He became a student of geodesy, a new scientific name for land surveying, which led to a position as surveyor for the Prussian government. He moved to Switzerland in 1829, then emigrated to the United States in 1834, his motives obscure. For a time he found employment with the U.S. Coast Survey, but was unemployed by 1841 thanks to a reduction in funds appropriated by Congress. The opportunity to serve Frémont may have seemed to be a godsend at the outset, but Preuss was in no way prepared for the hardships of a lengthy expedition. His own account of the trips, *Exploring with Fremont,* was written in German but translated and edited by Erwin and Elizabeth

Guddle.³ Preuss emeges in it as a reasonably cultivated European, apparently of melancholic disposition, a poor fit with the barbaric voyageurs in the party; not ready, like them, to eat mule or dog when more attractive food was unavailable (which was frequent), in no way a happy camper. It must be that, given his outlook, only high professional standards inspired him to produce continually maps of a high order. In the few years that remained for him following the expeditions, Preuss experienced declining health, and one is not entirely surprised to learn that, in 1854, he hanged himself from a tree.

Frémont's first western expedition was a trip to the Rocky Mountains in the summer of 1842, Colorado and Wyoming in particular. Susan McKelvey believed that Frémont, if an inexperienced collector, did not do badly with plants during the trip. He was not, to begin with, a professional scientist. But it is possible that he had acquired some knowledge of the techniques of collection and preservation of plants by watching Karl Geyer, who had been in the service of Joseph Nicollet during the two summers that Frémont had assisted Nicollet. Frémont had also learned enough about Geyer's offensive personality to eliminate him from any consideration as a member of the expedition. Preuss may not have been a jolly addition to that crew, but he was unquestionably a hard worker and could provide professional help. Not only does his diary provide an indispensable comparison with Frémont's account, as Preuss recorded events that went wrong, which Frémont usually concealed; but his descriptions of the botanical work could surpass those of Frémont, thus inviting the conjecture that Preuss must have collected some of the plants attributed to Frémont. The enigmatic aspect of so much in Frémont's career carried over into his botanical record, leaving questions that most likely will never be resolved.⁴

On 19 June 1842, early in the trip, while the party was still in Kansas, Preuss noted, "we have started to botanize." Since in the entire party only Frémont and Preuss had had any education, the *we* had to refer to them alone.⁵ By 5 August 1842, when the party would have been along the Sweetwater River in Wyoming, Preuss complained that Frémont was roaming through the hills, keeping everyone waiting for lunch: "that fellow knows nothing about mineralogy or botany. Yet he collects every trifle in order to have it interpreted later in Washington and to brag about it in his report."⁶ Indeed, one cannot read the entire journal without being struck by Preuss's evident opinion that Frémont was an immature, unreliable leader. In the long run, botanists would simply be grateful that Frémont had brought back so much material collected under difficult circumstances, and his lack of professionalism did not become an issue.

In fact, it even proved to be an asset. Frémont set out in 1842 without knowing about the customary arrangements for the determination and publication of plants. His plants would ultimately be sent to John Torrey simply on the basis of a friend's recommendation, and without Torrey's prior agreement to determine them. Fortunately for Frémont, as Stanley Welsh wrote, Torrey and Gray had begun publication of the North American flora and were eager to receive plants from the West. The best part of all was that they received the plants unbaptized, leaving them free to designate any new taxa they perceived without fear of contradiction. Unfortunately for Frémont, Torrey's attempt to honor him with a new genus (*Fremontia*) failed, as *Sarcobatus* had already been described in 1841; but there were no Nuttallian squabbles to stain the beauty of the bonanza.

Frémont's itinerary in 1842 took him through areas already crossed by collectors. Consequently, many plants he brought back had already been described by Pursh, Nuttall, Hooker, and others. There were two regional exceptions. When the expedition reached the forks of the Platte at the beginning of July, Frémont took a small detachment of men up the South Platte heading for Fort St. Vrain, a trading post established in 1837 about six miles northwest of the present town of Platteville (Weld County, Colorado). The main portion of the expedition was ordered to proceed up the North Platte to Fort Laramie.

Not until Frémont departed from Fort St. Vrain, with the intention of rejoining the rest of the expedition, did he pass through country previously unexplored. The trek was short. The detachment left Fort St. Vrain on 12 July 1842, starting down the South Platte. After crossing Thompson's Creek, a tributary, they reached what Frémont called the Cache-à-la-Poudre at noon, having crossed fields of various flowers. They then moved along the east side of what are now called the Laramie Mountains, camping that night on what they thought might be Crow Creek. Shortly after midday on 15 July 1842, they regained the North Platte about thirteen miles below Fort Laramie. The day being very hot, they rested the horses, riding on only at the end of the day and reaching the point where the Laramie joins the North Platte. All the plants collected during those four days belonged unequivocally to Frémont, as Preuss had not accompanied him on the side trip.[7]

The intense heat that July, and the consequent drought, not only limited forage for horses and mules, but limited plants for collection as well, as the party moved up the North Platte. Conditions only improved when they turned westward into the Sweetwater valley, finding substantial numbers of plants on 3 August 1842. When crossing South Pass on 7 August 1842, Frémont commented in particular on asters.

After turning northeastward into the valley along the west side of the Wind River Range, 10 August 1842, Frémont entered a second area that had not been previously explored except by John McLeod superficially. The five days in the Wind River mountains produced a collection of more than sixty taxa, the most productive period for collections on any of Frémont's expeditions.[8] "The depths of this unexplored forest," Frémont recorded, "were a place to delight the heart of a botanist. There was a rich undergrowth of plants, and numerous gay-colored flowers in brilliant bloom." He made a gratifying collection that evening, 12 August 1842, while supper was being prepared.[9]

Frémont aspired to climb the highest peak in the Rocky Mountains and apparently believed it must be in the Wind River Range. That belief suggests that his study of earlier western expeditions had been superficial. In any case, having selected what appeared to be the highest mountain in the range, a small party made the difficult ascent. Reaching the top on 15 August 1842, Frémont calculated the elevation to be 13,750 feet. The party left the summit at two o'clock that afternoon, and would soon begin their homeward journey.[10] The traditional assumption that Frémont climbed the mountain in Fremont County named for him, 13,745 feet, has proved to be incorrect. His own description much better fits Mount Woodrow Wilson, 13,500 feet, in Sublette County, a mountain not named until 1924, after one of its climbers remarked that it seemed to have fourteen points.

Turning homeward after 15 August 1842, Frémont's party was out of Wyoming after 5 September 1842. Despite the apparent haste, considerable numbers of plants were collected in that period. Frémont reached Washington in October, and the plants were farmed out to John Torrey, who apparently went to work on them without delay, as he had a plant list ready by March 1843. Among the fifteen plants Torrey believed represented new species, several would not stand after publication; and several others, published without descriptions, would require later republication. The survivors included:

Sium ? incisum Torr. in Frém., *Rep. Exped. Rocky Mts.* 90. 1845. Weld County, Colo. 12 July 1842→*Berula erecta* (Huds.) Cov. var. *incisa* (Torr.) Cronq.
Senecio fremontii Torr. & Gray, *Fl. N. Amer.* 2:445. 1843. Sublette County, Wyo. 15 August 1842
Senecio spartioides Torr. & Gray, *Fl. N. Amer.* 2:438. 1843. Sweetwater River near Jeffery City, Fremont County, Wyo. 21 August 1842
Ipomaea leptophylla Torr. in Frém., *Rep. Exped. Rocky Mts.* 94. 1845. Near Glendo, Platte County, Wyo. 22 July 1842
Abronia (*tripterocalyx*) *micranthum* Torr. in Frém., *Rep. Exped. Rocky Mts.* 96. 1845. Near Independence Rock, Natrona County, Wyo. 1 August 1842→ *Tripterocalyx micrantha* (Torr.) Hook.

Several additional new taxa were published subsequently from Frémont's Rocky Mountain collections in 1842, listed here alphabetically:

Actinella grandiflora T. & G. in Gray (1845). Wind River Mountains, Sublette County, Wyo. 15 August 1842.→*Hymenoxys grandiflora* (T. & G.) Parker
Amarella ventorum Rydb. (1913). Wind River Mountains, Sublette County, Wyo. 4 August 1842.→*Gentianella amarella* (L.) Boerner ssp. *acuta* (Michx.) J. M. Gillett
Mimulus jamesii T. & G. ex Benth. var. *fremontii* Benth. in DC. (1846). Horse Creek, Laramie County, Wyo. 14 July 1842→*Mimulus glabratus* Kunth var. *jamesii* (T. & G. ex Benth.) Gray
Penstemon strictus Benth. in DC. (1846). Wind River Mountains, near South Pass, Fremont County, Wyo. 7 August 1842.

While Frémont's second trip, in 1843–1844, concentrated primarily on the Great Basin and California, he began it in the Rocky Mountains. He entered Colorado on the South Platte, reaching the Denver area and going southward along Fountain Creek in El Paso County before returning to Mr. St. Vrain's fort in Weld County. Rather than proceeding to Fort Laramie, he determined to seek a passage up the Cache la Poudre, reaching the mouth of its canyon late in July of 1843, by which time the volume of water flow would have greatly diminished. At the top of the Poudre canyon, the party turned northward, descending the Laramie River. From the site of the present Woods Landing, they continued northward along the eastern base of the Medicine Bow Range until reaching the North Platte, then resumed the westward trek on the Oregon Trail.[11]

Frémont's own description of his return passage through the Rocky Mountains in 1844 is both difficult to follow and misleading.[12] Susan McKelvey, fortunately, has provided a succinct and accurate itinerary. Frémont's party emerged from the Great Basin in Utah in early June, arriving at the Green River in Moffat County, Colorado. They then ascended the Little Snake River into southern Wyoming, evidently going over the Park Range (known today as the Sierra Madre in Wyoming), and coming down to the North Platte near the present site of the town of Encampment. At that point, they opted to turn southward in order to explore the three great parks in Colorado, known to hunters and trappers, but as yet unknown to science. The parks surrounded the headwaters of three great river systems: the North Platte, the Grand River fork of the Colorado, and the Arkansas.

Following the North Platte into North Park (then New Park), Frémont's party headed for Muddy Pass. Descending into Middle Park (then Old Park), they reached the present site of Kremmling on 21 June 1844. Their attention was immediately consumed by the presence of warring Utes and Arapahoes; neither group seemed likely to be friendly. Proceeding across the Grand, they traveled up the Blue River and crossed a high pass into South Park on 21 June 1844: this was evidently Hoosier Pass rather than Fremont Pass, as traditionally presumed. There is no question that Frémont reached Pueblo on the Arkansas on 29 June 1844.

During the entire trip, about fourteen hundred species had been collected according to Frémont's count, and the collecting had been interesting in particular through the mountain parks in central Colorado. Frémont's good fortune did not last. The party camped on the Smoky Hill Fork of the Kansas River in Logan County on 13 July 1844. A series of thunderstorms during the night produced a flash flood that covered the party's baggage. The herbarium, as Preuss lamented, was in deplorable condition; and an attempt was made the following day to dry the collection, but most of it was damaged beyond recall.[13]

Among the few survivors from the Rocky Mountain portion of Frémont's second trip, Torrey judged only one plant to be new; and it would be reduced to synonymy. A few others were subsequently recognized and published:

Gilia stenothrysa Gray (1870). Duchesne County, Utah, n.d. 1844

Lithospermum multiflorum Torr. ex Gray (1875). Near head of Fountain Creek, El Paso County, Colo., 29 July 1843

Penstemon fremontii Torr. & Gray (1862). Uinta County, Utah, 5 June 1844

Penstemon pachyphyllus A. Gray ex Rydb. (1917). Duchesne County, Utah, 31 May 1844

Penstemon secundiflorus Benth. in DC. (1846). In the Rocky Mountains, n.d. 1844

Senecio multilobatus Torr. & Gray in Gray (1849). Uinta County, Utah, n.d. 1844

Frémont's primary objective during his third expedition, 1845–1847, was again to reach California. He entered southern Colorado from Kansas in late July 1845, remaining at Bent's Fort in Otero County from 2 to 16 August 1845. He then followed the Arkansas River to its headwaters in South Park, either Chaffee or Lake County, the collection site of a new *Eriogonum* on 2 September 1845. He collected in Eagle County from 4 to 11 September, then passed through Rio Blanco County, Colorado, and Uinta County, Utah, between 12 and 25 September 1845. At the beginning of October, Frémont was on the Provo River in Wasatch County, Utah; from there he left the Rocky Mountain region in the direction of the Donner Pass in California.[14] A few new Rocky Mountain taxa collected during the third expedition in 1845 would be subsequently published:

Eriogonum corymbosum Benth. in DC. (1856). Eagle County, Colo.

Eriogonum umbellatum Torr. var. *majus* Hook. (1856). South Park, Lake or Chaffee County, Colo.

Lepidium alyssoides A. Gray (1849). Otero County, Colo.

Pedicularis prosera A. Gray (1862). Otero County, Colo.

Penstemon watsonii A. Gray (1878). W. Colo. and Utah mountains

Sidalcea candida A. Gray (1849). Site unclear; could be either Colo. or Utah

Frémont's fourth and fifth expeditions yielded nothing botanical from the Rocky Mountain region, but concluded the exploratory portion of his career in 1854. Anyone familiar with his later political and military record might reasonably assert that his major accomplishments were achieved during the first half of his life. His subsequent defeats and failures, in fact, contributed to speculation that Frémont's record of notable expeditions had tended to obscure those limited capacities already evident during his earlier years. In any summing up, his botanical record may fairly be cited as a valuable achievement. Despite his want of formal training as a naturalist, Frémont took undeniable interest in collecting plant specimens, working to preserve them in the field under daily conditions so arduous that only extreme dedication and courage enabled him to prevail. The loss of so many specimens in the Kansas deluge must have been exceptionally heartrending and continues to be re-gretted by those knowledgeable of its magnitude. Stanley Welsh has calcu-lated that, from the five expeditions, a total of 2,129 specimens survived for scientific study.[15]

Those of us blessed with four-wheelers, a ready supply of fresh and palatable food, and effective insect repellants should keep our own exertions in perspective.

7

Geyer and Burke

TWO GARDENERS ABROAD

*L*ittle biographical detail remains for either Karl Andreas Geyer (1809–1853) or Joseph Burke (1812–1873). The name Geyer, at least, is well known to botanists of the Rocky Mountain region; but it may come as a surprise that he was not a trained naturalist, but a gardener from Dresden who had come to America looking for adventure. We have met him already in the service of Joseph-Nicolas Nicollet as a collector and preserver of plants, and know that Frémont probably learned such techniques by watching Geyer. We also know that when Frémont was assembling the party for his first expedition, he refused to engage the available Geyer, having found him obnoxious as a traveling companion. How Geyer was obnoxious Frémont did not reveal.

By 1842, the Engelmann-Gray partnership to promote botanical exploration had been formed. Engelmann recruited two German gardeners for them to sponsor—the Saxon Geyer and Friedrich G. J. Lüders from Hamburg, a man now obscure. Arrangements were made to attach them to the party of Sir William Drummond Stewart, whose luxurious pleasure trips into the Rocky Mountains had brought him fame. The Scottish nobleman, a former army officer and an avid hunter, was a horticulturalist of some merit, which accounted for his desire to retain four gardeners (always referred to as botanists) for the trip he made in 1843. It seems probable that Sir William had no inkling of Geyer's temperament.

The Stewart trip of 1843 seems to have been the most glamorous of his adventures: the wagons with red tops, the tents crimson, furnished each evening with Persian carpets spread by servants. Stewart's route was similar initially to that used by Frémont: traveling westward up the Platte valley across Nebraska to Fort Laramie; following the North Platte to its juncture with the Sweetwater (known to Geyer as the Eau Sucrée); continuing on to the Wind River Mountains; and crossing South Pass to the Green River at the mouth of the Big Sandy (or Grande Sableuse). Stewart had Jean-Baptiste Charbonneau as a guide—the son of Toussaint Charbonneau and Sacagawea—whose remarkable career provides an arresting account of successful assimilation through imaginative schooling.[1]

As for the four "botanists," only Geyer was making substantial collections that would survive the trip. Lüders apparently collected conscientiously, but later he would upset his canoe on the lower Columbia and lose everything. For reasons unclear, but presumably by choice, Geyer separated on the Green River from the Stewart safari, which proceeded northward into Yellowstone country. He joined a party of Jesuits bound for their mission among the Flathead Indians, the Chamokane Mission in northern Idaho. His exact route thereafter has always been unclear because of imprecise information on his collection labels. He would cite regions and months of collections, but never exact dates.

On occasion, a geographical reference has permitted the clarification of a location, such as Geyer's description of a solitary cliff near the junction of Ham's Fork and Black's Fork, the site of the present Granger in southwestern Wyoming. He called it one of the most productive areas on his trip, especially for plants in the Chenopodiaceae and the Onagraceae.[2] From that area, it would appear that the Jesuit party went northward into western Montana, up the Bitterroot River, and crossed the Bitterroot Range into Idaho sometime in November of 1843.

Geyer passed the winter at the Chamokane Mission, perhaps exposing his motive for having joined the Jesuit party in western Wyoming. Accordingly, he was able to renew his fieldwork in Idaho when spring so permitted. He began in the region of Coeur d'Alene Lake, Kootenai County, working his way south into Nez Perce County. He was in the Clark Mountains of Idaho into the autumn, then passed out of our range, skirting the Blue Mountains to reach Fort Walla Walla in October of 1844.

Geyer's destination was Fort Vancouver. The Oregon region was not only jointly occupied by the Americans and the British at that time, but it was a region of Sir William Hooker's continuing interest. Once Geyer began to enjoy the hospitality of the Hudson's Bay Company there, he was soon persuaded that his plants ought to be sent to Hooker rather than to his patrons, Engelmann and Gray. As a consequence, Geyer's collection was sent to Hooker by ship from Fort Vancouver, and he wrote to Engelmann that he would not be returning to the United States. The first Engelmann-Gray effort to promote exploration, in sum, yielded them absolutely nothing.[3]

Geyer estimated that he had collected between nine and ten thousand specimens. Hooker would note that Geyer had organized his plants into twenty sets, the largest sets containing about six hundred numbers, the smaller sets ranging from two to three hundred numbers. Hooker offered the extra sets for sale from Kew, which accounts for their distribution. Gray, already angry about Geyer's betrayal, steamed over his need to pay Hooker for a set.[4] The incident left a lasting impression on Gray of the probable untrustworthiness of field collectors.

His great adventure completed, Geyer left Fort Vancouver in 1845 and returned home to Dresden. Inasmuch as botanists have been primarily interested in Geyer's collection, and as he left his plants to be determined and published by others, his own essay, written from Dresden and published in serialized snippets by Hooker in his *London Journal of Botany,* seems largely to have escaped notice in later years. His comments on the phytogeography of the regions he passed through, occasionally mentioning the sites of plants observed, must have been of help both to Hooker and others who published Geyer's new species later. They remain a valuable and underutilized source of information for ecologists interested in past records.[5]

The first publication of Geyer's new species was undertaken by Hooker in the *London Journal of Botany* in 1847. Several from the Rocky Mountain region still stand, albeit sometimes transferred, probably joyfully, by Asa Gray:

Vesicaria geyeri Hook. 6:70. Upper Spokane valley, Idaho→*Physaria geyeri* (Hook.) A. Gray (1848)

Phaca annua Geyer ex Hook. 6:213. Upper North Platte, Wyo.→*Astragalus geyeri* A. Gray (1864)

Eryngium articulatum Hook. 6:232. Coeur d'Alene and Skitsoe Lakes, Idaho

Angelica verticulata Geyer ex. Hook. 6:233. High plains of Nez Percé Indians, Idaho→*Ligusticum verticulatum* (Geyer ex Hook.) Coult. & Rose (1895)

Peucedanum farinasum Hook. 6:234. Coeur d'Alene Mountains, Idaho→ *Lomatium farinasum* (Hook.) Coult. & Rose (1900)

Helianthus quinquenervis Hook. 6:247. Upper North Platte, Wyo.→*Helianthella quinquenervis* (Hook.) A. Gray (1883)

Scorzonella nutans Hook. 6:253. Coeur d'Alene Mountains, Idaho→*Micoseris nutans* (Hook.) Schultz-Bip. (1866)

Thanks to the distribution of Geyer's sets by Hooker, several of Geyer's familiar Rocky Mountain plants were published later by others:

Allium geyeri S. Wats. (1879). Collection no. 226, Clearwater River, northern Idaho

Aster laevis L. var. *geyeri* A. Gray (1884). Collection no. 638, Spokane and Columbia valleys

Cerex geyeri Booth (1846). Collection no. 332, Rocky Mountains

Ranunculus alismafolius Geyer ex Benth. (1848). Collection no. 306, Coeur d'Alene, Idaho

Salix geyeriana Anderss. (1858). Collection no. 286, Rocky Mountains

In 1894, Edward Lee Greene would name a handsome blue larkspur, commonly known by stockmen at that time as poison-weed, because it produced a fatal bloating in cattle, *Delphinium geyeri* Greene. The suggestion of a double-edged honor is unavoidable given Geyer's negative reputation. On the other hand, most larkspurs are toxic to some degree; and Greene, at the same time, published *Delphinium burkei* Greene to honor Joseph Burke, about whom little personal information had survived.[6]

Fifty years earlier, Geyer had left Idaho, proceeding to Fort Walla Walla, Washington, a Hudson's Bay Company post. On 27 October 1844, he met Joseph Burke there. Considering that Burke collected plants in the West during the favorable months from 1844 to 1846, it is surprising how little remains known of him. His trip was sponsored not only by Sir William Hooker, but by Edward Geoffrey Smith Stanley, the Earl of Derby, for whom Burke had gardened at Knowsley (east of Liverpool), with its great park. Such associations guaranteed Burke the cooperation of the Hudson's Bay Company, with whose agents he frequently traveled. Derby's interest dated from an extended tour he had made through Canada and the United States in 1824 in the company of several other milords.

When Burke reached Jasper House, in southwestern Alberta, in March of 1844, he meant to explore country not previously visited by Thomas Drummond. While Burke did collect in the Jasper region and as far north as the Peace River valley, late frosts and an unusually cold and rainy summer that year hampered the full development of plants, especially disappointing for a horticulturalist meaning in particular to collect seeds for shipment to England. In mid-September, he turned southward to Fort Walla Walla, where he met Karl Geyer in October. We can only suspect that Geyer's ultimate decision to send his collection to Hooker may have had its genesis in that meeting.

After spending the winter of 1844–1845 at Fort Hall in Idaho, Burke joined a trading party that went southward through the Bear River valley into Utah, as far south as Utah Lake. In early summer, he reversed course, traveling through the Blackfoot country to reach the headwaters of the Missouri. He was at Three Forks, Montana, on 31 July 1845; on the Yellowstone on 12 August 1845; and at Thomas Fort, Wyoming, 24 September 1845. Then he returned to Fort Hall for the winter of 1845–1846. In the summer of 1846, Burke worked west of the Rocky Mountains, in the Blue Mountains and around Walla Walla.[7]

After such immense labor under difficult conditions, the results were disappointing. Burke had somehow failed to be in places at times when seeds were developing; and after his return to England in 1847, it was soon perceived that his plant material was mostly familiar. That material, to be sure, contributed to the knowledge of plant distribution, but Burke's collections were never published as a group. His patrons revealed their displeasure, leading him to resign his position at Knowsley and emigrate to the United States with his family in 1848. He settled in Independence, Missouri, for a happier ending. His one monument remains *Delphinium burkei* Greene, based on a specimen he collected in "Snake country," Idaho.[8]

8

Concluding the 1840s

WISLIZENUS, FENDLER, AND STANSBURY

*B*iographical information about Frederick Adolph Wislizenus (1810–1889) has been elusive. He devoted only a few introductory pages about himself to a journal that remained unpublished until long after his death.[1] As he would become a friend of George Engelmann, some information about Wislizenus has been gleaned from Engelmann's correspondence. His birthplace was the Bavarian mountain town Königsee. During his time at several major universities—Jena, Göttingen, and Tübingen—he appears to have acquired the German liberal-nationalist convictions fashionable at the time.

In the aftermath of the July Revolution in Paris in 1830, the liberal-nationalist ferment in German universities caused Metternich to induce the Diet of the German Confederation at Frankfurt to impose the Six Articles, aimed at suppressing such liberal-nationalist activity (1832). In response, an international group of conspirators made an attempt on the Frankfort Diet in 1833, bent on the creation of a united Germany, probably a liberal republic. The attempt was easily overwhelmed; and Wislizenus, who apparently had been a participant, prudently fled to Zurich. He completed his medical studies there. Already a refugee when he obtained his medical doctorate, Wislizenus moved to America, settling in Mascoutah, Illinois, in 1835, only a few miles southeast of Saint Louis. He established a medical practice within the German community already predominant in the region and soon became acquainted with Dr. Engelmann.[2]

What little about Wislizenus's career can be documented makes one suspect that we have lost the history of a venturesome spirit with a lively mind—by no means the story of the student radical who matures into stolid conventionality. In the spring of 1839, for instance, he set out to visit the Rocky Mountains for apparently no other purpose than to see the vast new country. He joined a party of fur traders who were bound for the annual rendezvous at Ham's Fork on the

Green River in Wyoming. From there he accompanied another party as far as Fort Hall in Idaho. His journal indicates that he as yet had no particular interest in plants, especially unfortunate as, on his return trip, he passed through country not yet explored. Notably, he crossed the Park Range in northern Colorado into North Park; he then crossed the Medicine Bow Range somewhat north of the Cache la Poudre River, emerging roughly at the place Frémont would enter later, in 1844.

It is apparent that Dr. Engelmann, in the aftermath, became determined not to let such an opportunity go wasted in the future. By the time Wislizenus found a second opportunity to go exploring, Engelmann had impressed on him his obligation to reap a collection of plants. In fact, Wislizenus wished to study not only natural history, but also geography, geology, and mines. Thus, in 1846, at the time of the Mexican War, he attached himself unofficially to the expedition of the Missouri militia en route to the Southwest, led by Colonel Alexander W. Doniphan; this was the same Doniphan who had gained some repute from his negotiations for the Mormon evacuation of Missouri in 1838.

This expedition crossed Kansas into southeastern Colorado, heading for Santa Fe. During the week of 10–17 June 1846, they crossed the plain between the Arkansas and the Cimarron, where Wislizenus was struck by a large population of *Gaillardia pulchella* Foug., in an otherwise desolate region without water. They passed into New Mexico at week's end. In Moro County on 23 June 1846, he collected a specimen of *Opuntia arborescens* Engelm. in Wislizenus (1848), which would prove to be a synonym of *Opuntia imbricata* (Haw.) DC. Two days later, in the mountains near the town of Las Vegas, he collected material from two species of pine that he thought had not yet been described. One became *Pinus brachyptera* Engelm. in Wislizenus (1848), now recognized as *Pinus ponderosa* Dougl. ex Lawson & C. Lawson var. *scopulorum* Engelm. in S. Wats. The other still stands as *Pinus Edulis* Engelm. in Wislizenus (1848), the piñon pine, which, he noted, had seeds that were roasted and eaten.

In August, the expedition moved southward out of our range, Wislizenus with it. When his account was published in 1848,[3] with a scientific index and three maps, the botanical index had actually been supplied by George Engelmann. It would later be reprinted by William Trelease and Asa Gray.[4] Engelmann honored the plant collector with a new genus, *Wislizenia* in the Capparaceae, the type species being *W. refracta* Engelm., known in New Mexico as jackass clover. He also dedicated a new species to him: *Dithrea wislizenii* Engelm. in Wislizenus (1848),[5] later transferred to be *Dimorphocarpa wislizenii* (Engelm.) Rollins, known predominantly in New Mexico and Arizona in the Cruciferae. The live oak, *Quercus wislizenii* A. DC., is only known from California into Baja California.[6]

The wanderlust exhibited by Wislizenus was also characteristic of his German contemporary Augustus Fendler (1813–1883), another man deracinated early in life and never fully rerooted in the passing years. We know more about Fendler, because, late in life, he became a friend and correspondent of William Canby. After Fendler's death, Canby wrote a short article, "An Autobiography and some Reminiscences of August Fendler," based on material Fendler had sent him. The material had been meant for publication in *The Botanical Gazette* in 1885, but Asa Gray, who saw the article before publication, used the material to write a piece of his own and hurried it into print before Canby's appeared. At the time, Gray also knew that Engelmann had begun to write a notice of Fendler's life but had died (1884) with it unfinished on his worktable.[7] Whatever else the incident reveals, it tells us that Fendler, if hardly remembered today, was regarded by knowledgeable contemporaries to be unusually intelligent and reliable.

Fendler was born at Gumbinnen in eastern Prussia on 10 January 1813. Despite the loss of his father soon after, he had the benefit of instruction in the local gymnasium until the age of sixteen. He was then apprenticed to the town clerk; but his interest in mathematics and chemistry had been aroused at school, and he obtained, through examination, admission to the Royal Polytechnic School in Berlin at the age of twenty-one. At the end of a year, he withdrew because of deteriorating health, the ailment unspecified. Within a year, he had determined to start anew in America, and sailed from Bremen to Baltimore in 1836, virtually penniless.

Of necessity, Fendler took menial jobs in Philadelphia and New York, making his way to the German community in Saint Louis in 1838. Once again, odd jobs were his lot, until he was moved to take possession of an uninhabited island in the Missouri River, some three hundred miles upstream from Saint Louis. He lived a hermit's life for about six months; then a great rise in the river during spring threatened his cabin. He took to his canoe and floated back downstream to the city, where he still had no interesting prospects.

Fendler's fortune changed only when, in 1844, he made a trip back to eastern Prussia. In Königsberg, he had the luck to meet Ernest Meyer (1791–1858), a local botanist of considerable distinction who had published on the plants of Labrador. Meyer made Fendler aware that, in Saint Louis, he was well positioned to collect plant specimens in relatively unexplored country, and that dried specimens could be sold for herbaria. Back in Saint Louis, Fendler began to collect plants, taking his specimens to Dr. Engelmann for assistance in determining them and receiving encouragement as well.

Engelmann was not slow to perceive that here was another German collector who might do for Gray and him what Karl Geyer had failed to do. In 1846, they took the opportunity of the Mexican War to arrange for Fendler to be transported, with his equipment, with U.S. troops being sent to occupy Santa Fe. In the autumn, Fendler began collecting near Bent's Fort (on the Arkansas River near the present town of La Junta), reaching the base of the Raton Mountains on 27 September 1846. He admired in particular the tall ponderosa pines and what he called the elegant *Pinus concolor* Gordon, which we know today as *Abies concolor*

(Gord. & Glend.) Hildebr. (1861). By then, Wislizenus had left that region, moving toward northern Mexico.

Fendler passed the winter in Santa Fe. His principal collections in that vicinity were not made until 1847, between April and August, and, when leaving that region homeward bound via Fort Leavenworth, he crossed the mountains from Santa Fe to Las Vegas. He returned with the most substantial collection of plants, 1,026 numbers, to have been collected in northern New Mexico. Yet, the experience had not been pleasurable for Fendler. He had suffered from illness during that summer of 1847 and had been accompanied by his feeble-minded younger brother, whose need for constant care was a distraction. Those factors account for the fact that Fendler did not venture far from town to collect, and for his longing to return home by July.[8]

Engelmann saw the collection, and admired its quality, before the plants were sent on to Asa Gray for publication. Although Gray was immensely pleased by Fendler's plants, he took the time to describe and publish only 462 of his numbers. The remaining novelties were published later either by Gray, or by Edward Lee Greene, Amos Arthur Heller, or Paul Standley. The following new species are found in the initial major publication:[9]

Berberis fendleri A. Gray 4:5
Argemone hispida A. Gray 4:5
Nasturtium sphaeracarpum A. Gray 4:6→*Rorippa sphaerocarpa* (A. Gray) Britt.
Streptanthus micranthus A. Gray 4:7→*Pennellia micrantha* (A. Gray) Nieuwl.
Streptanthus linearifolius A. Gray 4:7→*Schoencrambe linearifolia* (A. Gray) Rollins
Cardamine cordifolia A. Gray 4:8
Vesicaria fendleri A. Gray 4:9→*Lesquerella fendleri* (A. Gray) S. Wats.
Lepidium alyssoides A. Gray 4:10
Sidalcea neomexicana A. Gray 4:23
Sidalcea candida A. Gray 4:24
Ceanothus fendleri A. Gray 4:29
Astragalus cyaneus A. Gray 4:34
Potentilla crinita A. Gray 4:41
Oenothera fendleri A. Gray 4:45→*Calylophus hartwegii* (Benth.) Raven ssp. *fendleri* (A. Gray) Towner & Raven
Cereus fendleri Engelm. 4:51→*Echinocerus fendleri* (Engelm.) F. Seitz
Opuntia phaeacantha Engelm. 4:51
Cymopteris fendleri A. Gray 4:56→*Cymopteris acaulis* (Pursh) Raf. var. *fendleri* (Gray) Goodrich
Galium fendleri A. Gray 4:60
Brickellia fendleri A. Gray 4:63
Erigeron canus A. Gray 4:67
Erigeron flagellaris A. Gray 4:68
Townsendia fendleri A. Gray 4:69

Townsendia eximia A. Gray 4:70
Sanvitalia abertii A. Gray 4:87
Hymenopappus flavescens A. Gray 4:97
Actinella argentes A. Gray 4:100→*Tetraneuris argents* (A. Gray) Greene
Senecio fendleri A. Gray 4:103
Cirsium ochracentrum A. Gray 4:110

Shortly after the appearance of Gray's article, several of Fendler's ferns were recognized:

Notholaena fendleri Kunze (1851)→*Argyrochosma fendleri* (Kunze) Windham
    (1987)
Cheilanthes fendleri Hook. (1852)

Additional Fendler plants, familiar in the Rocky Mountains, were published subsequently, including two new genera:

Oxypolis fendleri (Gray) Heller (1897)
Hieracium fendleri Schaltz-Bip (1861)
Fendlera Engelm. & Gray (1852), the type being *Fendlera rupicola* Gray
Fendlerella Heller (1898), the type being *Fendlerella utahensis* (S. Wats.) Heller
Hydrophyllum fendleri (Gray) Heller (1897)
Cryptantha fendleri (Gray) Greene (1887)

To keep the record straight, it must be noted that *Fendlera* Engelm. & Gray was based on a plant actually collected by Charles Wright in 1849; and *Fendlerella* Heller was based on a plant collected by Sereno Watson in 1873.[10] The *Sanvitalia* was dedicated by Gray to James William Abert, a topographical engineer in Frémont's service, who had been detached in northern New Mexico from Frémont's third expedition in 1845 and who had made a second trip up the Arkansas River in 1846, collecting as far as Bent's Fort. His small collections were given to Torrey for determination.[11]

Fendler never again collected in the American West. His biographical sketch portrays a life of wandering thereafter, not only in the United States but in Panama and Venezuela, his feeble-minded brother his only companion. In 1873, he made an attempt to settle in Wilmington, Delaware, which is when William Canby befriended him; but that residence was only brief. Asa Gray remembered Fendler as a quick and keen observer, an admirable plant collector, always courteous and amiable; but also as delicately refined, excessively diffident and shy, as perhaps never having been in good health.[12] Fendler would never find a comfortable home in this world.

While the exploration of Captain Howard Stansbury (1806–1863) was not to the Southwest, but rather to Utah, he was among that group, including Wislizenus and Fendler, whose trips occurred in the decade before midcentury. Like Frémont, he was a topographical engineer rather than a botanist, yet he was interested in the plants he saw and returned with a collection.

Stansbury's primary assignment was to explore and survey the Great Salt Lake, as well as the region around it, for the purpose of determining a potential route for a transcontinental railroad. His effort to obtain the collaboration of a natural scientist was unsuccessful, leaving him no option but to make natural observations the best he could.

Stansbury's name is usually associated with the Great Basin, outside of our range. Yet, he began his westward trip in 1849 along the Oregon Trail, across Nebraska to Fort Laramie, then to Fort Bridger in southwestern Wyoming. The route he found through the Wasatch Mountains into the valley of Great Salt Lake ultimately became the chosen rail route. Most of the plants he collected were evidently found on his return journey, which began in August of 1850. His narrative, while certainly not rich in technical references to plants, makes it clear that he was observing them.[13]

Stansbury's collection was given to John Torrey for determination. Torrey's paper on the plants appeared as appendix D in Stansbury's report.[14] Because Torrey found so few new species in the lot, his judgment likely contributed to the growing conviction in the East by midcentury that most of the Western flora had become known. In fact, the relatively small size of the Stansbury collection made it by no means a thorough plant survey of the region, nor had any such claim been made. The following few species were novelties that still stand in some form:

> Streptanthus crassicaulus Torr. 383. 1852.→Caulanthus crassicaulus (Torr.) S. Wats.
> Phaca mollissima Torr. var. utahensis Torr. 385. 1852.→Astragalus utahensis Torr. & Gray
> Cowania stansburiana Torr. 386. 1852.→Purshia stansburiana (Torr.) Henr. (Despite the difference in carpel numbers, the submersion of Cowania into Purshia was based on the easy hybridization between the two genera.)
> Heuchera rubescens Torr. 388. 1852

On 25 October 1849, Stansbury made an observation along the north end of Great Salt Lake. On the slope of a ridge he counted thirteen distinct, successive benches, or watermarks, which had evidently been washed by the lake at some time in the past: the highest was about two hundred feet above the valley. The marks suggested to him that "there must have been here at some former period a vast inland sea, extending for hundreds of miles."[15] This seems to have been the first observation of the saline phenomenon subsequently known as Lake Bonneville. That discovery would be of immense significance for students of ecology and phytogeography.

9

The New Era of Intensive Botanizing

CHARLES PARRY IN COLORADO

*M*uch of what we know about Charles Parry's personal life depends on a ten-page biographical essay published in 1893 for the Davenport (Iowa) Academy of Science by C. H. Preston, a colleague and friend. Charles Christopher Parry (1823–1890) was born in Gloucestershire, England, the descendant of a long line of Anglican clergymen. Preston asserted that Parry himself was a deeply religious man, which may have been true; but anyone reading the brief Parry narratives, as collected and republished by William A. Weber, will search in vain for any expression of religious sentiment or conviction.[1] It is remarkable, in fact, that, for a man so frequently praised as friendly and warm hearted, Parry never mentioned in his field notes traveling companions or any other specimens of western humanity he encountered over many years.

His immediate family moved in 1832 to a farm in Washington County, New York—that is, northeast of Albany near the Vermont border. He attended Union College in Schenectady for undergraduate work, where he was first introduced to medical botany; and he completed his medical doctorate at Columbia College, where he must have come under the influence of John Torrey. Parry went west to Davenport in 1846 to establish his medical practice.

From a report he made later in life to the Davenport Academy of Science, we can infer that the practice of medicine did not long compete with Parry's passion for botanical fieldwork. During the summer of 1847, anxious to secure the flora of central Iowa, he attached himself to a federal surveying party working under Lieutenant John Morehead in that area. During the following summer, 1848, he accompanied D. D. Owen's geological survey in the old Northwest, collecting especially up the Saint Croix River as far as Lake Superior. Beginning in 1849, Parry had an appointment to the Mexican Boundary Survey as a botanist, the details of which occupied him into 1853. Thereafter, he returned to Davenport, whether to active medical practice is unclear; and Davenport would remain his home even after he resumed botanical fieldwork.[2]

In retrospect, we may think of 1860 as a botanical watershed. In earlier years, botanists—notably those on railway surveys—had often crossed from the plains to the Pacific in a single season. During his work on the Mexican Boundary Survey, Parry became convinced that he needed a more intensive focus on a limited geographical area.[3] Beyond this, he tells us specifically why that new intensive research was feasible for the first time, and why Colorado was his choice for more intensive study:

> Within the past few years, . . . the discovery of gold deposits in this portion of the mountain range has attracted thither an adventurous and enterprising population, settling with wonderful celerity its picturesque valleys and introducing into its wild recesses many of the arts and comforts of civilized life. These various social movements have afforded facilities for the prosecution of researches in natural history which were not enjoyed by the early pioneer explorers of this region.[4]

In particular, Parry had in mind the new mining settlements of Empire City and Georgetown, which enabled him to occupy a simple cabin as a base for botanical exploration. No imperial splendor did he observe, except for that of the surrounding mountains! The cabin he built was in Georgetown, and he anticipated returning to it during subsequent summers.

Early in 1861, Parry notified John Torrey that he would set out toward Pike's Peak early in May. At the beginning of 1862, Torrey received the first batch of Parry's plants, 417 numbers, which Torrey passed on to Asa Gray. Given the extent of Parry's learning and prior field experience, it is difficult to account for the fact that many of his plant labels were unnumbered and frequently offered no locality data. No precise itinerary can be deduced from them, although one can tell that Parry botanized through the Clear Creek drainage and as high as the Continental Divide, from which he could look down into Middle Park. Before publishing the list, "Enumeration of the Plants," that was appended to Parry's "Physiographical Sketch," Gray somehow gave all of the plants numbers. It seems probable that he worked from several sets in order to obtain the fullest information possible.[5]

The following new species emerged from Gray's "Enumeration of the Plants" in *The American Journal of Science and Arts,* ser. 2:

no. 83. *Trollius albiflorus* Gray 33:241. 1862→*Trollius laxus* Salis. ssp. *albiflorus* (Gray) A. & D. Löve & Kapoor

no. 96. *Draba streptocarpa* Gray 33:242. 1862

no. 178. *Trifolium parryi* Gray 33:409. 1862

no. 193. *Astragalus parryi* Gray 33:410. 1862

no. 251. *Pedicularis parryi* Gray 34:250. 1862
no. 311. *Primula parryi* Gray 34:257. 1862

Additional new species from Parry's trip in 1861 were identified later and published by Gray and others:

no. 10. *Arnica parryi* A. Gray, *Am. Nat.* 8:213. 1874
no. 81. *Ranunculus adoneus* A. Gray, *Proc. Acad. Phila* 15:56. 1864
no. 142. *Claytonia arctica* M. F. Adams var. *megarhiza* Gray. Parry had used the name *megarhiza* in his sketch, and the name could be restored to specific rank.→*Claytonia megarhiza* (Gray) Parry ex Wats., *Bibl. Ind.* 1:118. 1878
no. 360. *Juncus parryi* Engelm., *Trans. St. Louis Acad. Sci.* 2:446. 1866
no. 417. *Aster foliaceus* Lindl. In DC. var. *parryi* (Eaton) A. Gray, *Syn. Fl.* 1(2): 193. 1884

Other names derived from that summer's exploration as well.

> In my solitary wanderings over these rugged rocks and through these alpine meadows," Parry recalled, "resting at noon-day in some sunny nook, overlooking wastes of snow and crystal lakes girdled with mid-summer ice, I naturally associated some of the more prominent peaks with distant and valued friends. To two twin peaks always conspicuous whenever a sufficient elevation was attained, I applied the names of *Torrey* and *Gray*; to an associated peak, a little less elevated but in other respects quite as remarkable in its peculiar situation and alpine features, I applied the name *Mount Engelmann*. Thus, following the example of the early and intrepid botanical explorer, Douglas, I have endeavored to commemorate the joint scientific services of our *triad* of North American botanists by giving their honored names to three snow-capped peaks in the Rocky Mountains.[6]

Not sharing the fate of *Dr. James's peak*, Parry's names have survived, all of them in Clear Creek County: Torreys Peak, 14,264 feet; Grays Peak, 14,274 feet; and Engelmann Peak, 13,037 feet.

Parry returned to Colorado for the summer of 1862, this time accompanied by Elihu Hall and J. P. Harbour, two plant collectors now obscure. It seems probable that they were Illinois farmers without botanical training, but with an interest in plants and quite aware that there was a market for sets of plants. Their specimens would lack information about collection dates and sites, but, according to Asa Gray, they were zealous and enterprising when collecting with Parry. *Heuchera hallii* Gray, apparently endemic to central Colorado, and *Penstemon hallii* Gray honor the one; while *Penstemon harbourii* Gray and *Harbouria trachypleura* (A. Gray) Coult. & Rose honor the other.

As in 1861, the exact location of collection sites in 1862 cannot be ascertained from plant labels. Apparently Parry sent an account of some sort to Engelmann, which enabled Engelmann to calculate the elevations of various points along the route.[7] From this, William Weber reconstructed an itinerary of the party. It appears that they went westward from Denver to what is now Bergen Park, and then southward to the present site of Conifer. Along the current route of Highway 285, they passed through Bailey, over Kenosha Pass, to Jefferson. From Jefferson, they took a side trip northward to Georgia Pass and Mount Guyot, then west of that pass, where they had their first encounter with alpine flora. It was Parry who named Mount Guyot to honor the Swiss-American savant Arnold Guyot, geologist and friend of Louis Agassiz. Returning to Jefferson, the party turned southeastward to Tarryall and then eastward to Colorado Springs.

Their ascent of Pike's Peak occupied 1 July 1862. Parry wrote an extensive account of it to John Torrey, who caused it to be published.[8] The only other botanist known to have made the ascent was Edwin James, who had visited the peak on 14 July 1820. Parry had read James's account of the climb in preparation for his own ascent. He found the account had been both truthful and graphic on the basis of what he now found. Yet, he also noted that James, paying careful attention to *Pinus flexilis,* had also mentioned in a cursory way the presence of *Abies balsamea, A. Canadensis, A. alba, A. nigra,* and *A. rubra,* trees common in the eastern part of North America, but not one them occurring in the Pike's Peak region. (That observation would be confirmed by George Goodman in 1995.) Parry understood this to be a common error that derived from confusing or confounding analogous species, easy to do if one has not collected specimens for closer observation. Parry might well have added that such an error could result from a supposition that eastern species were to be expected in the West.

Following the climb of Pike's Peak, the party returned to Denver, after which Parry was on his own for the remainder of the summer. His major field trip thereafter was from Empire City, over Berthoud Pass, and into Middle Park as far as Hot Sulphur Springs in Grand County. On his return trip, Parry climbed both Mount Engelmann and Grays Peak before coming to rest in Georgetown.[9] His collection of plants during 1862, again submitted to Asa Gray, included duplicates from Hall's and Harbour's collections. Gray's publication of them the following year was a plant list, the new species indicated, but only defined in footnotes.[10]

> no. 49. *Vesicaria montana* Gray 15:58. 1863→*Lesquerella montana* (Gray) s.
> Wats. (1888)
> no. 66. *Paronychia pulvinata* Gray 15:58. 1863
> no. 205. *Heuchera hallii* Gray 15:62. 1863

no. 256. *Aplopappus lyallii* Gray 15:64. 1863→*Tonestus lyallii* (Gray) A. Nels. (1904)

no. 257. *Aplopappus (Pyrracoma) croceus* Gray 15:65. 1863→*Pyrrocoma crosea* (Gray) Greene (1894)

no. 259. *Aplopappus (Pyrrocoma) parryi* Gray 15:65. 1863→*Oreochrysum parryi* (Gray) Rydb. (1906)

no. 268. *Helianthella parryi* Gray 15:65. 1863

no. 272. *Helenium hoopesii* Gray 15:65. 1863

no. 293. *Linosyris (Chrysothamnus) parryi* Gray 15:66. 1863→*Chrysothamnus) parryi* (Gray) Greene (1904)

no. 299. *Artemisia scopulorum* Gray 15:66. 1863

no. 318. *Senecio soldanella* Gray 15:67. 1863

no. 321. *Senecio bigelowii* Gray var. *hallii* Gray 15:67. 1863

no. 450. *Polemonium confertum* Gray 15:73. 1863

no. 632. *Muhlenbergia pungens* Thurber in Gray 15:78. 1863

Additional new species from Parry's trip in 1862 were published elsewhere:

no. 359. *Campanula langsdorffiana* Fisher 15:70. 1863→*Campanula parryi* Gray, *Syn. Fl.* 2nd ed. 2 (1): 395. 1886

no. 388. *Penstemon hallii* Gray, *Proc. Am. Acad. Arts & Sci.* 6:70. 1862

no. 396. *Penstemon harbourii* Gray, Ibid. 6:71. 1862

no. 480. *Asclepius hallii* Gray, Ibid. 12:69. 1876

no. 470. *Gentiana parryi* Engelm., *Trans. St. Louis Acad. Sci.* 2:218. 1863

The reader may have noted that compassionate descriptions of Indian life by botanists, prominent in the Lewis and James accounts, ceased thereafter. The Jeffersonian era had passed and the idea of assimilation with it. By Parry's time, permanent settlements enabled him not only to take up residence, so to speak, but to contemplate the feasibility of agriculture, as well. Parry became the first of the botanical explorers in the Rocky Mountains to dwell on issues within the realm of economic botany. Most any student of the plant sciences would have been aware, of course, that wherever man has gone he has set himself to growing food, for a fear of famine and starvation lurks in the memory of the race. But it is probable that Parry published, in Chicago in 1863, a popular article on the potential for agriculture in a region above four thousand feet in elevation, based on observations he had made in Middle Park the previous summer.

There is no echo here of the better-known, pessimistic assessments made by Stephen Long and Edwin James. Parry recognized that, given the uncertain rainy season, irrigation from the mountain streams would be necessary for agriculture at such elevations. Success would also depend on the development of adequate knowledge about the variability of the different seasons. But, given that knowledge, Parry foresaw the raising of garden vegetables of excellent quality and, in the larger bottomlands, in considerable quantities. His prediction was applicable not just to Colorado but to the whole Rocky Mountain region below eighty-five hundred feet in elevation.[11]

Parry's trip to Colorado in 1864 provided another opportunity for considerable fieldwork, but it is evident that he collected much less than in prior seasons. He does not appear to have offered an explanation for the decline, leaving it to others to infer that the flora of Colorado had become virtually entirely known. During June of 1864, Parry botanized in northern Boulder County, especially on the upper reaches of Left Hand Creek. In the vicinity of the mining town of Gold Hill, he came upon a series of small ponds bearing rushes and other aquatic plants. From one of them, he collected what he believed to be an undescribed species in bud, returning later in the summer to find it in full bloom. It proved to be the type for *Nuphar polysepalum* Engelm., *Trans. Acad. Sci. St. Louis* 2:282. 1865, the yellow pond lily.

During the interim, in July, Parry returned to Middle Park and the area around Hot Sulphur Springs, and then in August was back in Boulder and Larimer Counties. With a small party, he made an attempt to climb Long's Peak. By their own calculation, they fell six hundred feet short of success, and Parry consoled himself with the conviction that the peak itself was probably inaccessible. A visit to the open basin valley of Big Thompson Creek, then occupied by only one family, moved Parry to a lyrical description of luxurious grasses, immense herds of wild game, and a stream abounding in delicious trout; and he had no doubt that, once a road could be built from Denver, Joel Estes's park would become a pleasure resort.[12]

In 1867, Parry signed on as botanist for the Kansas Pacific Railroad survey, led by General William Palmer. The party passed through southeastern Colorado and northern New Mexico, but was within our range only briefly, when they traveled up the Huerfano River valley west of present-day Walsenburg to Sangre de Cristo Pass. Parry published his report (1868) independently from that of the expedition and published a plant list in 1870. The one new Rocky Mountain species, collected in northern New Mexico, was published even later: *Oxytropis parryi* Gray, *Proc. Amer. Acad. Arts Sci.* 20:4. 1884.[13]

Parry also presented a paper to the Saint Louis Academy of Sciences in 1867; it made him the first of the Rocky Mountain botanical explorers to attempt to explain the phenomenon of timberline.[14] Barometric measurements he had recorded between 1861 and 1864 had shown him that timberline, albeit with slight local variations, marked a very uniform elevation that gradually lowered as one moved northward. He wondered whether that feature, in other parts of the globe as well, was connected to a certain range of mean annual temperature—without speaking of what that mean might be.

On the basis of his observations in the Rocky Mountains alone, Parry was inclined to refer the limitations of tree growth to a certain range of minimum temperature. He was also inclined to define *true timberline* as that point beyond which tall conifers ceased to grow tall, thereafter becoming dwarfed or stunted. The species in his descriptions were exclusively *Picea engelmannii* and *Pinus aristata*. Above the timberline, these species became deformed, forming dense mats or creeping through rocky fissures. The elevation of their growth depended on local peculiarities and would be fairly irregular; but Parry deemed this a *false timberline*.

The only way those species could survive beyond the line of minimum temperature, Parry asserted, was to submit to a thick covering of winter snow, which accounted for their bent and twisted forms. His principle was further illustrated by the pattern of shrub growth above timberline; the survival of shrubs at the highest elevations depended on the protection provided by the accumulation of heavy snow. Shrubs of the genus *Salix* seemed to attain the highest of elevations, notably species that grow low and are easily bent. *Salix reticulata,* a prostrate willow that roots from the nodes, was evidently the highest climber.[15]

The phenomenon of photosynthesis would not be recognized until late in the nineteenth century; and the general view today is that photosynthesis is a temperature-dependent process. There comes a point at which temperatures are too low during the growing season to sustain the level of photosynthesis required by large plants. Heat deficiency is the primary cause of arctic and alpine tree lines. Thus, Parry's concept of a minimum temperature was on the right track.

The same paper was notable in that it was accompanied by a list of plants Parry had found above timberline. "In this list," he explained, "I confine the term *alpine* to such plants as are met with on the bald exposures above the timber line." What is more, he stated that "the subjoined localities, wherever given, denote that the species referred to is not peculiar to the Rocky Mountains, but is also met with in the different regions [of Europe and Asia]."[16]

From this context, it must be inferred that Parry was aware he was deviating from the traditional use of the word *alpine*. In time, his limited use of the word would become conventional, but not without causing the confusion engendered by the abrupt change in meaning of *any* word. Howard V. Knox, who studied the matter early in the twentieth century, concluded that the derivation of the name *Alps* was uncertain. He found that, at least traditionally, that name applied exclusively to high mountain pastures, not to the peaks and ridges of the chain. In Switzerland in particular, the inhabitants of the high mountain valleys used the word *alp* to mean the summer pastures situated above the plains, but below the snow line. That usage becomes more comprehensible if one notes that the Alps are not a continuous mountain barrier, like the Himalayas or the Andes, but are formed by numerous ranges, divided by deep valleys, that extend from southeastern France virtually to the borders of Hungary.

A second potentially confusing factor today is that many species found above timberline are referred to as *alpines,* when they may be merely reduced or dwarfed specimens of species that are really subalpine or even occasionally montane. In such cases, the plants are not true alpines according to the usage revised by Parry and now generally accepted, including in Europe. Accordingly, the true alpine species are considerably fewer than a casual observer might suspect.

For the traditional, pre-Parry use of the term *alpine,* turn to Linnaeus, the definer of botanical nomenclature. Certainly he used the term *alpine,* as had Casper Bauhin in the seventeenth century. Three examples of plants now found in the Rocky Mountains, their names dating from *Species Plantarum* (1753), are cited below to illustrate Linnaeus's use of the adjective to define both plants and habitats:

1. *Thalictrum alpinum* L., 1:545, habitat Lapland (or Lappland), citing Robert Morison's *Thalictum montanus minimum praecox* as a synonym. In the Rocky Mountains the species ranges from the high montane throughout the subalpine.
2. *Astragalus alpinus* L. 2:760, habitat Lapland and Switzerland. Here, the plant ranges from the lower montane into the subalpine.
3. *Aster alpinus* L., 2:872, habitat Austria, Switzerland, and the Pyrenees. This is a true alpine of the northern Rockies with rare collections as far south as Colorado.

Evidently, Linneaus's use of *alpine* referred to mountainous location, often below timberline. In 1834, Thomas Nuttall gave the name *Bolophyta alpina* Nutt. to a new genus and species he had found "in the Rocky Mountain range; latitude about 42°, 7,000' elevation on summit of lofty hill, near place called 'Three Butes' by the Canadians, towards the sources of the Platte." While he may appear today to have misnamed it, he was perfectly correct. The description of the site suggests the Oregon Trail near Alcova, Wyoming, where the plant has again been found, albeit as transferred to *Parthenium* by Torrey and Gray. Nuttall had sought to segregate *Bolophyta* from *Parthenium,* noting a dissimilar habit, making it perfectly distinct when compared to the *Parthenium integrifolium* L. he had seen in Arkansas.[17] It remains to be seen whether *Bolophyta* will again rise from the dead, as have other distinctly Western genera in recent years.[18]

It is curious that Parry, when describing his restricted use of the word *alpine,* in 1867, neglected to cite any rationale for his decision. We have to assume that he was reflecting new knowledge about plant distribution emanating from Europe, knowledge of which his friends, Gray and Engelmann, were cognizant. Louis Agassiz, Engelmann's fellow student at Heidelberg and Paris, is probably best known for the announcement before the Swiss Society of Natural History, in July 1837, that he had discovered evidence that a prehistoric ice sheet, in the Pleistocene period, had covered the world from the North Pole to the borders of the Mediterranean and Caspian Seas. The sheet had then receded, leaving many traces of the ice masses, including the glaciers in Switzerland, which still moved. The announcement was expanded to book length in 1840 in Agassiz's *Etudes sur les glaciers.*[19]

As Agassiz's discovery provided a key to the geographic distribution of animals and plants, Darwin, who admired Agassiz's work, was perplexed by his apparent unwillingness to pursue the implications of the evidence he had published. When Darwin later devoted a chapter to geographical distribution, he commented that, as early as 1747, J. G. Gmelin, then beginning publication of his *Flora sibirica* in St. Petersburg, had indicated the remarkable fact that many of the plants in the snowy regions of the Alps or Pyrenees had also been found in the extreme northern parts of Europe. Gmelin had presumed these same species must have been independently created at several distinct points. Darwin learned, moreover, from Asa Gray that the plants in the White Mountains in New England were the same as those in Labrador, and nearly the same as those in the loftiest mountains of Europe.

Darwin remarked that it still would have been possible to accept Gmelin's interpretation had it not been for Agassiz and others calling attention to the Glacial period, which, "as we shall immediately see, affords a simple explanation of these facts." He expressly added that he referred to the effects suffered under an arctic climate.[20]

Subsequently, Darwin referred to the far-northern plants both as *arctic* productions and as *Alpine* productions, although in a striking way:

> But with our Alpine productions, left isolated from the moment of the returning warmth, first at the bases and ultimately at the summits of the mountains, . . . it is unlikely that all the same arctic species will have been left on mountain ranges distant from each other, and have survived there ever since; they will, also, in all probability have become mingled with ancient Alpine species, which must have existed on the mountains before the commencement of the Glacial epoch, and which during the coldest period will have been temporarily driven down to the plains. Their mutual relations will thus have been in some degree disturbed; consequently they will have been liable to modification; and this we find has been the case.[21]

In the immediate aftermath of the publication of *Origin,* Darwin's close friend, Joseph Dalton Hooker, who had earlier taken an interest in plant distribution (as had Asa Gray), presented a lengthy paper, "Outlines of the Distribution of Arctic Plants."[22] Asa Gray at once wrote a notice of Hooker's paper for the *American Journal of Science and Arts,* calling attention not only to the facts advanced by Hooker, but to the recent Darwinian hypothesis based on which the facts were discussed.

In passing, Gray made note of an even earlier paper by the British naturalist Edward Forbes (1815–1854), who had prepared the way with an essay in 1846,

"On the connexion between the distribution of the existing Fauna and Flora of the British Isles, and the Geological Changes which have affected their Area, especially during the epoch of the Northern Drift." The connections illustrated were those between various groups in Great Britain and isolated localities on the continent.

As Hooker put the matter,

> Mr. Darwin's hypothesis accounts for many varieties of one plant being found in various alpine and arctic regions of the globe, by the competition into which their common ancestor was brought with the aborigines of the countries it invaded. Different races survived the struggle for life in different longitudes; and these races again, afterwards converging on the zone from which their ancestor started, present there a plexus of closely allied but more or less distinct varieties, or even species, whose geographical limits overlap and whose members, very probably, occasionally breed together.

A further implication of the Darwinian hypothesis was that "the Scandanavian flora is present in every latitude of the globe, and is the only one that is so."[23] In these discussions, the words *alpine* and *arctic* were used interchangeably; and in retrospect, it could seem regrettable that Parry did not choose the word *arctic* to characterize our Rocky Mountain species above timberline, to avoid ambiguity. Hooker recognized that Lapland, if small, contained the richest of the arctic flora, virtually three-quarters of that known in Hooker's time. Lapland is the least frigid portion of the arctic zone and experiences the highest summer temperature.[24] Thus, Linnaeus's exploration of Lapland before his publication of *Species Plantarum* in 1753 proved to be fortuitous.

Parry's considerable fieldwork and his botanical insight won him not only the friendship, but the respect of Torrey and Gray. When the Smithsonian Herbarium was transferred to the Department of Agriculture in 1869 (where it would remain until 1896, when it was restored to the Smithsonian to form the National Herbarium), Torrey secured an appointment for Parry as botanist of the Department of Agriculture. Parry enjoyed the appointment, as it gave him access to numerous collections made at government expense but still untreated. He was also able, in his official capacity, to visit his native country; and at Kew he met the director, Sir Joseph Dalton Hooker, with whom he would maintain a long friendship.

Parry's dismissal in September of 1871 by Judge Frederick Watts, the commissioner of agriculture, was quite unexpected.[25] Asa Gray was at once distressed. Watts's failure to provide a reason for the dismissal could well have led to the suspicion that some grave ethical lapse on Parry's part had been uncovered and was being discreetly cloaked. Gray may also have worried that his judgment of Parry's capacity had been challenged. A series of letters on the subject passed between Gray and Judge Watts, at the end of which Watts granted Gray permission to publish the correspondence to remove any suspicion that anything unethical had occurred. The letters were published in the *American Naturalist* in 1872 to clear the air.

Despite the absolute courtesy of both correspondents, there was a hint of sarcasm in Gray's letters that may have reflected an annoying suspicion that he was getting the truth from Watts, but not the whole truth. His suspicion could have been rooted in the fact that he had not been entirely forthcoming. Gray had also written to Joseph Henry, America's leading physicist, at the Smithsonian, asking for an explanation, a fact he did not reveal to Judge Watts; and Henry's responses were not published along with those of Watts. The two explanations were dissimilar, and Henry's contained some implications that evidently were inconsistent with Gray's purpose.

In truth, even Watts's letter to Gray dated 8 November 1871 revealed that Parry had never performed the wide scope of duties expected from the botanist of the Department of Agriculture. He had devoted himself almost exclusively to the preservation of the herbarium, whereas the department was designed to make the developments of plant science available to farmers and horticulturalists: "The principles of vegetable physiology, their relations to climate, soils, and the food of plants, and the diseases of plants, which are principally of fungoid origin, it is clearly the duty of the botanist to investigate." Watts found no evidence that Parry had entered that domain, nor had he shed any light on cryptogamic botany: "The routine operations of a mere herbarium botanist are practically unimportant." Fair enough, Gray had to admit, leaving him no grounds for complaint beyond the impropriety of the abrupt dismissal without explanation.[26]

The botanical community was thus assured that Parry had not been guilty of any ethical lapse. Joseph Henry's investigation, however, put the incident in a different light, one consistent with the ethos of a bureaucracy. Henry found that there had been a quarrel between Parry and the chief clerk, "who artfully induced Judge Watts to believe that Dr. Parry was incompetent and unfit for his position, in as much as he was obliged to send plants out of the office to be named by other persons, and that his conduct was insubordinate and insulting to the commissioner. I think that Judge Watts is now convinced that he acted hastily."[27]

A few weeks later, Henry reported that, meanwhile, Parry had written Judge Watts an insulting letter regarding some of Parry's procedures that had been in violation of the department's protocol. During his years of employment, Parry apparently had not been greatly concerned with conforming to the bureaucratic protocol of the department; and, as in any clash between scholar and bureaucrat, the scholar rarely wins. Given the insulting letter, Watts could hardly reverse his regretted action.[28]

Parry made the best of his dismissal by spending the summer of 1872 in Colorado. The Grays, in California that summer, proposed to visit Parry on their return trip in order to climb Grays Peak. As Torrey was unexpectedly sent to California that summer as a member of a commission relating to the Mint, he and his daughter, Maggie, also decided to visit Georgetown; although Torrey, at seventy-six, would make no attempt to climb Torreys Peak.[29] Parry entertained the Grays at his cabin in preparation for the dedication of Grays and Torreys Peaks.

The celebration took place at the top of Grays Peak on 14 August 1872, and the account of it was published in the *Georgetown Miner* of 22 August 1872. Asa Gray, Jane Loring Gray, and Maggie Torrey were present, but John Torrey remained below. The party came to a total of twenty-one: present were friends from Davenport, Iowa; local worthies from Georgetown and Empire; and the Reverend Edward Lee Greene of Greeley, Colorado. The principal welcoming address to Gray was delivered by the Reverend Professor Weiser of Georgetown, and was as lengthy and ornate as both the epoch and the location required. Weiser placed Asa Gray in a long line of eminent scientists including Solomon, Theophrastus, Dioscorides, Fuchs, Clusius, Ray, Tournefort, Linnaeus, the Jussieus, and Candolle, among others.

"You with your honored teacher and lifelong friend Dr. Torrey," he continued, "have perhaps done more to simplify and enrich the science of botany than any of your predecessors." He did not mean to undervalue the work of Gray's predecessors, but rather to note that Gray had had the good fortune to be born in the nineteenth century, "when all the sciences began to assume a more practical form." Gray made a short, but appropriate, speech of thanks; after which the ladies present joined to sing the national air, "My Country, 'Tis of Thee, Sweet Land of Liberty." It was altogether a most exhilarating day, on a summit they believed had perhaps the most extensive and magnificent view in the world! The party reached Georgetown safely at eight o'clock that evening.[30]

Parry made a substantial collection in Colorado that summer, but none of the species turned out to be new, no doubt contributing to Gray's confidence that the flora of the Rocky Mountains all had been identified. Parry, moreover, felt free in 1873 to accept Captain William A. Jones's invitation to join an engineering party for the reconnaissance of northwestern Wyoming, in regions not thoroughly explored by Hayden. The opportunity for novelties was attractive. Jones meant to explore the headwaters of the Snake, Bighorn, Greybull, Clark's Fork, and Yellowstone Rivers.

The party assembled at Fort Bridger (Uinta County, Wyoming), departing from there on 11 June 1873. They proceeded northeastward, crossing the Green River and then going across South Pass. Once they had turned northward, with Yellowstone as the target, they passed along the eastern flank of the Wind River Mountains. As usual, Perry's record of collection sites and dates was imprecise and confusing. He did put some emphasis on crossing a low spur of the Owl

Creek Mountains, west of the present site of Thermopolis, an area little explored and the source of several species that proved to be new:

Aquilegia jonesii Parry, Am. Nat. 8:211. 1874
Stanleya tomentosa Parry, Am. Nat. 8:212. 1874
Astragalus grayi Parry ex S. Wats. 8:212. 1874

Evidently the route followed the South Fork of Owl Creek up until the party crossed into the valley of the Stinking Water, which would be the Shoshone River today. Following it to its source, the party then proceeded to the headwaters of the Yellowstone River, descending its valley into the Yellowstone basin. Yellowstone itself proved to be disappointing, as so much botanical material had already been included in the Hayden reports for 1871–1872. But on the return trip, at a high point in the Absaroka Range, from which he could look down into the Snake and Wind River valleys, Perry found *Draba ventosa* Gray, Ibid. 8:212. 1874. The descent was made along the Wind River, and *Townsendia parryi* Eaton, Ibid. 8:212. 1874, was collected in the Wind River Mountains. The trek ended at Camp Brown on 12 September 1873.[31]

Parry had named three Colorado peaks for eminent colleagues, and the nominations had all stood. The surveyor general, G. M. Case, returned the compliment. Parry Peak is located between Clear Creek and Grand Counties. At 13,341 feet in elevation, it is slightly less lofty than Engelmann Peak, making the designation botanically correct.[32]

10

Joseph Dalton Hooker

DARWIN'S CONFIDANT

*T*he study of plant distribution became a new emphasis for botanists in the nineteenth century, a logical development from the accumulation of vast plant collections from around the globe that dated from the eighteenth century. The earliest recognition of floristic affinities between East Asia and North America had appeared in a student thesis sponsored by Linnaeus in 1750, titled *Plantae Rariores Camschatcenses,* it may be found in the series known as *Amoenitates Academicae.* The thesis was probably written by Linnaeus, given the custom of that day, but would have been defended by the student, Jonas P. Halenius.

A large collection of plants, made the previous year in Kamchatka, had been brought to Linnaeus by a botanist now obscure, Lercke. Linnaeus had found among them plants already known to him from Lapland; there were also plants he recognized as having come from Canada and elsewhere in North America, namely, from collections made in eastern Canada by Jean-François Gaulthier, and in Virginia by John Clayton. While Linnaeus expressed surprise about the evidence of such widespread distribution of plants, his observation did not provoke any speculation about plant migration. As in the case of J. G. Gmelin, the conventional acceptance of species being fixed through independent creation had yet to be undermined.[1]

The topic—especially the matter of glaciation—was injected in the prior chapter solely to account for Charles Parry's restricted use of the term *alpine* in 1867. We shall return to the topic here for the context of Joseph Dalton Hooker's visit to the Rocky Mountains in 1877. Botanists today are familiar with the *Index Kewensis,* initially published in two large volumes from 1893 to 1895. They may be unaware that this indispensable index was published under Hooker's direction and made possible by a bequest from Darwin—a recognition of the contributions that plant taxonomy and phytogeography had made in the formulation of his revolutionary hypothesis.

The frequently made assertion that Hooker came to the United States at the invitation of F. V. Hayden to examine the Western flora is inaccurate. In fact, by 1877 Asa Gray had visited England four times, had become a friend of Hooker, and had repeatedly urged Hooker to visit America. The two botanists had, in particular, a strong interest in plant distribution, and Darwin had been aware of their observations before 1859. Gray's awakening to the mysteries surrounding disjunct plant populations seems to have dated from 1839, when he received a copy of the *Flora Japonica*. Based on the collection of Philipp Franz Siebold, of Leyden, the work was arranged and prepared for publication by J. G. Zuccarini, of Munich, and published in Leyden between 1835 and 1839.[2]

Having read of Siebold's collection, Gray also became aware of earlier collections in Japan by Karl Peter Thunberg, a student of Linnaeus, who had provided evidence that a substantial number of species known in eastern North America had also been found in eastern Asia. Thunberg had been in Japan at the time of Linnaeus's death in 1778 and would not publish his *Flora Japonica* until 1784. Gray published a brief paper in 1840 to call attention to the striking analogies between the flora of Japan and that of the temperate part of eastern North America, but made no attempt to account for the disjunct plant populations.

Gray's opportunity to study the phenomenon more closely came when it fell to him to examine specimens collected by Charles Wright, botanist on the North Pacific Exploring Expedition following the "opening" of Japan; as well as plants collected by S. Wells Williams, the missionary engaged by Commodore Perry to act as an interpreter; and by Dr. James Morrow, whose task had been to demonstrate agricultural implements to the Japanese. The Wright collection was the most extensive of the three, as reflected in the title of Gray's paper. Hunter Dupree called this the most important paper of Gray's career.[3]

Of the 580 species determined from Japan, more of them were represented in Europe than in western North America. But far more of them were represented in eastern North America than in either of the other two regions. Rather than accept the idea of separate or double creation to explain the disjunct populations, Gray asserted that the common *temperate* flora had extended unbroken between Asia and North America during the Tertiary period. With the later advances of the glaciers in the northern hemisphere, this homogenous flora was driven southward and separated into two disjunct branches. When the glaciers later retreated, the temperate flora could again drift northward. The idea of a common ancestry and a single center of creation was congenial with Darwin's and Hooker's ideas.[4]

Hooker had been investigating independently the influence of the glacial period on the American flora, especially the hard division between the arctic floras of America and Greenland. When he came to America at Gray's invitation in 1877, Hooker, at sixty, had had long experience as a botanical explorer. The second son of Sir William Hooker, Joseph Dalton Hooker took his medical degree in 1839, then signed on as an assistant surgeon for Sir James Ross's Antarctic expedition and spent three years in the South Seas. On the basis of this expedition he published three major floras encompassing the Antarctic, New Zealand, and Tasmania. His next expedition was to the northern frontiers of India, from which came monographs on the flora of India (1855) and on the Rhododenrons of Sikkim Himalaya (1849). Hooker subsequently traveled in Palestine (1860) and in Morocco (1871).[5]

On the matter of plant distribution, Darwin had derived evidence from Hooker's experience with polar flora. Hooker had found that the plants on the Kerguelon Islands, though standing closer to Africa than to America, were primarily related to the plants of America. That is to say, they were clearly Fuegian. The islands had been stocked mainly by seeds brought with earth and stones on icebergs drifted by the prevailing currents. Even such remote islands did not have an independent flora.[6]

Hooker's scientific reputation had become immense. He succeeded his father, Sir William, as director of Kew Gardens in 1865, and he was knighted in 1877. By the time he came to America that year, he had become president of the Royal Society. Asa Gray, at sixty-seven, was seven years Hooker's senior; but in their exploration west, Gray was obviously the junior partner. Hooker sailed for New York on 28 June 1877, along with his old friends from India, Major-General Sir Richard Strachey and wife. Once there, he received an invitation from F. V. Hayden to join his survey party.

By then, both Hooker and Gray had independently associated disjunctive plant populations with the glacial period. But the question remained as to why the great mountain chains of the American West seemed to contain only a few "pockets" of East Asian types among plants of Mexican and more southern types. Hayden's invitation facilitated that inquiry; the trip was never meant primarily for plant collection, though plants would be collected. Gray and Hooker first went to Saint Louis, where they had a good discussion with George Engelmann, and where they were met by Hayden and his chief assistant, Captain James Stevenson.[7]

The trip was greatly facilitated by the new railroads in the West. The party left Saint Louis on 18 July 1877, taking the Santa Fe Railroad to Pueblo, Colorado, a trip that required two days and two nights. From Pueblo, they boarded the new Denver and Rio Grande Railroad for the trip up the Arkansas valley to Canon City, driving from there up to La Veta Pass, where a camp was established at about nine thousand feet in elevation. A photograph of the party taken there survives at the Gray Herbarium.

The distinction of the group becomes even more impressive if one notes the credentials of not only Hooker, Gray, and Hayden, but of Richard Strachey. Major-General Strachey had for many years been an eminent officer in the British administration of India, where he had become knowledgeable about the geology, botany, and physical geography of the Himalayas. He had also given much time to research in meteorological science, and was largely responsible for the establishment of the Indian Meteorological Department. As for the geologist, James Stevenson, he and his wife, the formidable Mathilda Coxe Stevenson, would soon undertake fundamental research on the ethnology of the Zuni in New Mexico. Whatever may have been of permanent value from this research, her intrusive tactics—especially her campaign to induce the Zuni to use soap—produced a hostility to anthropologists that has never entirely dissipated among the Zuni. The metallurgist, Dr. Robert H. Lamborn, also appears in the photograph. He was an officer of the Denver and Rio Grande Railroad at that time.[8]

On 26 July 1877, the party was in Fort Garland in the San Luis Valley, from where they made the ascent of Blanca Peak, 14,345 feet in elevation, the highest mountain in the Sangre de Christo Range. The effort was very fatiguing and generated much complaining. They spent a night around a huge fire at about thirteen thousand feet, botanizing on the heights the following day.

From the San Luis Valley the party proceeded to Colorado Springs in order to spend two days botanizing in the neighborhood of Pike's Peak, reaching Denver afterward on 1 August 1877. The next day, they went up Clear Creek Canyon to the Georgetown area for the mandatory climb of Grays Peak, Gray alone crossing over to the top of Torreys. Returning to Denver, they went north to Cheyenne, from where they would board the Union Pacific for Ogden.

By 8 August 1877 they were in Salt Lake City, enabling them to make brief jaunts into American Fork Canyon and Cottonwood Canyon. Hooker was eager to meet Brigham Young and secured an interview. Hooker's description of that encounter is either little known or infrequently quoted given the acidity of his remarks. After their stay in Salt Lake City, the party left the Rocky Mountain region for western Nevada and continued into northern California. The entire trip was not productive of new species, nor was it intended to be; but Hooker would return to England with nearly one thousand species of dried plants from the Rocky Mountain, Sierra Nevada, and Coast Range floras for his study of plant migrations.[9]

Almost immediately after returning to England that autumn, Hooker published a brief summary of his observations during the trip. First, he remarked on the clear contrast between the two humid floras in the United States, by which he meant the Atlantic-Mississippi flora and the Pacific flora. Both of them, he added, had been illustrated by Dr. Gray, a reference to Gray's "Contributions to North American Botany," which Gray had been publishing since 1846, and Gray's collaboration with W. H. Brewer and Sereno Watson on the *Botany of California,* a publication that had begun in 1876.

Second, Hooker emphasized that the relation of the dry, intermediate region to the above two humid floras, or to the floras of other countries, had not been similarly treated by anyone.

Third, Hooker stated that the vegetation of the middle latitudes of the continent "resolves itself into three principal meridional floras, *incomparably more diverse than those presented by any similar meridians in the old world;* in fact as far as the trees, shrubs, and many genera of herbaceous plants are concerned, absolutely distinct. These are the two humid and the dry intermediate regions above indicated."[10]

Having used the term *Rocky Mountain region* generally to include the area west of the forested Mississippi area and extending to the Sierra Nevada, Hooker recognized that he must divide that immense region into three floras: 1) a prairie flora, 2) a desert or saline flora, and 3) a Rocky Mountain proper flora—temperate, subalpine, and alpine. He added, moreover, that the Rocky Mountain region, if greatly distinct from both the Eastern and Western regions, did contain a few elements of the Eastern region and still more of the Western region.

Hooker emphasized that, throughout the trip, both Gray and he had been preoccupied with the probable influence of both glacial and warming periods in directing the migration of arctic forms southward and Mexican forms northward on the continent; as well as the effects of the great body of water that had occupied the whole saline region (as it appeared to them) during a glacial period.

Recognizing the significance of Hooker's observations, John M. Coulter at once published an extract from the article in his new journal;[11] and Coulter would be the first to provide a flora for the Rocky Mountain region, following his field experience with the Hayden Survey. An expanded version of Hooker's article, coauthored by Asa Gray, dealing exclusively with the Rocky Mountain region westward through the Wasatch Range, was then published in 1880.

Hooker and Gray proposed that thenceforth the designation *alpine district,* or *alpine zone,* be restricted to mountain summits that feature a "southward prolongation of arctic vegetation." If a considerable number of more temperate species, which had become alpestrine in dwarfed forms, were to be excluded, it meant that the alpine flora did not comprise a large number of species. In Hooker's opinion, the alpine species of North America seemed notably meager in number compared to those of Europe, a matter of geographical configuration and climate. The authors recognized that the botany of the European Alps was thoroughly known by 1880, whereas that of the Rocky Mountains remained "quite imperfectly so," implying that more genera and species remained to be found.[12] One is tempted to assume that Gray had been nudged into that latter assertion, as it was contrary to what he had earlier believed and inconsistent with his continuing disputes with E. L. Greene.

The authors recognized only three genera, as of 1880, that were endemic to the Rocky Mountain region:

Chionophila Benth., a genus in Scrophulariaceae that encompassed two species, either alpine or near timberline

Leucampyx Gray ex Benth. & Hook. f., a monotypic genus in the montane
Orogenia S. Wats., including two species in the Umbelliferae, also montane[13]

These examples may have been meant to illustrate the relative meagerness of the
Rocky Mountain flora, or may have implied that much remained to be found.

The problem of disjunctive genera and species became the second focus of
Hooker and Gray's article. That phenomenon, they asserted, poses no impossible difficulty for those who assume that all the members of a natural genus
were derived at some time or other from a common stock, an assumption by
then generally made in natural history. "A reference to the existing state of
things will seldom answer questions of this kind; but a reference to the past
may sometimes do so."[14]

However far back in time the vegetable paleontologist may go, Hooker and
Gray believed, the botanist of their era could take the Tertiary period for his
point of departure. As for the botanist of the Rocky Mountains in particular, he
must recognize that the arctic flora, between the Arctic Circle and the North
Pole, had extended southward during the glacial age. With the retreat of the ice-
cap and gradual amelioration, the arctic flora was carried back northward except for on the highest mountains, leaving the arctic-alpine vegetation of today.
Thereafter, that primeval stock was exposed to the vicissitudes and climatic
conditions peculiar to Europe, Asia, and North America, and survived in the
forms best adapted to meeting their situations.

Hooker and Gray concluded, finally, with an explanation for differences in
plant distribution that had earlier troubled Asa Gray. It now appeared that the
withdrawal of glaciation took place earlier on the Atlantic side of the continent
than in either the high central or the Pacific regions. Consequently, the Atlantic
side had been less disturbed by catastrophic occurrences, and its flora was probably more completely restored than the floras in the mountainous and Pacific
regions. But that deficit on the Pacific side was obscured by a replenishment
from the Mexican plateau. Hooker and Gray suspected that some East Asian
types, which they called the boreal-oriental element, must have appeared in
North America at a later date. Beyond the particulars in their presentation, they
made a general conclusion that, thenceforth, a satisfactory systematics would require greater research in paleobotany, ecology, and morphology.[15]

Given Hooker and Gray's knowledge of a boreal-oriental element in American flora, the reader may be surprised by the absence in their article of any reference to the Bering bridge. In the summer of 1728, Vitus Bering had sailed
through the strait between the Seward and Chulatka Peninsulas, demonstrating
that the New World was separate from the Old World. Later sounding would
reveal that much of the water in the strait is less than one hundred feet deep;
and, at their closest point, the two continents are separated by only about eighty
kilometers of open water. It is known today that there had been a land bridge
across the North Pacific connecting the two continents during the Tertiary pe-

riod, and another land bridge across the North Atlantic connecting North America to Europe.

Only in 1937 would Eric Hultén, the Swedish specialist on arctic flora, coin the term *Beringia* for the North Pacific land bridge in his doctoral thesis. He emphasized the importance of unglaciated Alaska as a refugium for arctic and boreal plants during the glacial periods. The great storage of water in the immense ice sheets lowered the level of the sea and *re-created* the land bridge, or Beringia, during the glacial periods. That is, the fluctuations of the glacier meant that periodically the ice-free bridge would reappear. When open, the bridge was a route for the interchange of biota, and it accounts for the patterns of plant distribution we recognize today. The final closure of the bridge occurred about ten thousand years ago.[16]

With our increasing awareness of disjunctive plant populations and the migrations of biota over millions of years, the difficulty of distinguishing reliably between native and naturalized has increased commensurately, at least for botanists. Popular use of *native* and *naturalized* has generally been indiscriminate, especially when they are lumped together as *wildflowers,* a word without scientific standing that could be expunged from our vocabulary without imperiling civilization. Popular usage of *native,* in particular, has been further distorted by social and political adaptation to imply either superiority or entitlement to precedence. That tactic is analogous to the adoption of the scientific word *race* in the nineteenth century to mean nationality, the better to make nationalist invidious comparisons that, in fact, quite lacked any scientific credibility.

If, in the search for evidence of nativity, one wishes to go back into the Tertiary period for vegetational history, as Hooker and Gray presumed would be necessary, there has been considerable study, not only of megafossil remains, but also of pollen and spore assemblages that constitute a microfossil record. Fossil flora records on plant distribution and ancestry are available from scattered sites in the Rocky Mountain region: the Green River and vicinity in northwest Colorado and northeast Utah; Kisinger Lakes in northwest Wyoming; Thunder Mountain in the Challis area of Idaho; the Creede site in Mineral County, Colorado; and the Florissant site west of Colorado Springs are notable centers of research. Many of the generic names that have been reported from them have a ring familiar to Rocky Mountain botanists today.[17]

In personal correspondence during the months following his trip to America, Hooker expressed his surprise at having found so many Asian types in western America that were not represented in the East. He suggested that this might indicate several different migrations at very different periods. A more astonishing proposal, however, he made in a note to Darwin: the Rocky Mountain flora would stand a very fair comparison with that of the Altai, which the Sierra Nevada flora would not.[18] As the Altai extend from south-central Siberia southward along western Mongolia into northwest China, Hooker's proposal meant that he quite accepted the possibility of extremely disjunctive plant populations.

Strange to say, no Rocky Mountain plant was named for Joseph Dalton Hooker. *Erigonum hookeri* S. Wats. (1879) did honor him and is found in various western locations; but it is a plant of desert habitat, usually below six thousand feet in elevation, inappropriate for a botanist and phytographer who reached greater heights himself. We can remember him as Darwin's most powerful and effective advocate, as expressed in particular in Hooker's *Flora Tasmaniae,* published several months after the appearance of *Origin.*

11

Sereno Watson

BOTANIST BY INADVERTENCE

*C*ompared to his contemporaries (Hooker, Gray, and Parry), Sereno Watson (1826–1892) remained nearly invisible during the entirety of his respectable career, an obscurity that has survived. To be sure, the *S. Wats.* appended to a remarkable number of western species testifies to the existence of a devoted botanical scholar; but very little of Watson's personality or character seems to have made a defining impression on his contemporaries. What evidence does survive allows the observation that he had cultivated obscurity deliberately and was more than content that notability had eluded him. Such an observation, of course, cannot account for why he had preferred to live in the shade.

It is known that Watson was born in East Windsor in northern Connecticut, that he graduated from Yale College, and that he studied medicine thereafter, training that would have given him some introduction to botany. For nearly the next twenty years, he drifted from vocation to vocation, failing to find any satisfaction: either in the practice of medicine, in teaching, in banking, in insurance, in editorial work, or in farming. Finally, at the age of forty, with his options running out, he enrolled in the Sheffield Scientific School at Yale, evidently in preparation for a move to California and its promise of a new life. Somewhat over a year later, in 1867, he reached California, and almost at once learned that the geologist Clarence King had just departed on his survey of the Great Basin along the fortieth parallel.

Lacking any other prospects, Watson set out to find King in the hope of employment. He rode the Central Pacific Railroad as far east as it went, and then set out to walk eastward along the fortieth parallel. In late July he caught up with the expedition, encamped on the Truckee River, and asked for a job. Being asked to hire a middle-aged man had to have been awkward for King. Only fairly young men, capable of tolerating the rigors of extensive exploration, were generally recruited for western expeditions. The botanist in the King party, William Whitman Bailey, only 24, was a typical example. Moreover, no staff positions were vacant. King, evidently out of pity, allowed Watson to remain with the expedition, but as a volunteer worker without pay.

Given Watson's diverse background, which included medical and scientific instruction, he was able to do many things, and became unexpectedly valuable. It is evident that he soon began to help Bailey with botanical work, as Bailey was apparently ailing, not bearing the strenuous life in the field well. Watson certainly had had some introduction to botany and would have readily learned more in assisting Bailey, as Bailey, a graduate of Brown and employed at M.I.T. at the time he signed on for the expedition, was a competent botanist. By December of 1867, Bailey would write to Asa Gray that Watson had already collected twice the number of specimens than he had, adding, "I cannot speak in terms of too high praise of this gentleman—always genial and kind—and ever persevering. He works early and late, and seems never tired or ruffled."[1] For Watson, life apparently began after forty.

After nine months in the field, Bailey surrendered to his ailments and resigned from the survey. Whether Bailey's decline was primarily physical or mental has never been clear, and he may have been tormented by a conviction that Watson's capacity was greater than his own. In any case, Clarence King was exceedingly fortunate to have a replacement immediately at hand, and Watson was appointed to the botanist's position, with a salary, in March of 1868. The appointment conferred on him the responsibility for writing the botanical section of King's final reports. Because the King survey was mainly confined to the Great Basin, the botanical collection necessarily featured that region. Only toward the end, in the summer of 1869, was Watson able to work in the Wasatch and Uinta Mountains. It was fortunate for Watson that Daniel Cady Eaton (1834–1895) of Yale visited the expedition that summer. An early student of Asa Gray, Eaton must have given Watson valuable professional guidance.

Back in Connecticut by the year's end, Watson sought additional help from Asa Gray in preparing his report, and Gray invited him to Cambridge to work on his collection. Watson described his work as a "Catalogue of the Known Plants of Nevada and Utah with descriptions of genera and species as do not occur east of the Mississippi." It was published as the fifth volume of King's report[2] and included new species in the Compositae named by Eaton. The following new taxa are well known in the Rocky Mountains:

Aquilegia flavescens S. Wats. 5:10. Wasatch Mts.
Caulanthus S. Wats. New genus. 5:27
Caulanthus crassicaulus (Torr.) S. Wats. (type) 5:27. East side of Salt Lake
Caulanthus hastatus S. Wats. 5:27. Wasatch & Uinta Mts.→*Chlorocrambe hastata* (S. Wats.) Rydb.
Astragulus jejunus S. Wats. 5:73. Bear River Valley near Evanston, Wyo.

Sedum debile S. Wats. 5:102. Wasatch & Uinta Mts.

Orogenia S. Wats. New genus. 5:120

Orogenia linearifolia S. Wats. 5:120. Wasatch Mts.

Cymopteris longipes S. Wats. 5:124. Wasatch Mts.

Angelica pinnata S. Wats. 5:126. Wasatch Mts.

Peucedanum bicolor S. Wats. 5:129. Wasatch Mts.→*Lomatium bicolor* (S. Wats.) Coult. & Rose

Aster kingii D.C. Eat. 5:141. Wasatch Mts.→*Tonestus kingii* (D.C. Eat.) Nesom

Erigeron ursinus D.C. Eat. 5:148. Above Bear River Canyon, Uinta Mts.

Tanacetum diversifolium D.C. Eat. 5:180. Wasatch Mts.→*Sphaeromeria diversifolia* (D.C. Eat.) Rydb.

Synthyrus pinnatifida S. Wats. 5:227. Wasatch Mts.

Mertensia brevistyla S. Wats. 5:239. Wasatch Mts.

Polygonum minimum S. Wats. 5:315. Uinta Mts.

Zigadenus paniculatus (Nutt.) S. Wats. 5:343. Wasatch Mts.

Prosartes trachycarpa S. Wats. 5:344. Uinta Mts.→*Disporum trachycarpum* (S. Wats) Benth. & Hook.

Calachortus gunnisonii S. Wats. 5:348. The collection by Creuzefeldt, 1853, from high mountains in Utah is evidently mislabeled; the site had to be southern Colorado.

Allium brevistylum S. Wats. 5:350. Uinta Mts.

Another Watson collection from the Uinta Mountains was published later: *Erigeron eatonii* Gray, *Proc. Am. Acad.* 16:91. 1880. Gray's recognition of a new species from the Rocky Mountains may not have seemed an extraordinary event in 1880, and one would have had to be familiar with Gray's review of Watson's monograph (1871) to even wonder whether Gray's habitual outlook had been altered. That review had been quite favorable, at least superficially; and the fact that Gray had retained Watson's services as an assistant in the Harvard Herbarium was additional evidence of respect. In retrospect, such evidence concealed ambiguities.

In the review, for instance, Gray asserted that one of Watson's most notable discoveries was *Parrya macrocarpa* R. Br., which we know today as *Parrya nudicaulis* (L.) Regel, a species originally published by Linnaeus as a *Cardamine* and located in Siberia. Watson had found the plant at about twelve thousand feet on one of the tallest peaks in the Uintas, illustrating the affinity of alpine and arctic plants in Asia and North America. Gray also noted the new genus, *Caulanthus* S. Wats., to accommodate species previously placed in both *Streptanthus* and *Thelypodium*—of which he obviously did not approve. *Caulanthus* has, of course, survived, as has the type species. It is curious, in fact, that Gray, in a fairly lengthy review of Watson's report, gave little evidence that he recognized the validity of most of Watson's novelties in our range, almost as if he did not expect them to stand.[3]

It remains possible, therefore, that Gray, approaching retirement from his professorship in 1874, sensed that Watson would prove to be an ideal assistant in the Herbarium: he was quiet and painfully shy, dutiful and energetic, having mastered the tools of plant taxonomy, but revealing no wider range of interests that could make him a troublesome innovator. By a curious set of circumstances, Sereno Watson had found his niche. Thereafter, he lived modestly in Cambridge, refused all offers to teach, and rejected all opportunities for greater scientific and social activity.[4]

It would be a mistake, however, to accept Watson's self-imposed limitations as a fair measure of his intellectual capacity. The Harvard Herbarium was simply an ideal refuge for a reclusive botanist. Watson was one of the few botanists of the later nineteenth century about whom Marcus E. Jones retained a favorable opinion. While Jones's views of others have often been challenged as unfair, in Watson's case the assessment was grounded on a close examination of Watson's botany of the fortieth parallel, a geographical area of which Jones had firsthand knowledge, and deserves to be taken as reliable. Jones judged Watson's volume to be the best book yet published on American botany, partly because Jones agreed with most of Watson's judgments on generic and specific limitations, partly because Watson had attempted to write an *ecological* botany for a region.[5]

Asa Gray had also been struck by those observations by Watson that had revealed a new character in Western botanical exploration: an interest in the viability of agriculture in a region often considered to be unsuitable, such as Parry had noted for Colorado. Watson had remarked that water supplies from the Uintas and the Wasatch already provided circumstances favorable for irrigated fields in eastern Utah. But he suggested that the low, shrubby, and perennial vegetation on the plains, which did well without irrigation—or more serviceable substitutes adapted to such conditions—might well be turned to profitable account by future settlers. He had in mind certain orchards, vineyards, or even tree cultures that would not require irrigation and would tolerate a moderate amount of alkali in the soil.[6]

A time would come in the writing of American history when famous careers would be founded on denouncing the introduction of any sort of agriculture into the arid regions of the West; whereas a legitimate protest ought to have exposed the various attempts to introduce crops unsuitable to regional circumstances. That particular mischief led to various abuses of the Western lands, the consequences of which are still unresolved today.

12

The Hayden Survey

BOTANICAL OPPORTUNITY

*F*erdinand Vandiveer Hayden (1829–1887) of Pennsylvania was not a botanist, but rather a geologist and paleontologist who had also obtained a medical degree. He became celebrated as the leader of the United States Geological and Geographical Survey of the Territories, which worked primarily in the northern and central Rocky Mountains between 1867 and 1879, now commonly known as the Hayden Survey. As most of the survey's publications, especially the annual reports, appeared under Hayden's name, the notable scientific personnel on his staff did not enjoy popular recognition; they cast a shadow, for instance, over the botanical contributions of Thomas Conrad Porter, John Merle Coulter, and Leo Lesquereux that has never entirely lifted.

Two recent, commendable biographies of Hayden leave no doubt about the remarkable accomplishments of the Hayden Survey during its summers in the field, especially in matters geological and geographical. Both biographers also endeavor to grapple with Hayden's complex and deeply flawed personality; it has long been known that he was *difficult,* but he has never before been exposed in such detail, yet sympathetically. Hayden emerges as a man of undoubted talents, who sought and obtained the leadership of a vast enterprise that achieved notable results, but also as that breed of man who should never be granted administrative authority over the lives and careers of other human beings.[1]

His administrative difficulties were compounded by the fact that such enterprises, funded by governments, have always been vulnerable to those whose political support for funding comes at the price of employing a favorite relative or client regardless of qualification. Hayden, without doubt, was successful in his intention to recruit men of established scientific authority for his staff. We also have evidence of volunteers occasionally joining the survey for limited periods, mature, responsible men hoping to contribute to scientific knowledge by collecting plants for determination by the chief botanist. George Nelson Allen, for example, had been a professor of natural history at Oberlin for nearly thirty years; he joined the survey in 1871, after retiring from teaching. Robert Adams, a Philadelphia attorney, had studied geology under Hayden at the University of Pennsylvania; he collected plants with George Allen in 1871.[2] But the wastrels were abroad, too, mostly young, out for a lark, and astonished to find that work was expected of them. Porter would frequently complain to Hayden about the fragmentary plant specimens such indifferent collectors would bring to him. Their names, and those of their patrons, have been treated at some length by James Cassidy.[3]

During the second summer the survey was in the field, 1868, Hayden made plant collections himself. He would have had at least elementary instruction in botany during his study for a medical doctorate. The experience probably convinced him of the need for a professional botanist on the staff. The survey crossed Wyoming that year along the Union Pacific Railroad, going as far as Fort Bridger, Uinta County; then it backtracked in order to work along the Front Range in Colorado. En route, two side trips were made: the first into the Medicine Bow Range to explore the "Last Chance" diggings; the second from Fort Sanders (Laramie) up the Big Laramie to the Old Cherokee Trail, which led them westward into North Park. Plant collections would be given to Porter after his appointment as chief botanist for the survey in 1869.[4]

Thomas Conrad Porter (1822–1901) has never loomed as a major figure. He graduated from Lafayette College, Easton, Pennsylvania, in 1840 and took an M.A. in 1843, also at Lafayette. His theological training took place at Princeton between those two degrees, and he did serve as pastor of the Second Reformed Church in Reading, Pennsylvania, for a time. But, in 1848, he accepted an appointment in the natural sciences at Marshall College (soon to become Franklin & Marshall), remaining until 1866. The tradition of the pastor-naturalist had been common since the eighteenth century. In such bifurcated careers, the faith in sciences frequently became dominant. Porter's appointment to a professorship at Lafayette College in 1866 signified recognition of his professional command of the natural sciences, and he held that appointment until retirement in 1897. In the interim, he was awarded the degrees of Doctor of Divinity (Rutgers, 1865) and Doctor of Letters (Franklin & Marshall, 1880). Service on the Hayden Survey occupied his summers from 1869 to 1874.[5]

The survey of 1869 was launched from Fort Russell (later Fort Warren), working southward across Colorado into New Mexico. Hayden had engaged Cyrus Thomas, brother-in-law to Senator John Logan, for the trip. Faced with the necessity of accommodating political pressure without threatening the professionalism required to accomplish his mission, Hayden could at least find some solace in the fact that Thomas had acquired some reputation as an entomologist (albeit self-taught) and had developed an interest in agriculture.[6] His primary mission on the survey, consequently, was to investigate the locust plague in the West, and he could presumably serve as a plant collector for Porter.

As Porter would never acknowledge that Thomas had been a significant collector (and he would be generous in such acknowledgments), it is fair to assert that Thomas's major contribution that year was his report entitled "Agriculture in Colorado," a twenty-two-page paper in Hayden's *Third Annual Report* for 1869. Settlers along the Front Range in Colorado told Thomas that streams had been producing greater volumes of water in recent years, an assessment verified by local Mexicans and Indians. Such testimony led Thomas to believe that the settlement of the territory—the development of roads and the cultivation of fields—had been followed by a gradual increase in rainfall.

In later years, the Hayden Survey would be held responsible for the thesis that rain follows the plow, and unfairly so, as that idea had earlier been advanced by Josiah Gregg and was already widely believed on the plains. Neither Thomas nor Hayden, moreover, was among those promoters who seized on the thesis in their eagerness to attract farmers to settle on the plains. Both men believed that irrigation would be required for successful farming on the plains. Later research would confirm that there had been some increase in moisture at the time of Thomas's report, the result of a climatic cycle. But before the thesis was discredited, many farmers were ruined by attempts to plant crops unsuitable to the conditions.[7]

The fourth survey, in the summer of 1870, was mainly of Wyoming. The party again set off from Fort Russell (Cheyenne), proceeded to Fort Fetterman on the North Platte (at its juncture with La Prele Creek), and then followed the traditional route up the Platte to the Sweetwater, and westward over South Pass to Fort Bridger—through a region, in other words, already well botanized. The return trip, beginning after mid-September, moved into the Uinta Mountains south of Henry's Fork of the Green River. Eastward bound, the party passed through Bridger's Pass (south of the present Creston Junction) in the Red Desert and crossed the Medicine Bow Range to reach Cheyenne. Most of the return trip was beyond the plant-collecting season. Porter did produce a plant list for the *Fourth Annual Report,* attributing the collection to Hayden, and padded the list with plants that Hayden had collected in North Park, Colorado, during August of 1868.[8]

Leo Lesquereux (1806–1889), the paleobotanist, joined the survey for the first time in 1870. Born in Neuchâtel, Switzerland, he had emigrated to the United States in 1848, settling permanently in Columbus, Ohio, in 1850. His work for Hayden, cataloguing fossil plants, would extend throughout the remaining history of the survey. His service provides an instance in which Hayden gave a staff member good treatment invariably, clearly recognizing that Lesquereux required and merited special care. In the first place, Lesquereux was sixty-five when he joined the survey, well beyond the age considered the upper limit for service on expeditions. He would not have gone at all without a substantial salary, as he had worked his entire life in science but had no provisions for his future. Lesquereux acknowledged that Hayden had paid him fairly, at five dollars a day, and had given him every encouragement in his work. That encouragement enabled Lesquereux to overcome his poor eyesight and to cope with total deafness. He had learned English only after becoming deaf, so he remained inarticulate and worked in total silence. "I have lived with nature, the rocks, the trees, the flowers," he wrote. "[T]hey know me, I know them. All outside are dead to me."[9]

The dependence was, in truth, mutual. As a geologist, Hayden took a special interest in the discovery of coal beds, both their location and dates. He had come to the conclusion that the lignites in Colorado and Wyoming were part of the same basin, which he called the Great Lignite, on the Upper Missouri, and that the coal beds were Tertiary in age. John S. Newberry, under whom Hayden had studied when a medical student, and who had conducted research in New Mexico, argued that the lignites were Cretaceous, extending that claim to include fossil plants collected in the Green River Basin. Once Hayden became aware, in 1870, that Lesquereux shared his opinion, all new fossil plants were given to Lesquereux for determination, and none sent to Newberry, for the next six years. As a consequence, Lesquereux wrote the sections on fossil plants for Hayden's annual reports and final report. Lesquereux's age caught up with him during the summer of 1873. Returning home exhausted, he knew he must not go out again.[10]

The Hayden Survey took aim at the Tetons and Yellowstone for the summer of 1871. The trip was launched from Ogden on 11 June, and the party headed northward through Idaho to Fort Ellis in Montana (near Bozeman), from where they turned south into the Yellowstone region. Porter published the lists of plants collected in 1871, including those collected on the headwaters of the Yellowstone River by George N. Allen and Robert Adams; in addition, there were a few plants collected on Grays Peak near Georgetown by Dr. George Smith, a naturalist from Pennsylvania who collected in Colorado in 1871.[11]

Porter acknowledged that, in his plant determinations, he had consulted with Torrey, Gray, Engelmann, S. T. Olney, E. A. Tuckerman, George Thurber, and Lesquereux on those orders of which they were specialists. That practice is so common among botanists, in the interest of precision, that botanists would have seen the statement as evidence of conscientious scholarship. As in the case of Charles Parry's earlier clash with the clerk in the Department of Agriculture, an outsider could interpret such a practice as an admission of incompetence. Consequently, the matter would be of no significance except as a *possible* explanation for Hayden's unexplained loss of confidence in Porter later that year.

Meanwhile, Porter's list contained several taxa worthy of note:

Aster haydenii Porter in Hayden. 485. 1872, from the upper falls of the Yellowstone River→*Aster alpigenus* (Torr. & Gray) A. Gray ssp. *haydenii*
(Porter) Cronq.
Porterella Torr. in Hayden. 488. 1872. The type species was *Porterella*
carnosula (H. & A.) Torr., from Yellowstone Lake, transferred from *Lobelia,*
the original specimen collected by John McLeod from Blackfoot River,
Snake Country, published by H. & A. 1839.

For the survey of 1872, Hayden decided to divide the expedition into two
parties. He would lead one group to resume the exploration of the Yellowstone
region south of Fort Ellis. The second group would be led by James Stevenson
from Ogden to Fort Hall, Idaho, and there turn eastward toward the Tetons, to
explore first the Teton Basin in Idaho. John Merle Coulter was present on the
survey for the first time and assigned to the Stevenson party. The celebrated
photographer William Henry Jackson was also in the Stevenson party.[12]

Coulter (1851–1928) had graduated in 1870 from Hanover College in Indiana with a B.A., and was only twenty-one at the time he joined the survey. His
interest in botany had suddenly blossomed during his senior year in college
thanks to the inspiring teaching of a newly appointed professor of natural sciences, E. Thompson Nelson. Coulter's employment on the Survey, however, was
owed to the influence of his geology professor, Frank H. Bradley, who served as
chief geologist for the Stevenson section in 1872 and took Coulter along as an
assistant in geology. Coulter's unwillingness to play cards during leisure hours
on the trip (a common pastime) led him to begin plant collecting. It is useful to
remember him as coming toward the end of that era when natural scientists
were trained liberally rather than professionally. Even when he would later take
his doctorate from Indiana University in 1882, his field was philosophy.[13]

Even though the actual route of the Stevenson party deviated somewhat from
the initial plan, its guiding purposes were faithfully served; and the party leaving Ogden in late May would rejoin the Hayden group on the Firehole River in
Yellowstone on 14 August 1872. The actual route enabled Coulter to collect
plants on both the western and eastern watersheds of the Continental Divide,
for the possibility of distinctive floras interested him. He found that the plants
common to the mountains and valleys along the Yellowstone River were not essentially different from those met along the Snake River. Slight differences
would be recorded, but were hardly sufficient to form two distinct floras.

The route offered initially the opportunity to explore the western flank of the
Wasatch Range; then it followed the stage road to Fort Hall; in July it took the
party up to the western slope of the Tetons. By August, they were moving up
Henry's Fork of the Snake to Henry's Lake, crossing the Divide into the drainage
of the Madison by way of Targhee Pass. Coulter found the Wasatch Range to
have few alpine plants, as the subalpine flora clothed the highest peaks almost

entirely. For the most part, the plants on the Wasatch were identical to those he collected at equal elevations on the Tetons. But because the Tetons rise so much higher in elevation than the Wasatch, and are exposed constantly to such severe cold from snow and winds, Coulter found a flora above ten thousand feet such as he saw nowhere else during the trip: it was a great opportunity to collect what he called *truly alpine plants*. He was struck by the abruptness with which tree life terminated at the *average* elevation of eleven thousand feet. Tall, straight conifers grew to the very edge of that line. "One step beyond and you enter an open, bleak world, the few trees stunted and twisted, usually growing in the shelter of a rock or steep bank."[14]

Coulter found the flora of the Firehole Basin in Yellowstone distinct for two reasons: the geyserite had created what he called *an unnatural soil,* and the hot springs produced an artificial warmth. Not all the plants there were species different from those in nearby valleys, but they became much ranker, grew to two to three times their usual size, and were sometimes discolored. Under those soil and temperature conditions, Coulter believed that species within the Compositae dominated.[15]

After the two sections of the survey were reunited in mid-August of 1872, Hayden became favorably impressed by what Coulter had accomplished since May; it does appear that the months in the field had been a graduate school for Coulter, who had worked hard and learned much. After mid-August, productive collecting declined rapidly, and it virtually ceased by September. Meanwhile, what Porter had been accomplishing remains unclear. For in the aftermath of the survey that year, Hayden, without any warning or explanation, replaced Porter as chief botanist with John Coulter. Porter was deeply hurt by the abrupt demotion. It was not only humiliating given his substantial seniority; but it meant that the plants collected that season, technically Hayden's, would be assigned to Coulter for publication of the record.[16]

While Coulter accepted that assignment, it is apparent that he managed his subsequent association with Porter with great tact, adopting the junior role as assistant to Porter. His great sense of propriety enabled the two to collaborate cordially into 1873 and 1874, and Coulter would publicly declare that it had been *his privilege* to assist Porter in compiling the first flora of Colorado. In the meantime, Coulter published the botanical results of the 1872 survey, a report not notable for its new species, but rather for its emphasis on ecological factors, and for a generous inclusion of difficult taxa that one would have no reason to expect from a beginning collector. Numerous grasses, fungi, mosses, and lichens brought the total collection to over twelve hundred species.[17] The lichens, sixty-six of them, were published separately by a specialist.[18]

For the next four years, 1873 to 1876, the survey was in Colorado, an area already well botanized by Parry, Harbour, Hall, and others. Accordingly, Porter believed that the time had come to publish an overview of the flora of Colorado, based not only on the collections they would make during the summer of 1873, but on those of their predecessors. Working together, Porter and Coulter collected widely, but mainly in central or interior Colorado. Collection sites ranged from the Arkansas Valley northward through Jackson County, also including Clear Creek and Boulder Counties and the Long's Peak area. Even though Frémont and Hayden had been in North Park earlier, Porter and Coulter were the first to collect successfully in that vast mountain park and into the Sierra Madre Range in Wyoming.[19]

Porter and Coulter's book was published officially as a product of the Hayden Survey.[20] The authors acknowledged a number of prior collectors and their collecting dates in Colorado, most notably Parry, Hall, and Harbour, whose published plant lists could be studied. Also included were amateurs, botanophiles whose names are long forgotten, but whose specimens were frequently available for actual examination:

Dr. William Abraham Bell of Manitou Springs, Colorado, a railroad executive who collected along railroad routes

Ferdinand Hayden in 1868

Benjamin Hayes Smith of Denver, who collected plants in 1869 for his father's herbarium in Pennsylvania

Dr. George Smith (the father), founder of the Delaware County Institute of Science, who collected in Colorado in 1871

William B. Canby of Wilmington, Delaware, who collected in South Park in 1871

Thomas Meehan, botanist-horticulturalist in eastern Pennsylvania, who collected in Colorado in 1871 and 1873 for the Academy of Natural Science of Philadelphia

Josiah Hoopes, nurseryman of West Chester, Pennsylvania, who collected in Colorado in 1873

John Howard Redfield, businessman affiliated with the Academy of Natural Sciences in Philadelphia

Townsend S. Brandegee, civil engineer, in Canon City, Colorado, beginning in 1871

Reverend Edward Lee Greene of Pueblo, Colorado, in 1872 and 1873

Porter and Coulter were given no time to prepare an introductory article that could have provided helpful information. The title of their book, *Synopsis,* unfortunately suggests the usual plant lists published in official reports. In fact, the *Synopsis* was a real flora and remains a valuable reference work. Collection locations were given, along with the name of the collector, for every species included. Although there is no glossary from which to verify their definitions, one can deduce from their use of *alpine* and *subalpine* that the authors had been introduced to the new, restricted usage of *alpine.* Thanks to the inclusion of plants collected by amateurs, the *Synopsis* remains of interest to those studying phytogeography.

Porter's New Species

Astragalus scopulorum T. C. Porter, *Syn. Fl. Colo.* 24. 1874. South Park
Astragalus brandegei T. C. Porter, Ibid. 24. 1874. Arkansas River near Canon City
Rosa arkansana T. C. Porter, Ibid. 38. 1874. Abundant in the Rocky Mountains
Aplopappus integrifolius Porter ex Gray, *Syn. Fl. Colo.* 1:128. 1884→*Pyrrocoma
    integrifolia* (Porter ex Gray) Greene. Colo., Wyo., Mont. Collected by Coul-
    ter on Henry's Fork of the Snake, 1872
Aster ericoides L. var. *strictus* Porter, *Syn. Fl. Colo.* 56. 1874→*Aster porteri*
    Gray, *Proc. Am. Acad.* 16:89. 1881. Mountains of Central Colo.
Erigeron coulteri Porter, *Syn. Fl. Colo.* 61. 1874. Mountains of Colo.
Actinella grandiflora Torr. & Gray var. *glabrata* Porter, Ibid. 76. 1874→*Actinella
    brandegei* Porter ex Gray, *Proc. Am. Acad.* 13:373. 1878.→*Tetraneuris bran-
    degei* (Porter ex Gray) Parker. Southern Colo., alpine
Senecio renifolius Porter, *Syn. Fl. Colo.* 83. 1874. nom. illeg.→*Senecio porteri*
    Greene, *Pitt.* 3:186. 1897. Ouray County, 13,000', White House Mountain
Melica bulbosa Geyer ex Porter & Coulter, Ibid. 149. 1874. Geyer's collection
    from upper North Platte, Wyo.
Melica mutica Walt. var. *parviflora* Porter, Ibid. 149. 1874→*Melica porteri*
    Scribner. Glen Eyrie, El Paso County, Colo.

Completion of this flora terminated the two authors' affiliation with the Hayden Survey. For the summer of 1875, Hayden hired Townsend S. Brandegee of
Canon City, Colorado, as a topographer-botanist. Brandegee (1843–1925), a
graduate of Yale in 1870 and by training a civil engineer, has been primarily remembered for his later years of residence in Berkeley and San Diego, when he
had become chiefly a botanical explorer; and for having founded the botanical
journal, *Zoe,* in San Francisco in 1890. It would become an outlet for the publication of new Western species. But between 1871 and 1879, he had been employed as the city and county engineer in Canon City, where he began to botanize
for his own amusement. He became known in the East by sending duplicates
from his collections to the major herbaria, accounting for why Asa Gray recommended him to Hayden when the Survey reached southern Colorado in 1875.
Hired primarily as a topographer, Brandegee would not be able to collect as thoroughly as he would have desired; but after 1875, he accepted several assignments
to do railway surveying, which enabled him to become better acquainted with
the plants of Colorado. *Allium brandegei* S. Wats, for instance, was collected by
Brandegee in the Elk Mountains, Gunnison County, in July of 1881.[21]

As for the itinerary in 1875, the survey left from Pueblo, crossed the Sangre de
Cristo Range over Mosca Pass, reached the Rio Grande about fifteen miles upstream from Del Norte, proceeded up that valley to Wagon Wheel Gap, and
crossed the San Juan Mountains into the Animas River valley. Brandegee was able
to explore the Mesa Verde area and was evidently in the valleys of the La Plata, the

Mancos, and the San Juan Rivers. He necessarily limited his collecting to what he thought had not been previous published, given the constraints on his time.

Yet, he also devoted a lengthy passage in his report to describing known plants in the various geographical regions through which he passed, providing good information for later ecologists. He was, in fact, quite aware that southwest Colorado, never having been the residence of the white man, had not yet been invaded by certain plants commonly introduced from eastern seeds. He mentioned the pesky cocklebur, *Xanthium strumarium* L., already introduced on the eastern slope by cattle from Texas, predicting that it would become apparent on the western slope as well, on ditch banks, as soon as farmers began to irrigate. He predicted that cultivation, irrigation, or large herds of cattle and sheep would produce great changes in the plant population.[22]

Brandegee's published list of plants indicates that he collected in areas not on the route of the Hayden Survey. Many of the plants were determined for him by Gray, Engelmann, Watson, Porter, and Eaton; and, if new species, published elsewhere before appearing on Brandegee's list:

no. 234. *Polygala acanthoclada* A. Gray. San Juan River in Utah near border

no. 234. *Trifolium brandegei* S. Wats. Sierra La Plata

no. 235. *Astragalus humillimus* A. Gray ex Brandeg. Mesa Verde

no. 235. *Astragalus haydenianus* A. Gray. La Sal Mountains→*Astragalus bisulcatus* (Hook.) A. Gray var. *haydenianus* (A. Gray) Barneby

no. 235. *Astragalus pattersonii* A. Gray ex Brandeg. Gore Range, Grand County

no. 237. *Mentzelia chrysantha* Engelm. ex Brandeg. Canon City

no. 238. *Aster coloradoensis* Gray ex Brandeg. San Juan Pass→*Machaeranthera coloradoensis* (Gray ex Brandeg.) Osterhout

no. 239. *Dicoria brandegei* Gray. San Juan River, Utah

no. 240. *Gilia haydenii* A. Gray. Mesa Verde

no. 241. *Gilia brandegei* A. Gray. Wagon Wheel Gap→*Polemonium brandegei* (A. Gray) Greene

no. 242. *Grayia brandegei* A. Gray. San Juan valley→*Zuckia brandegei* (A. Gray) Welsh & Stutz ex Welsh

Toward the end of his sojourn in Canon City, Brandegee undertook a study of the growth patterns of conifers on the Crestones, high pinnacles of rock in the Sangre de Cristo Range. The Crestones rise as high as fourteen thousand, two hundred feet in elevation, and the timberline is at roughly twelve thousand feet. Brandegee recorded the approximate elevations reached by the local conifers—eight species of pine, fir, spruce, and douglas fir—but made no attempt to explain the phenomenon of timberline. Instead, the brief report serves as an illustration of the increasing interest in ecology characteristic of botanists in the later nineteenth century.[23]

The contemporary work of Joseph Trimble Rothrock (1839–1922) can be cited as a notable example of the new emphasis. A Pennsylvanian, Rothrock graduated in 1864 from Harvard, where he was a student of Asa Gray; and he completed his medical doctorate at the University of Pennsylvania in 1867. That background enabled him to serve on the survey led by Lieutenant George M. Wheeler between 1873 and 1875, in Colorado, New Mexico, Arizona, Utah, and Nevada, as both surgeon and botanist. As a collector, he became responsible for the general botanical report, much of which he wrote himself.[24] During 1873, Rothrock had as his assistant John Wolf (1820–1897), a botanist-naturalist little remembered today. It is known that he lived in Canton, Illinois, and was evidently an associate of Elihu Hall, who had botanized with Parry and Harbour. Rothrock acknowledged that Wolf did most of the collecting that summer in Colorado.[25]

A number of species associated with the names Rothrock or Wheeler were, in fact, published elsewhere and were not Rocky Mountain plants. Examples are: *Artemisia rothrockii* A. Gray, *Nama rothrockii* A. Gray, and *Potentilla wheelerii* S. Wats., all published in 1876. The *Erysimum wheelerii* Rothr. (1878), reported from Colorado mountains, is today generally held to be a form of *Erysimum capitatum* (Dougl. ex Hook.) Greene. That section of the report written by Daniel C. Eaton, "Ferns of the Southwest," largely featured species out of our range.[26]

While the plant collection reported from the Wheeler expedition was very extensive, comparatively few new species were found for such a lengthy period in the field. Yet, the magnitude of the collection was an important contribution to phytogeography, all the more so given Rothrock's report on economic botany, which indicated his breadth of interest, and which remains valuable for ecologists today.[27] The few new Rocky Mountain species were all from Colorado, and John Wolf was the likely collector:

Atriplex wolfii S. Wats., *Proc. Am. Acad.* 9:112. 1874. Central Colo.
Salix wolfii Bebb ex Rothrock, *Bot. Wheeler Exp.* 6:241. 1878. South Park, Colo.
Ribes wolfii Rothr., *Am. Nat.* 8:358. 1874. Mosquito Pass, Lake County, Colo.
Townsendia rothrockii Gray ex Rothrock, *Bot. Wheeler Exp.* 6:148. 1878. South
    Park, Colo.
Trisetum wolfii Vasey, *USDA Monthly Report.* Feb.–Mar. 156. 1874. Twin Lakes,
    Lake County, Colo.

The Hayden Survey in 1876 did not employ botanists, and thus dispensed with plant lists and reflections on economic botany. But Cyrus Thomas, the entomologist from Illinois, was on board, resulting in observations and proposals pertaining to agriculture in the West beyond what he had written in 1869. It has been pointed out that the men with Hayden who had farming experience all came from regions where streams were of a different character from those in the arid West—men who had had no experience with desert conditions.

Hayden estimated in 1876 that 4.5 million acres in the Rocky Mountain West were tillable, 7 percent of the entire area. He believed that there was enough water to irrigate without creating reservoirs, and that irrigation would be indispensable. This proved to be a major overestimation of what could be irrigated from direct flow. It has to be added in all fairness that there had not yet been any measurement of stream flow, nor was even the annual precipitation known for any considerable period. Evaporation was an unknown factor.

Although a charitable case has been made to exonerate both Hayden and Cyrus Thomas for the invention of the "rain will follow the plow" theory, the evidence remains that Thomas in particular was prone to advocate proposals regarding the use of western water that were far from his area of expertise. He was, for instance, the author of a scheme to join the Arkansas and South Platte Rivers by a two-hundred-mile canal in eastern Colorado. The combined waters from the two rivers were then to be backed up into a series of lakes, not only for irrigation, but to modify the climate and increase the rainfall. The proposal appeared in the Hayden report for 1876 along with Hayden's disclaimer attributing the idea to Thomas alone. Hayden called the project magnificent and worthy of being ranked with the Great Wall of China as an expensive folly.[28]

John Coulter, meanwhile, after his experience on the Hayden Survey, joined the faculty of Hanover College (Indiana) in 1874. There he established his *Botanical Bulletin* in 1875, soon renaming it the *Botanical Gazette*. The journal would go with him to Wabash College in 1879. Both Hanover and Wabash were decent schools, but both were deficient in libraries and laboratories. It seems probable that Coulter sensed such employment to be a threat to his professional development, and that he used editing a journal to counteract intellectual isolation.

Since the days of the rebellious Nuttall, all the Rocky Mountain plant collectors had deferred to the authority of Torrey, Gray, and Engelmann. The deference derived in part from a legitimate regard for their professional stature; but also from their control of the limited patronage available, and from the fact that opportunities for publication were virtually limited to Philadelphia, New York, and Washington, where the patrons' influence was paramount. When John Coulter founded his journal, and did so in Indiana, he inadvertently opened the first breach in the established monopoly. It was not an act of hostility; Coulter would always be on good terms with Asa Gray. But, henceforth, Coulter's precedent would encourage those who craved independence to found their own journals within the West itself; and theirs would be a generation that would actually settle in the West (Rydberg being the exception), thereby losing a sense of dependence on the East.[29]

Coulter remained at Wabash for a dozen years. One of his students, Joseph Nelson Rose (1862–1928), became Coulter's assistant and ultimately his collaborator. While in Crawfordsville, Indiana, they published an important monograph on umbels, in which appeared *Ligusticum porteri* Coult. & Rose, collected along the headwaters of the South Platte and in the Sierra Madre Range by Coulter in 1873.[30] Rose moved on to the U.S. Department of Agriculture as a botanist in 1888, moving again in 1896 to the United States National Museum, where he remained until his retirement in 1912.

The haste that had been imposed on Porter and Coulter in preparing their *Synopsis of the Flora of Colorado* for publication with the Hayden report had left Coulter in particular with an urge to rectify what he believed to be the book's shortcomings. Not only did the *Synopsis* lack what he called a convenient organization, but its coverage was limited to Colorado. What was needed was a manual for the entire Rocky Mountain region.

Coulter wrote such a book while still at Wabash College.[31] Ever mindful that he was primarily a geologist, Coulter not only recalled the privilege he had had in assisting T. C. Porter, but acknowledged the encouragement and criticism he had received from Gray and Watson and his debt to the work of M. S. Bebb on *Salix* and L. H. Bailey on *Carex*. With several deviations, Coulter's plant order followed that of Bentham and Hooker's *Genera Plantarum,* the last of the great prephylogenetic linear systems; it was a system that Hooker, in particular, thanks to his association with Darwin, had recognized to be outmoded. A notable feature of the new manual was Coulter's separating native plants as much as possible from those introduced by placing all introduced plants in footnotes.

A suggestive illustration of Coulter's adherence to Asa Gray was Coulter's acceptance of Gray's transfer of *Phellopterus montanus* Nutt. to *Cymopteris montanus* (Nutt.) Torr. & Gray; whereas Rydberg and Nelson would retain *Phellopterus* into the twentieth century. A similar example would be Coulter's preference for *Parthenium alpinum* (Nutt.) Torr. & Gray over *Bolophyta alpina* Nutt., whereas M. E. Jones, Rydberg, Nelson, and W. A. Weber all would remain loyal to *Bolophyta* as a good genus.[32]

Coulter's professional advancement was delayed further when he accepted the presidency of Indiana University in 1891, remaining for two years, and then the presidency of Lake Forest College, a small private school probably more congenial to Coulter's strong religious views. After three more years, he received an appointment (1896) to the young University of Chicago with a mission to build a new department of botany, and he took the *Botanical Gazette* with him to Chicago.[33] He would be instrumental in 1907 in inducing the University of Chicago to place its herbarium in the Field Museum to give Chicago one great herbarium rather than two competing ones. The precedent had been the recent merger of the Columbia University herbarium with that of the New York Botanical Garden.

Coulter's arrival, so to speak, turned his attention away from the Rocky Mountain region; and the two genera named to honor him, *Coulterella* Vasey & Rose and *Coulterophytum* Robinson, are not represented in our region. His religious commitment remained unaltered. The young man who had taken to plant collection rather than play cards was a devoted member of his church in his Chicago years, teaching a large Sunday School class for the men of his church every Sunday morning without fail.[34]

13

Edward Lee Greene

BOTANIST-HISTORIAN

*E*dward Lee Greene seems to have irritated most of his contemporaries most of the time. Baffled equally by his behavior and his taxonomic principles, they could not respond by ignoring him, as the magnitude of his work commanded attention; and his mastery of languages and history, coupled with exhaustive fieldwork, surpassed most of theirs. If the requisite materials were available, a full-scale biography of him would be an irresistible project. The surviving record encompasses scattered correspondence, his herbarium, publications, mere traces of his clerical years, plus the inevitable recollections left by acquaintances who generally knew him superficially, but felt driven to make definitive pronouncements about him. The most reliable summary of Greene's life, based on primary sources, occupies only twenty-seven pages; but it provides an admirable alternative to the received ideas about the man.[1]

Even from such fragmentary evidence, it is possible to perceive a remarkably consistent pattern in Greene's life, beginning in childhood, of which he was quite conscious, and against which he made no protest. He was born in Rhode Island in 1843. Even in much later years, he retained a fond memory of an old garden on the family property, recognizing it to have been an earthly paradise for him as a child. His mother, who was a devoted gardener, had a copy of Mrs. Lincoln's elementary textbook on botany in her library.[2] The book was generously peppered with religious messages meant to convince the novice of the absolute propriety of botanical study and the sublimity of science. Greene would recall that he had found the book at about the age of six and had been inspired by it. As a child, he would give evidence of strong religious conviction, and his mother's garden became that other Eden, perhaps reflecting the aura at home created by his mother.

By the age of eleven, when the family moved briefly to Illinois before settling in southern Wisconsin, Greene recalled having already become an avid searcher for plants in the field. Such an early immersion in plants and religion, if conducive to a precocious knowledge of vegetation, surely suggests a childhood obstructive to normal social development. It could explain why Greene's later social life, although he was not unfriendly or reclusive, seems to have been confined to matters botanical and to religious issues. His passion extended no further.

The move to Albion, Dane County, Wisconsin, quite inadvertently served to cultivate Greene's predisposition. A Swedish naturalist, Thure Kumlien, had settled nearby. Kumlien, a graduate of the University of Uppsala, had studied with Elias Fries, one of Europe's most eminent botanists, known especially for his fundamental work in the classification of cryptogams. In 1859, at the age of sixteen, Greene entered the Albion Academy, a coeducational school founded by Seventh Day Baptists, but having a nonsectarian religious emphasis. The curriculum was classical, but considerable training in natural science was available. Kumlien occasionally took groups of students on field trips, and Greene would remember him as his earliest teacher and companion in botanical study. Kumlien also impressed on him the importance of language study, and Greene's later facility in languages would help him in the study of both botany and botanical history.

Greene's junior year at the academy was interrupted by his deciding, along with his father and two brothers, to join the Union Army; and he served as a private in the Thirteenth Wisconsin Infantry for nearly three years (1862–1865). Throughout the war, he and Kumlien kept up a correspondence, from which it has been deduced that Greene carried a copy of Alphonso Wood's *Classbook of Botany* (1845) in his pack,[3] and that he collected plants during moments of leisure. It is a most curious fact that Greene's letters revealed no interest in the political or military issues of the day or in the war itself. With the end of the war, he returned to Albion Academy to complete his studies, graduating in 1866 with a Bachelor of Philosophy degree.[4]

Between 1867 and 1870, Greene taught in rural schools in Illinois, always working at his plant collecting and pursuing his study of Latin. He had earlier been alerted to the botanical opportunities in the West, when he read the reports of the Pacific Railway Survey with Kumlien, and by 1870 Greene had determined that he ought to spend the summer in Colorado. He wrote to both Gray and Engelmann for advice, receiving it in a cordial manner along with requests that he send them duplicates from his collections. He spent that summer, as planned, botanizing between Denver and the mountains to the west. Greene was quite aware that he was an exceptionally strong man, contributing to his readiness to venture out alone in a remote, rugged country.

It may be suspected, moreover, that, at twenty-seven, he used this period of isolation to resolve the religious uncertainties that had preoccupied him since childhood. Despite his early religious inclination and its association with flowers, Greene does not seem to have received any religious instruction at home.

The family had been nominally Baptist, but he had been left free to visit various denominations to find his right place. During the time he was teaching in Illinois, he attended a Methodist church. The religious history of any individual is inevitably obscure. Formal adherence to a particular denomination is, to be sure, suggestive of faith, but is no assurance of actual religious belief. It appears that, by the time Greene was botanizing in Colorado, the choice was between the Roman Catholic and the Episcopal Churches—meaning that he was not a Low Churchman.

Once he had decided in favor of the Episcopal Church, Greene entered the new Jarvis Hall seminary in Golden, Colorado. He was admitted to the Sacred Order of Deaconry in 1871, whereupon he moved to Greeley to take charge of the congregation there. Only after his ordination as a priest in 1873 did he move on to Pueblo; and he subsequently served in various mission churches: in Empire, Georgetown, Canon City, and Silver City, New Mexico. Greene's separation from his family in Wisconsin troubled him considerably at the outset; but the family moved to Colorado in the fall of 1871, buying a farm near Denver. In 1881, Greene was called to Berkeley for what would prove to be his last mission.[5]

Meanwhile, his missions in Colorado and New Mexico served as bases for renewed botanical study. The specimens he had been sending Gray and Engelmann since the summer of 1870 had convinced them that Greene was a keen-eyed collector. When Gray reached Colorado in the summer of 1872, to be the guest of Charles Parry in Georgetown, Gray wrote to Greene from Denver, 6 August 1872, inviting him to join the party that would climb Torreys Peak and Grays Peak on 12 and 14 August, respectively. A phrase in Gray's letter would stick in Greene's mind for a long time: "I hope you may find some new things; but you will be sharp if you do." That was Greene's first inkling that Gray believed that little was left to be found in the Colorado region. The celebration in Georgetown delighted Greene: he liked Asa Gray, and Parry would remain a longtime friend.[6]

His pleasure radiated from his first article, which was not a botanical treatise, but rather a testimonial to the beauty of the local flora and landscape, written in a highly aesthetic key. While the purpose of the article was to call attention to the collections made by Parry, Hall, and Harbour, the young Reverend Greene, as he was already called, added personal observations. He had found the most beautiful local flowers at just the tree line, calling *Primula parryi* Gray "altogether the finest plant of the Rocky Mountains." Was it not strange that such a species should have selected its home so near the everlasting snows in a region so remote from man? And he ranked *Mertensia alpina* (Torr.) G. Don as one of the most elegant tenants of the heights.[7]

A second article reflecting his mood during his sojourn in Greeley described a trip he had made north of town in May of 1872. The article was an appreciation of the spring flora along Crow Creek and near Cheyenne, and the aesthetic tenor reappeared. He judged the handsome yellow bloom of *Thermopsis fabacea* (Pall.) DC. (which must have been *Thermopsis rhombifolia* [Nutt. ex Pursh] Nutt. ex Richards.), growing amidst *Oxytropis multiceps* Nutt., to be one of the most rare and charming of all the plants peculiar to the Rocky Mountains.[8]

The E. L. Greene evoked by such articles—written when he was approaching the age of thirty—seems quite consistent with his character in childhood and youth; it also seems a far cry from the E. L. Greene fellow botanists would later come to know. If one can describe the gradual transformation of Greene's personality, to explain the reasons for it is quite another matter. The evidence is simply too scanty. One can imagine a series of short stints as a pastor in rough frontier towns awakening a sense of hopelessness and deracination, even though Greene was more than capable of coping with any physical threats without fear. His continued botanical study, of course, provided needed diversion; but it is possible that, as in the cases of other pastor-botanists, a moment of questioning arrived about which calling was paramount.

Greene had learned early in his collecting career in Colorado, probably from Parry, that no new proposed species could get published in an American journal unless Gray had seen and approved it. Within four or five years, as Greene became familiar with the flora of Colorado through work in the field, he developed a keen sense of the liabilities of being primarily a closet-botanist. That is, his own proposals for new species were proving unacceptable to Gray, raising the suspicion that Gray, not believing there were new species to be found, resolutely refused to recognize exceptions to his rule. Once that suspicion dawned, Greene's resentment of his subservience to Gray began to fester as an intolerable intellectual censorship. It is clear that by 1880 Greene had become determined to publish independently.[9]

In June of that year, and without obtaining Gray's prior approval, Greene published his first new species in Coulter's *Botanical Gazette: Asclepias uncialis* Greene, *Bot. Gaz.* 5:64. 1880. The species still stands and is known from New Mexico into southwestern Wyoming. One might anticipate that in Hunter Dupree's fine biography of Asa Gray, one would find an interpretation of the developing Gray-Greene controversy favorable to Gray, and such is the case. By omitting the fact that Greene's *Asclepias* still remains a good species today, and even misstating the place of publication, Dupree was able to imply that Greene's real motive had been selfish, not scientific. Publishing independently, in Dupree's opinion, was meant to add the fame of authorship to the botanical immortality gained in plant names. The obvious issue of censorship, a primary concern for anyone pursuing new knowledge, entirely escaped him.

Dupree's doubt about Greene's integrity was also founded on a later remark by Greene, when he was publishing independently, that he was publishing more new things than all the Eastern botanists combined—an assertion construed by Dupree as indicating a quest for fame.[10] Was not Greene quite plainly saying that he was publishing more than they because the Easterners could not, or would not, see the existence of many novelties in the West?

The move in 1881 to take charge of the parish in Berkeley opened up a new frontier for conflict. During the prior decade, serving a variety of missions, Greene does not seem to have aroused any doctrinal opposition, suggesting perhaps the prevalence of indifferentism in the raw communities. In Berkeley, in what was meant to be a more permanent position, Green's high church views soon provoked doctrinal strife in the parish. He came to recognize that his Catholic teaching could not be imposed on resolute Protestants. In 1884, aware that his bishop would remove him if he did not resign, Greene did more than resign from his post. He abandoned the Episcopal Church and became a Roman Catholic layman.

In 1885, Greene secured an appointment to the Department of Agriculture at the University of California. A separate Department of Botany was created only in 1890, with Greene its first chairman; he would remain until 1894.[11] Meanwhile, after Greene's arrival in California, Gray and he remained at least superficially congenial. Greene was still sending Gray unusual plants and providing help on the manuscript on which Gray was working: *The Synoptical Flora of North America,* which had begun to appear in 1878 (Gray would live until January of 1888). Even so, Greene had begun to expose his bases for the segregation of species by criticizing Gray for excessive dependence on such characters as flower color, pappus, and achenes, while overlooking differences of plant habits and chemical properties, indicated by the odors of herbage. The latter Greene regarded as one of the best characters available for technical distinction.[12] Reliance on the odors of herbage was a privilege reserved for field botanists and served to highlight the disadvantages of closet-botany.

Greene's gradual emergence as a lone eagle was exhibited in ways other than his well-known penchant for splitting. To facilitate his independence and his separation from the Eastern establishment, he launched new journals. *Pittonia* first appeared in 1887, following Greene's employment by the university. Even the choice of the name was pointed, as it honored Joseph Pitton de Tournefort, the eminent seventeenth-century French botanist, and thus a pre-Linnaean. The first volume of *Erythea,* named to honor Sereno Watson's new genus in the Palm family, was dated 1893.

It had been decades since anyone had challenged the taxonomic authority of Asa Gray, and no one doing fieldwork in Rocky Mountain botany could be indifferent to the clash. The pungent character of Greene's prose, reflecting a burgeoning exasperation over the various oppositions he had met since reaching California, often turned mere doubters into bitter enemies. Easily overlooked is evidence that Greene had sympathizers, too, quieter perhaps, but encouraging. Charles Parry may have taken pains to remain on good terms with Gray, but he declined to break with Greene, suggesting that he retained a favorable opinion of Greene's knowledge and abilities.[13] T. C. Porter wrote to Greene to offer support for his taxonomic efforts.

In addition to Greene's particular views on taxonomy, he had been developing ideas in Berkeley on priority in plant nomenclature that contributed immensely to the confusion of issues in dispute. Greene's campaign to reform botanical nomenclature was publicized in his new journals, *Pittonia* and *Erythea*. It must be emphasized that Greene did respect the utility of binomial nomenclature, its practical use dating from Linnaeus. His objection to the Linnaean reform was based on its procedure—namely, the wholesale elimination of traditional plant names in order to achieve rational order. He thought, in other words, that to wipe the slate clean and begin anew, as he claimed Linnaeus had done in *Species Plantorum* in 1753, was to risk losing all memory of the historical past, a great injustice to the long tradition of botanical scholarship dating from Theophrastus. Most botanists, grateful for the rational order that Linnaeus had provided, were unmoved by Greene's agitation for the recovery of the historical past.

It is probable that Greene's wish to preserve botanical tradition lends insight into his dedication to the church of long tradition, not to speak of antagonism to anyone acting to disrupt continuity. Be that as it may, Greene was surely correct in his supposition that a loss of historical perspective weakens any intellectual or political institution. It is only fair to add that Linnaeus, in rationalizing botanical nomenclature arbitrarily, used prior, familiar names whenever feasible; and he customarily listed, for each species, the nomenclature used by several prior authors—thereafter known as synonyms—as a useful reference. In truth, not all had been lost.

There was an additional aspect to the nomenclature campaign fought by Greene. His passion for historical justice made him an opponent of the Kew Rule as then practiced by Bentham and Hooker. That rule permitted authors, when transferring a species from one genus to another, to ignore the original trivial name if they preferred a new one. Greene believed strongly in the absolute priority of the original trivial name as proper recognition of the initial author. It must be preserved in any generic transfer. He found support from Nathaniel Lord Britton of the New York Botanical Garden.[14] Greene would apply that principle in his botanical publication despite lack of international agreement on nomenclature usage. This, and other issues, would not be definitively resolved until the Fifth International Botanical Congress in Cambridge, England, in 1930; and the story of the wrangles and compromises necessary to reach unanimity would require a separate and wearisome chapter.

In view of Greene's unexplained decision to leave the University of California after only ten years, and well before retirement age, one can only speculate that by 1895 he had reached a point at which he was overcome by a desire to seek a more congenial ambiance for his remaining years. The years of doctrinal disputes within the Berkeley parish had been followed by strife within the California botanical community as Greene became its preeminent figure. Publication of new species he had found in California aroused the ire of those who believed that much of the flora was already known. Others supposed that he did not accept the concept of evolution on religious grounds, and that his consequent belief in the fixity of species dating from the Creation accounted for his habitual splitting. That argument barely concealed the opinion that conversion to Roman Catholicism was clear evidence of mental deficiency.

Such criticism was not restricted to interoffice intellectual gossip but appeared in print. Katharine Brandegee, who was affiliated with the California Academy of Sciences until 1893, published her highly negative opinion of Greene's work. She predicted that not more than one in ten of Greene's California species would prove to be tenable, "that perhaps one in fifteen or twenty would be nearer the mark," a prediction that turned out to be well off target. Rogers McVaugh found that 70 percent of Greene's taxa—that is, those described while he still lived in California—have stood the test of time; and certainly Greene's student, Willis L. Jepson, believed that Greene's best work was done during his Berkeley years. How, then, is one to account for Hunter Dupree's comment that few of Greene's species have won the approval of botanists?[15]

Not only did fierce loyalty to Asa Gray generate such an inability to cope with the evidence, but an unsubtle campaign to destroy Greene's personal reputation had been launched in Berkeley by those who disagreed with him. Without doubt, Greene had become highly independent during his years of wandering as a plant collector. Many have testified that Greene could be an affable friend of those who agreed with him or treated him fairly. But his sense of independence made him less than sociable with those who increasingly disagreed with him. To complicate the record, he was unmarried: he was a strong and attractive man with no history of love affairs. The two passions of his childhood, religion and plants, remained his sole interests throughout his life.

In the eighteenth century, it was not uncommon for botanical explorers, in foreign lands or overseas during extended periods, to remain unmarried and childless: this was a vocational celibacy almost as routine and unquestioned as that of the clergy. By the end of the nineteenth century, thanks to the emergence of an academic field called psychology, the celibate botanist became vulnerable to the suspicion of homosexuality. After working in the Brandegee botanical materials, Joseph Ewan indicated in 1942 that the rumor of Greene's homosexuality had been hatched within the Brandegee circle. The charge seems credible inasmuch as Marcus E. Jones, a friend of the Brandegees, would become the most vitriolic of the purveyors of that rumor, even claiming that homosexuality had been the cause of the strife in Greene's parish. There was, in fact, no documentary evidence to support such charges, and none has surfaced in more recent years.[16]

The question of Greene's alleged rejection of evolution amounts to a second unsubstantiated rumor. The rumor cannot have been based on anything he wrote or published, but rather on the assumption that such a splitter *must* have believed in the fixity of species. To bring to mind any of the contemporary taxonomists well known for a penchant for splitting, but who quite accept the principle of evolution, is to recognize the inadequacy of that proof. Indeed, it could be argued, as Rogers McVaugh has done, that a splitter might well see slight alterations in character as evidence of evolutionary change. While Greene's writing never pronounced specifically on the matter of evolution, there *are* passages that clearly indicate the opposite of fixity: a given species will show variation depending on changes in soil, climate, elevation, or other conditions.

As support for her criticism of his taxonomy, Katharine Brandegee claimed that Greene had argued for the fixity of species in her presence, apparently citing religious grounds. In retrospect, her own taxonomic judgment does not compare favorably with his at that time. As for her personal castigation of Greene, it may well have been founded on her failure to attract Greene before she married Mr. Brandegee, as Joseph Ewan suggested after his examination of the Brandegee papers.[17] The taxonomic dispute concealed personal spite.

The very failure of Greene to publish on the question of evolution offers an explanation quite antithetical to conventional opinion. Since the issue has necessarily been a matter of conjecture to begin with, further conjecture is not out of order. Assume for a moment that Greene, who had worked intensely in the field over many years, was quite sufficiently perceptive to have seen evidence that the Darwinian hypothesis was sustainable; but assume that for personal reasons, recognizing the traditionalism of his coreligionists, he chose to remain noncommittal on the issue. Botany may have been his profession, but the botanists themselves had grouped themselves into embattled factions. As Greene's religious quest had refined and narrowed over the years, the Church had emerged as his true community. Anyone, a century later, who has experienced the futility of debating creationism with those impervious to the facts of nature should have some insight into a resolution of silence serving as a key to civility. In any case, we are given a possible explanation for Greene's sudden resignation from the University of California in April of 1895. He was awarded an honorary Doctorate of Laws in June from the University of Notre Dame, and he joined the faculty of Catholic University of America that August.

Despite Greene's ultimate reputation as an extreme splitter, an important distinction must be pointed out, as did Rogers McVaugh. While Greene was still active in the field and had seen, or could see, existing plant populations, his work was remarkably sound. He did not make much use of the category *varieties,* which encouraged the creation of entirely new species, and some of them have been subsequently reduced to varieties. But the differences he perceived were not invalidated. Only after he left Berkeley for Catholic University, where he would remain for nine years, and *especially* after he became, in 1904, an associate of the National Museum, the Smithsonian Institution, where he had to work entirely on herbarium material, did he begin to publish greater and greater numbers of new species that his contemporaries could not see in nature. A new publication, his *Leaflets of Botanical Observation and Criticism,* launched in 1903, dated from that final, and unfortunate, period.

If one looks only at Greene's new species in the Compositae that have survived, and are characteristic of the Rocky Mountain region, it soon becomes apparent that they were published before 1904:

Antennaria neglecta Greene, Pitt. 3:173. 1897
Antennaria media Greene, Pitt. 3:286. 1898
Arnica rydbergii Greene, Pitt. 4:37. 1899
Artemisia franserioides Greene, Bull. Torr. Bot. Club 10:42. 1883
Bidens vulgata Greene, Pitt. 4:72. 1899
Chrysopsis [Heterotheca] fulcrata Greene, Bull. Torr. Bot. Club 25:119. 1898
Chrysothamnus linifolius Greene, Pitt. 3:24. 1896
Crepis modocensis Greene, Erythea 3:48. 1896
Erigeron eximius Greene, Pitt. 3:298. 1898
Erigeron formosissimus Greene, Bull. Torr. Bot. Club 25:121. 1898
Erigeron simplex Greene, Fl. Francisc. 387. 1897
Grindelia decumbens Greene, Pitt. 3:102. 1896
Grindelia fastigiata Greene, Pitt. 3:102. 1896
Grindelia inornata Greene, Pitt. 3:102. 1896
Grindelia subalpina Greene, Pitt. 3:297. 1898
Machaeranthera leucanthamifolia (Greene) Greene, Pitt. 3:61. 1896
Machaeranthera linearis Greene, Bull. Torr. Bot. Club 24:511. 1897
Nothocalais Greene, n. g. Bull. Calif. Acad. Sci. 2:55. 1886
Petradoria Greene, n. g. Erythea 3:13. 1895
Psilostrophe bakeri Greene, Pl. Baker. 3:29. 1901
Senecio atratus Greene, Pitt. 3:105. 1896
Senecio carthamoides Greene, Pitt. 4:122. 1900
Senecio dimorphophylus Greene, Pitt. 4:109. 1900
Senecio flavulus Greene, Pitt. 4:108. 1900
Senecio mutabilis Greene, Pitt. 4:113. 1900
Senecio pudicus Greene, Pitt. 4:188. 1900
Senecio wootonii Greene, Bull. Torr. Bot. Club 25:122. 1898

If one next looks at transfers Greene made from Gray's species in the period before 1900, the character of the disagreements between the two will be clarified for those knowledgeable of Rocky Mountain plants. The illustration is divided into six generic groups:

1. *Chrysothamnus* was a Nuttall genus not recognized by Gray.
   Chrysothamnus greenei (Gray) Greene, Erythea 3:94. 1895 [from *Bigelovia* DC.] Greene's collection on Huerfano Plains, Colorado, 1872

Chrysothamnus parryi (Gray) Greene, *Erythea* 3:113. 1895 [from *Linosyris* T. & G.]

Chrysothamnus vaseyi (Gray) Greene, *Erythea* 3:96. 1895 [from *Biglovia* DC.]

2. *Erigeron eliator* (Gray) Greene, *Pitt.* 3:167. 1897. Gray had made this Parry specimen a variety of *Erigeron grandiflorus* Hook., whereas *eliator* is very distinct.

   Erigeron aphanactis (Gray) Greene, *Fl. Francisc.* 389. 1897. Gray had made this a variety of *Erigeron concinnus* (Hook. & Arn.) T. & G.

3. *Machaeranthera pattersonii* (Gray) Greene, *Pitt.* 3:63. 1896 [from *Aster pattersonii* Gray]

4. *Cryptantha crassisepala* (T. & G.) Greene, *Pitt.* 1:112. 1887 [from *Eritrichum* Schrad.]

5. *Cryptantha fendleri* (Gray) Greene, *Pitt.* 1:120. 1887. Gray had put this Fendler plant in *Krynitzkia* Fisch. & Mey.

6. *Cryptantha watsonii* (Gray) Greene, *Pitt.* 1:1120. 1887. A Watson plant put in *Krynitzkia* Fisch. & Mey.

7. *Lotus wrightii* (Gray) Greene, *Pitt.* 2:143. 1890 [from *Hosachia* Dougl. ex Benth.]

8. The issue of *Haplopappus* Cass., a large genus of nearly 150 species: All have yellow flowers, the phyllaries imbricated in several rows, a pappus of few to many bristles, and alternate leaves. Henri Cassini based his type species (*Aplopappus glutinosus* Cass., *Dict. Sc. Nat.* 56:168–169. 1828) on a dried specimen presumably brought back to France from Chile by Jules Dumont d'Urville during a circumnavigation of the globe for scientific purposes, 1822–1825. The genetic name referred to its simple pappus, distinguishing it from *Diplopappus* Cass., which he had named in 1819, and which proved to be a synonym of *Aster* L.

All the species subsequently placed in the genus are in the western cordillera of both North and South America, none in Eurasia. But the species differ greatly from each other in size and general appearance; and, it now appears, in both morphology and cytology. W. J. Hooker and Nuttall were the first to attempt some segregation within the North American species, to Asa Gray's disapproval. Gray held this position to the end of his life, whereas Greene took the same route as Hooker and Nuttall had.

Those species within *Haplopappus* whose leaves have spinulose-tipped teeth; their involucral bracts papery, their tips green; he put in *Machaeranthera* Nees. *Machaeranthera bigelovii* (Gray) Greene, *Pitt.* 3:63. 1896

Two of Greene's other machaerantheras, *commixta* and *mucronata*, are considered good species by some taxonomists, but are reduced to varieties of *bigelovii* by others.

Those species within *Haplopappus* whose leaves had spinulose-tipped teeth, but whose involucral bracts were more or less foliaceous, Greene put in *Pyrrocoma* Hook.

Pyrrocoma crocea (Gray) Greene, *Erythea* 2:69. 1894

Pyrrocoma integrifolia (Porter ex Gray) Greene, *Erythea* 2:69. 1894

Pyrrocoma lanceolata (Hook.) Greene, *Erythea* 2:69. 1894

Pyrrocoma uniflora (Hook.) Greene, *Erythea* 2:60. 1894

Greene also accepted *Oonopsis* Nutt., which included those species within *Haplopappus* without spinulose-tipped leaves; the involucral bracts not foliaceous; the stems leafy.

Oonopsis multicaulus (Nutt.) Greene, *Pitt.* 3:45. 1906

Oonopsis wardii (Gray) Greene, *Pitt.* 3:46. 1906

Those species within *Haplopappus* with the same characters as *Oonopsis,* except for having stems scapose, at least naked above, he put in *Stenotus* Nutt. The only species he transferred likely to be found in the Rocky Mountains is *Stenotus lanuginosus* (Gray) Greene, *Erythea* 2:72. 1894, in Idaho and Montana.

Greene was fifty-one when he decided on the move to Washington, D.C. What he could not leave behind him were unresolved controversies over priority in nomenclature and the arbitrary selection of 1753 as the beginning of botanical nomenclature; and, if anything, he became increasingly arbitrary himself as he aged. The avalanche of new species that he triggered during his Washington years were only in part the result of his separation from fieldwork and his reliance on dried herbarium specimens. His judgment was increasingly unleavened by common sense, and he gave evidence of a gnawing resentment that he had been inadequately appreciated: a certain megalomania in him exposed a mind predisposed to see differences rather than similarities and inclined to be quarrelsome. The keenness of perception, which had served him so well in earlier years, gradually eroded into a heightened sense for grievances. It may be that the wounds from earlier battles never healed but remained running sores.

When Aven Nelson's revision of John Coulter's first flora of the Rocky Mountain region appeared, Greene published a review of it that was markedly autobiographical and demeaning to all other workers in that field. He called Nelson's work an exercise in the suppression of others' species. His claim that the original Coulter had been almost wholly based on others' books and monographs was both unfair and unwise, given his fieldwork and collaboration with Porter; and although Greene welcomed Nelson's revision as an *advance,* to be an advance of a worthless book—Greene's evident view of the original Coulter—could be taken as faint praise. Recalling his own fieldwork in much of Colorado, Wyoming, California, Arizona, and New Mexico, Greene asserted that he "had acquired a fuller knowledge of far western botany than had ever before been gained by an individual botanist." Given the tone of the review, one must suspect Greene was confident that no one since had matched his achievement.[18]

Greene's outlook was undoubtedly darkened by the decline of his financial situation. The years at Catholic University had proved to be a time of troubles and misunderstandings, accounting for his decision to move to the National Museum as an associate in 1904. Aven Nelson learned directly from Greene in 1912 about the sad state of his personal affairs. His title at the National Museum carried no stipend despite the fact that he gave, in his estimation, several thousand dollars worth of service each year. In order to earn a living, he was obliged to do additional work, earning a hundred dollars a month from the drudgery of identifying Forest Reservation plants. Such labor seriously cut into his time for scholarly work and fed his resentments.[19]

Given the circumstances, it is astonishing that Greene had been writing botanical history of a very high order during that period. He had, to be sure, a personal goal in trying to revive botanists' interest in the history of their profession; but his historical writing entirely lacked the polemical tone one had come to expect from Greene. In designing his *Landmarks of Botanical History,* Greene did not mean to write a comprehensive history of botany, but only to focus on a few landmarks in the development of botanical knowledge from Theophrastus into the seventeenth century. Consequently, the two parts featured a selected group of herbalists, all pre-Linnaean, whose remarkable work deserves to be recalled as foundational to plant science. Among the qualities that set Greene apart from all other botanical explorers of the Rocky Mountains were his sense of history and his profound knowledge of languages, which contributed to his wide knowledge of plants. Only the first part of *Landmarks* was published in 1909; the remainder was left in manuscript. The work makes good reading and more than merited the republication in its entirety in 1983 sponsored by the Hunt Institute for Botanical Documentation.[20]

The rationale for several of Greene's well-known positions may be found in his treatment of, and admiration for, Andrea Cesalpino (1519–1603). Unlike any of his botanical predecessors, who were satisfied simply to publish plant descriptions, Cesalpino attempted to group plants into natural orders based on natural affinities. This first attempt was made in his book *De Plantis,* published in Florence in 1583. The affinities between genus and genus, Cesalpino claimed, could be detected in the structure of the flower and the fruit, especially in the fruit and its seed.

From these characters, he perceived a natural order of plants, a linear series with the highest plant organisms at one end and the lowest at the other end. Even though Cesalpino expressed his views in a narrative rather than devising a descriptive chart, his work amounted to the beginning of systematic botany. Such a descriptive chart was constructed in 1953 and introduced by the editor into the 1983 edition of *Landmarks* for clarity. It shows a recognition of thirty-two groups with the Glandiferae first—the acorn-bearers as he called them, a family group that included the oaks, the chestnuts, the beech, and the hazel—and the Cryptogamae at the end. The woody plants were placed ahead of the suffructicose and the herbaceous plants. As Cesalpino was an avowed Aristotelian with an expressed teleology in his reasoning, it may well explain why Greene, as a conservative Roman Catholic, preferred Cesalpino's system to that of Engler and Prantl.

Within the order of woody plants, Cesalpino made a major division between genera with one-seeded fruits, and genera with several-seeded fruits. Further subdivisions, of course, were necessary: these included grouping by fruit structure, such as the number of placentae; or by the position of the "blossoms," superior or inferior. One need go no further into a literary description of the key to demonstrate that this first attempt at systematics was impressive. And Greene, by citing the well-known Linnaean aphorism that, if the genera are confused, all is confusion—which Linnaeus attributed to Cesalpino—implied that modern botany began with Cesalpino, not with Linnaeus.[21] Inasmuch as Cesalpino did not accept the sexuality of plants, most historians of botany would not concur. Indeed, given the remnants of a medieval outlook in Linnaeus (his reliance on essentialism), the issue illustrated the folly of attempting to define beginnings and endings precisely in history.

In a paper prepared to commemorate the Linnaean bicentenary, Greene did not raise the matter of his quibble with Linnaeus as a nomenclator. Instead, he praised Linnaeus's genera concept as almost perfect, as it enabled Linnaeus to develop the art of generic diagnosis. Generic diagnosis, as represented in *Genera Plantarum* (1737), was, in Greene's opinion, the most priceless of Linnaeus's several principal contributions to phytography. Greene left no doubt about his highest regard for Linnaeus as a botanical genius.[22]

The memorial lecture was soon expanded into a short book, *Carolus Linnaeus* (1912), in which the final chapter, "Linnaeus as an Evolutionist," is of particular interest. In reading *Species Plantarum,* Greene had been struck by a remark at the end of the treatment of *Thalictrum lucideum* L. Linnaeus had added: *Planta, an satis distincta, a T. flavo? Videtur temporis filia*—that is, "a plant sufficiently distinct from *T. flavo*? perhaps at some time related." Greene's interpretation of Linnaeus's meaning was: "It seems to be the product of its environment." He believed he had stumbled on evidence that Linnaeus accepted the possibility of the descent of some species from others. What is also significant is that the chapter revealed none of Greene's alleged denial of evolution. Instead, he found his discovery *electrifying.*[23]

Greene indicated that he had been reading the 1764 edition of *Species Plantarum,* but the speculative phrase Linnaeus added to his description of *Thalictrum lucideum* was also evident in the first edition of 1753. The two species are still held to be good and distinct today, and with the great affinity that Linnaeus's question implied. As of 1753, both species had been found in Spain; and, in addition, one in northern Europe, and the other around Paris. Given the similarity of habitat, it is understandable that Greene found the phrase *videtur temporis filia* to imply that Linnaeus had wondered whether the difference between the two species had occurred over time, suggesting evolutionary change.

Consequently, it must be noted that, by 1764, Linnaeus had developed his cortex-medula theory and expressed it in *Genera Plantarum* of that year. He proposed that external changes in the cortex of a plant might occur, thanks to environmental circumstances; but the *essence* of the species, borne internally within the pistil, would be inherited without essential change. That concept was incompatible with what we understand evolution to be.[24]

While there can be no doubt that Linnaeus's binomial nomenclature was a blessed reform, bringing rational order out of threatening chaos, the inadvertent result that Greene feared also came to pass. Few botanists today have any knowledge of their science that antedates Linnaeus, 1753, much less regret for what has been lost. That circumstance sheds light on those apparent inconsistencies in Greene's career that irritated his contemporaries. He was widely believed to be radical in his taxonomy and in his growing antagonism to the authority of the closet-botanists in the East. That perception obscured the fact that he was deeply conservative in both his religious choices and his respect for botanical tradition.

What Greene's turbulent career ultimately illustrated was that the botanical exploration of the Rocky Mountains had crossed, in its final phase, an intellectual watershed. Henceforth, the major figures would continue to explore and to collect in the confidence that their region was unique. The issues of evolution, ecology, and plant distribution had come into sharper focus. Greene's new taxa and transfers of the 1880s and 1890s had verified the observations published by J. D. Hooker in 1877 and 1880, sparking as well a revived interest in the proposals of Thomas Nuttall.

14

Marcus E. Jones of Utah

*M*arcus E. Jones (1853–1934) is apt to be remembered as a plant collector in the Great Basin. In fact, his collecting sites were widespread throughout the West; and, in time, he came to harbor the notion that the entire region was his personal botanical domain, which did not require the intrusion of others. It seems inevitable that he should have collided with his older contemporary, E. L. Greene, who developed similar ideas. As they grew older and experienced, both men exhibited what may be politely called a polemical spirit.

In other respects, they were opposites: Greene, though possessing unusual physical strength and endurance, was the refined, High Churchman. Jones, often gross in manner and expression, had been reared in the Congregationalist community of Grinnell, Iowa. There he had fallen under the influence of the famed revivalist Dwight L. Moody, an influence that shaped him permanently, about which more later.

Despite his territorial claims, there were, in truth, large regions of the West that Jones never saw. As for the Rocky Mountain region, he would explore most noticeably the mountains of central Colorado, all of eastern Utah, into western and southeastern Idaho, into only western Montana, and very little into western Wyoming.

To account for his life as a botanist, Jones would later recall his mother's love of flowers and his early access to Mrs. Lincoln's elementary flora. Yet, when he emerged from college in Grinnell in 1878 with an M.A., he was prepared to be a Latin teacher, not a natural scientist. His biographer has found evidence that Jones by then had become preoccupied with his health. At this late date, it is hard to know whether his occasional ailments were unusual for that day and age. But the severe headaches from which he suffered, and would continue to suffer for the remainder of his life, suggest emotional stress that may well have been a byproduct of the insalubrious religious instruction he had received, a brand inspiring fear. If he had come to suspect that an outdoor occupation would be beneficial, it could account for his decision to collect plants in Colorado during the summer of 1878.

The venture was primarily commercial. When he returned to Grinnell that October, Jones brought back eleven hundred different species, but a total collection of at least forty thousand specimens, obviously meaning to sell many sets. As a novice, he sought the help of Charles Parry of Davenport. The latter assured him that he had identified many species correctly, but recommended sending uncertain ones to Gray or Engelmann for determination. Jones returned to Colorado in the early summer of 1879, initially to teach during the summer session at Colorado College, a congenial Congregational institution. In mid-July, at the end of the session, he set out for the region around Salt Lake City to resume plant collection. Once again, he was mainly concerned in preparing sets for sale and collected in quantity.[1]

Back in Grinnell for the winter of 1879–1880, he had the assistance of Anna Richardson in arranging sets of specimens for shipment to purchasers. Richardson was a member of the local Congregationalist community and was being courted by Jones. Only after their marriage, in early 1880, did Jones decide to move to Salt Lake City to settle permanently. He accepted a teaching position at the Salt Lake Academy, evidently an anti-Mormon outpost. Some might find in Jones's choice of Salt Lake City—as he was vigorously hostile toward Mormons—a possible insight into his personality.

That summer, 1880, Engelmann and Parry visited Jones, and the three botanized together in City Creek Canyon northeast of the city. That visit was the occasion of Engelmann's near death in Great Salt Lake.[2] For reasons obscure, Jones lost his teaching position before the end of the school year. It was a time when Jones, not yet thirty, began to exhibit abnormal behavior that would earn him a bad personal reputation and be detrimental to his career. At the time, for instance, both Coulter and Jones had in mind the composition of a Rocky Mountain flora. Jones, learning of Coulter's project, wrote to Coulter to warn him "off his ground." The more experienced Coulter paid no attention, publishing his flora in 1885.

Out of a job, Jones ventured off on a visit to California for the spring and summer of 1881. In April, he joined Charles Parry and Cyrus G. Pringle of Vermont for a field trip into Baja California. Jones and Pringle, at least, got as far south as Ensenada. On the return trip, the party camped by the hot springs at Tijuana. As the following day was a Sunday, Jones refused to move on, insisting on spending the day in religious meditation. Consequently, the rest of the party drove on toward San Diego without him. This necessitated sending their teamsters, John and Charles Orcutt, back to get him the next day. At the point of a revolver, Jones ordered the Orcutts out of their wagon and drove off without them.

News of the incident was communicated in two ways. The newspaper in San Diego published a story on it; and the furious Charles Parry wrote to Asa Gray:

Jones has behaved *shamefully* on the trip, capping the climax of his conceit and ignorance by *drawing a pistol* on an inoffensive young man of the party to whom we were under great obligation. . . . Of course, I have *cut him*, and shall have no more to do with him. Pringle, who takes the same view, will do the same. Jones has indicated that he will *steal a march* on us in the publication of n[ew] sp[ecies] of which I give you warning. He has got nothing of any consequence that we have not got *better* specimens of, as he is a miserable collector.

Parry also wrote to Engelmann about a new rose that Jones would claim as his own. They had all seen it from the wagon at the side of the road. Jones may well have been the first out of the wagon, but all three botanists had examined the plant. By sending a specimen to Engelmann, Parry hoped to avoid having a "horrid" name attached to the beautiful plant. "Our wish is that you should give it a good characteristic name . . . hoping our *darling* may not be prematurely cursed by a *Jones* at the end of it." It would be published as *Rosa minutifolia* Engelm., and Jones would charge that it had been stolen from him.[3]

Jones's biographer believed that events relating to the Ensenada trip not only were critical to Jones's reputation, but affected his psyche permanently. Perhaps the incident made matters worse, but the critical damage to that psyche surely dated from earlier years. Jones had long since been living with the fear of eternal damnation and had been plagued by frequent violent headaches. One of the immediate results of his notoriety was the closure of publication opportunities. Coulter closed off the *Botanical Gazette* to Jones; and Parry, with the compliance of Asa Gray, endeavored to close off the *Bulletin of the Torrey Botanical Club* to Jones. Lee Lenz attributed Parry's reaction to jealousy of a newcomer intruding on his domain, quite overlooking the fact that Parry had been the first to encourage Jones.[4]

One has to suspect, on the basis of what we can reliably know about a man long dead, that the torments Jones inflicted on others were rooted in the torments the poor man had long experienced himself. Anyone reading the non-botanical parts of his biography, moreover, ought to be struck by Jones's endless financial difficulties, his relentless pursuit of wealth through mining ventures, his publication of religious tracts, and his troubled domestic life, which add up to a gothic tale. Jones became increasingly engaged in religious activity, especially after switching from his Congregationalist affiliation to the Baptist Church.

Jones's grand design was a flora reaching from the eastern base of the Rocky Mountains to the Pacific Ocean. Yet, throughout his botanical career, Jones's energy was usually diverted by a need to earn money. Most plant collectors gathered enough replicates to sell sets or to exchange them in order to build their herbaria;

most also had private means from a successful business or a fortuitous inheritance, or held a salaried governmental or academic post. Jones for the most part was without any such financial resources.

In 1882, Marcus and Anna opened a kindergarten in Salt Lake City; it soon seemed profitable enough to be converted, in 1883, into the Jones High School. Both of them were employed with the teaching. This enterprise was closed inexplicably in about 1888. Lenz found evidence that Jones had become increasingly depressed and morose, whether from worry about finances or because of his incapacitating religious preoccupations. That would account for Anna's decision to lease a large, three-story house in 1890, enabling her to open a boarding house and turn the large, well-lighted, third-story attic into a herbarium and study where Jones could devote himself exclusively to the preparation of his flora. The arrangement might have had the further convenience of putting him out of the way.

That same year, T. S. Brandegee founded his journal, Zoe, in California, providing Jones an outlet for publication. His papers were generally published as "Contributions to Western Botany," whether in Zoe or, later, independently; and some of his new taxa would be published under that title in the Proceedings of the California Academy of Science. Jones did not meet the Brandegees until July of 1902, when he went to San Diego to see their herbarium. He found them to be congenial, and the subsequent friendship may have been founded on mutual hostility toward E. L. Greene.[5]

In 1894, Jones accepted a commission from F. V. Coville, the botanist at the U.S. Department of Agriculture, to collect plants from March through December at a salary of one hundred dollars a month. He was directed to follow the Colorado River downstream from Grand Junction and to explore the lower San Juan and the Little Colorado (Colorado Chiquita) valleys, ending in the Eldorado Canyon in Nevada. Jones meant to make the commission an opportunity to collect additional sets for himself. The conflict of interests was soon evident to Coville, provoking exchanges of violent, embittered letters before the episode came to an end short of Eldorado.

While this is not the place for any detailed review of Jones's mining ventures, it is appropriate to note that his botanical research was considerably curtailed after 1900 by his search for wealth. He had acquired some knowledge of geology as a college student in Iowa and had pursued the subject, after moving to Utah, as the key to earning money. Especially after the turn of the century, he became involved in a variety of western mining enterprises that occupied too much of his time. They evidently brought in some money, but no real wealth, providing instead considerable opportunity to suffer from the conviction that he was being cheated by the large mining companies. The truth of that matter is elusive.

Despite such distractions, Jones began to publish new species in 1891. Though we concern ourselves here only with his new Rocky Mountain species, the reader should be aware that the total number was considerably larger for the entire West. Such a list, arranged alphabetically by genus, is available in the Lenz biography, which included the updated nomenclature of taxa that did not stand. A more chronological arrangement adds the advantage of indicating approximate itinerary. The initial publication was in *Zoe:*

Astragalus asclepioides Jones 1:238. 1891. Grand Co., Utah
Astragalus cottoni Jones 2:237. 1891. Carbon Co., Utah
Astragalus desperatus Jones 2:243. 1891. Grand Co., Utah
Astragalus sabulosus Jones 2:239. 1891. Grand Co., Utah
Cleomella palmerana Jones 2:236. 1891. Grand Co., Utah
Cymopteris megacephalus Jones 2:14. 1891. Cosonino Co., Ariz.
Astragalus wetherilli Jones, *Zoe* 4:34. 1893. Mesa Co., Colo. (an Alice Eastwood collection)
Eriogonum bicolor Jones, *Zoe* 4:281. 1893. Grand Co., Utah
Astragalus eastwoodae Jones, *Zoe* 4:369. 1894. Grand Co., Utah
Phlox albomarginata Jones, *Zoe* 4:367. 1894. Lewis & Clark Co., Mont.
Asclepius labriformis Jones, *Proc. Calif. Acad. Sci.* (2) 5:708. 1895. Wayne Co., Utah
Aster glaucus Torr. & Gray var. *wasatchensis* Jones, Ibid. (2) 5:694. 1895. Piute Co., Utah→*Aster wasatchensis* (Jones) Blake
Astragalus cymboides Jones, Ibid. (2) 5:650. 1895. Emery Co., Utah
Astragalus musiniensis Jones, Ibid. (2) 5:671. 1895. Emery Co., Utah
Astragalus serpens Jones, Ibid. (2) 5:641. 1895. Wayne Co., Utah
Astragalus argophyllus Nutt. ex T. & G. var. *panguicensis* (Jones) Jones, *Contra. W. Bot.* 8:5. 1898. Garfield Co. Utah
Astragalus coltoni Jones var. *moabensis* Jones, Ibid. 8:11. 1898. San Juan Co., Utah
Astragalus feensis Jones, Ibid. 8:12. 1898. Santa Fe, N.M.
Astragalus oocalycis Jones, Ibid. 8:10. 1898. San Juan Co., N.M.
Peucedanum juniperinum Jones, Ibid. 8:29. 1898. Summit Co., Utah→ *Lomatium juniperinum* (Jones) Coult. & Rose
Allium fibrillum Jones, Ibid. 10:24. 1902. Washington Co., Ida.
Allium geyeri Wats. var. *tenerum* Jones, Ibid., 10:28. 1902. Washington Co., Ida.
Eriogonum batemanii Jones, Ibid. 11:11. 1903. Carbon Co., Utah
Eriogonum ostlundi Jones, Ibid. 11:12. 1903. Piute Co., Utah
Penstemon cleburni Jones, Ibid. 12:62. 1908. Sweetwater Co., Wyo.
Astragalus detritalia Jones, Ibid. 13:8. 1910. Duchesne Co., Utah
Astragalus duchesnensis Jones, Ibid. 13:9. 1910. Duchesne Co., Utah
Astragalus lutosus Jones, Ibid. 13:7. 1910. Uintah Co., Utah
Cymopteris duchesnensis Jones, Ibid. 13:12. 1910. Duchesne Co., Utah
Townsendia mensana Jones, Ibid. 13:15. 1910. Utah Co., Utah

By 1910, the Jones marriage had deteriorated to a point at which a separation was the only solution. The truth of the couple's domestic situation has never been clear. Anna had made sacrifices for many years to enable Marcus to complete his great book, enduring his frequent headaches and periods of depression. By the time of their separation, she must have suspected that the book would never be born. Since there is reason to believe that Marcus was happier in the field than at home, their incompatibility had to have been more complex than we can know. They lived separately in Salt Lake City after 1910. Anna would die in 1916 at the age of sixty-three, her health no doubt undermined by profound disenchantment.[6]

A different disenchantment was visited upon Jones around 1922, during the last months he would live in Salt Lake City. Certain events and statements have been recorded that indicate his traditional religious fundamentalism had become incompatible with what he had learned from his work in geology and from his reading of Darwin. Arguments on such issues within his congregation, including with the pastor, drove him to the conclusion that his study of the Bible forced him "to discard the fundamentals of Christianity as being fraudulent," leaving him in a mental wilderness. He would later write to Alice Eastwood that he would give anything to regain his childlike faith of younger days, happy in the thought that he was on solid ground. "Now it is all bunk to me."[7]

Fortunately, by that time Jones had virtually completed his monograph on *Astragalus*. He had worked for most of his life toward a flora of the Great Plateau, by which he meant everything from the eastern base of the Rocky Mountains to the Pacific coast, probably an impossible task, as it had to be based on his personal library and herbarium. It would remain far from finished by the time of his death. Consequently, the monograph—*Revision of the North American Species of Astragalus* (1913), which he had to publish personally in Salt Lake City—proved to be his major work. Arthur Cronquist described it as "an exasperatingly idiosyncratic but fundamentally sound work, which remained the standard treatment for forty years. How appropriate that Jones so well understood the loco weeds!"[8]

As far as the Rocky Mountain astragali are concerned, Jones had already published most of his novelties by 1910. The monograph introduced only three additional taxa:

> *Astragalus argophyllus* Nutt. ex T. & G. var. *martini* Jones, *Rev. Astrag.* 207.
> 1923. Franklin Co., Idaho
> *Astragalus campestris* (Nutt.) Gray, var. *crispatus* Jones, Ibid. 75. 1923→
> *Astragalus miser* Dougl. ex Hook. var. *crispatus* (Jones) Cronq. Rivalli
> County, Mont.
> *Astragalus osterhoutii* Jones, Ibid. 25. 1923. Grand County, Utah

During the half-dozen years following Anna's death, Jones repeatedly contemplated selling his herbarium. He was over sixty and had limited provisions for later years; and the very idea of giving up his collection must have been a signal that he had become tacitly reconciled to the improbability of completing his major work given his location. Only in 1923 did Jones receive an offer that met his price, worked out by Philip Munz of Pomona College. The collection was sold to Pomona for twenty-five thousand dollars, with the understanding that Jones would move to Claremont to continue his work. The California botanists, of course, were delighted that the herbarium came West rather than East; and Jones could not have had a more satisfactory arrangement.[9]

He may have left the scene of his troubles for good, but his character remained unaltered by the new environment. Jones may have been a happier botanist in California, having shed the burden of his Christian fundamentalism; but the rancor over having lost it was far from buried, and his polemical temperament remained undimmed. Jones's passionate and publicized hatred of E. L. Greene was too extreme to have been simply a reflection of their differences in taxonomy and nomenclature, no matter that such differences did make enemies within the American botanical community by the turn of the twentieth century. Had those issues been at the base of his anger, he surely would have directed his wrath toward Rydberg as well.

In 1929, fourteen years after Greene's death, Jones published the following words in his *Contributions to Western Botany:* "He was a renegade clergyman, a sodomite socially and a stench in the eyes of all decent people. The most charitable thing we could say of him was that he was insane." Even if any proof of such charges had come to light (and it never has), such lines would be, in the words of Jones's biographer, unpardonable.[10]

Because Jones, unlike Greene, never engaged in open conflict with Asa Gray, one might assume that Jones had been untroubled by Gray's disinclination to recognize the distinctiveness of the Western flora. On the contrary, while he admired the immense amount of work Gray had accomplished, Jones believed that Engelmann was the more perceptive botanist of the two. In his later years, Jones indicated that, had it not been for the death of both Gray (1888) and Watson (1892), he would certainly have collided with Harvardian conservatism.[11] Aside from Greene's later proclivity to splitting, Jones and he had much in common in their appreciation of the Western flora, and many of their species have stood. Although Thomas Nuttall might not have claimed either of them, any more than they claimed each other, they were his spiritual descendants.

Jones's slanderous remarks about Greene, if never thereafter equaled in venom, stimulated him to write additional sketches under the rubric "Botanists I Have Known," published in numbers 16 and 17 of *Contributions to Western Botany* in 1930. Additional impressions were published after Jones's death by his daughter, Mabel Jones Broaddus, or were left more charitably unpublished in manuscript. On occasion he expressed a favorable opinion of a contemporary; and some of his judgments, if severe, have been sustained in the long run. But as a group, the sketches illustrate why Jones had always been remembered for his sharp pen. If his invective had a singular cutting edge, it must be recognized that his character had been forged much earlier in religious controversy and hatreds; and that bitterness boiled easily to the surface when a fellow botanist did not see the light exactly as did Marcus Jones. He had absolutely no use for the opinions of others with whom he disagreed.[12]

On the last day of his life, 3 June 1934, Jones was botanizing in the San Bernadino Mountains. Returning to Claremont, he was killed in an automobile accident. An appraisal of his life was published the following year by Mabel Broaddus, the work of a loyal daughter. She revealed nothing directly about the character of her father's marriage. Yet, by recognizing that her mother had probably exhausted herself in an effort to enable Marcus to complete his lifework, she provided a veiled account of the marriage. A second remark—that, with other scientists, Jones "was usually sharp and caustic, although he did not himself take criticism very well nor tolerate difference of opinion"—amounts to a confession that Jones had been a very difficult man. As for his need for religion, she took notice of the collapse of his fundamentalism, when he was about seventy, after a dispute over the significance of fossils found in the Wasatch. But if he repudiated the Church as an institution in some anger, he retained his faith in God and his belief in the efficacy of prayer.[13]

With the passage of time, those who did not encounter Jones in person have been able to remember him more kindly. Rupert Barneby dedicated a recent volume to the memory of Marcus Eugene Jones, pioneer botanical explorer and monographer of American *Astragalus*: "His name is imperishably associated with many of the most strikingly individual plants of the region."[14]

15

The Heightened Attention to Grasses

*A*fter so much focus on embattled botanists, the reader should welcome the assurance that botanical knowledge has not been advanced only by calumny and bloodshed. The West did enjoy quieter botanizing in the latter part of the nineteenth century, carried on more modestly by explorers devoid of a sense of competition. William Marriott Canby (1831–1904) was one of them, a banker from Wilmington, Delaware, whose financial independence may have contributed to his pacific bent. For the degree to which intellectual life has been subverted or perverted by the scramble for research and travel assistance is a topic worthy of study by students of psychopathology. Beginning around 1880, the federal government began to take a more organized approach in the promotion of botanical research, doing so primarily through three federal agencies: the United States Geological Survey, founded in 1879; the United States Department of Agriculture (USDA), concerned with learning about the grasses of the Western region in detail; and the United States Herbarium, as an ally of the agriculture department.

Canby, because of his financial independence, was never an employee of a federal agency. What is more, his botanizing was not limited to the Rocky Mountain region. For three decades he traveled widely in the United States and Canada. Both Gray and Engelmann regarded him as a friend, and the Western botanists in general, even Marcus Jones, came to have a high opinion of his botanical knowledge and his collecting skills. His apparent indifference to publication suggests how completely an amateur he was and accounts, at least in part, for how little we know about his lengthy botanical odyssey. His plants were published by others, primarily from specimens given to the National Herbarium in Washington; and his herbaria ultimately came to reside in the New York Botanical Garden.

Within our range, Canby first appeared in Colorado in 1871, collecting in South Park in particular. Ten years later, he attached himself to the Northern

Transcontinental Survey as a companion to Charles Sprague Sargent, the director of the new Arnold Arboretum. But Canby became best known for an exploration, made independently in 1883, starting in Helena, Montana. His exact route as he worked his way through rugged mountain terrain has been difficult to trace. Obviously he crossed the Continental Divide into the valley of the South Fork of the Flathead River, crossed Cutbank Pass, and returned eastward over Lewis and Clark Pass. One of the new species named for him, *Ligusticum canbyi* Coulter & Rose, he recorded as collected at the headwaters of the Jacko River in Montana.[1]

Most of the species named to honor Canby were actually collected by others:

Lomatium canbyi (Coulter & Rose) C. & R., known from Oregon and Washington into Idaho, was first collected by T. J. Howell.

Aster foliaceus Lindl. ex DC. var. *canbyi* (Vasey) A. Gray was collected on the White River in western Colorado by George Vasey.

Other taxa in his eponomy are only known in areas outside the Rocky Mountain region:

Canbya Parry ex A. Gray, in Papaveraceae, is known only in desert areas of California and Oregon.

Angelica canbyi Coulter & Rose is limited to the Pacific Northwest, a collection of W. N. Suksdorf.

Frank Tweedy (1854–1937), a topographical engineer, also began to collect plants when a member of the Northern Transcontinental Survey, 1882–1883. A New Yorker, Tweedy had taken a degree in civil engineering at Union College in 1875; and he would become a permanent employee of the United States Geological Survey in 1884, remaining until his retirement in 1915. In both 1884 and 1885, he was in Yellowstone National Park; and his *Flora of Yellowstone National Park* was based largely on his own collections.[2]

Tweedy's itineraries cannot be precisely deduced from his collection numbers, since he began renumbering his plants every year he was in the field rather than numbering them sequentially. In 1891, he was again in Yellowstone and in Montana; and his largest collection of Yellowstone plants, after the publication of his flora, dates from that year. Despite his efforts, and those of Coulter and Parry before him, the southeastern quadrant of the park remained practically untouched. In the decade after 1891, Tweedy's numbers reflect collections in both Colorado and Wyoming.[3] The Tweedy eponomy consists of new species collected by him, all of them published by his contemporaries:

Erigeron tweedyi Canby, *Bot. Gaz.* 13:17. 1888. Trail Creek, s.w. Mont.

Gilia tweedyi Rydb., *Bull. Torr. Bot. Club* 31:634. 1904. Encampment, Wyo.

Penstemon tweedyi Canby & Rose, *Bot. Gaz.* 15:66. 1890. Beaverhead County, Mont.→*Chionophilia tweedyi* (Canby & Rose) Henderson (1900)

Plantago tweedyi A. Gray, *Syn. Fl.* 2nd ed. 2:390. 1886. East Fork Yellowstone River

Salix barrattiana Hook. var. *tweedyi* Bebb ex Rose, *Contr. U.S. Nat. Herb.* 3:572. 1896. Big Goose Creek, Big Horn Mts., Wyo.→*Salix tweedyi* (Bebb ex Rose) Ball (1905)

Juncus tweedyi Rydb., *Mem. N. Y. Bot. Gar.* 1:90. 1900. Yellowstone Park

Stipa comata Trin. & Rupr. var. *intermedia* Scribn. & Tweedy, *Bot. Gaz.* 11:1886. Yellowstone Park, Junction Butte

After midcentury, the ecological and economic implications of permanent settlements in the West had been publicized by a number of botanical explorers. Following the census of 1890, there was an official recognition that the frontier no longer existed, implying that settlement would become denser thereafter. The Department of Agriculture became active in Western botanical exploration, grasses being the primary focus of such exploration. Areas in northern Idaho received early attention, the initiative coming from George Vasey (1822–1893); the choice was probably a response to the admission of Idaho to the Union in 1890.

Most of the participants in the USDA expedition to Idaho (1892), although qualified professionals, are now little known and would probably be quite forgotten were not their names linked to new species published in the aftermath. George Vasey had apparently had an interest in botany since his boyhood in Illinois, but he attended medical school and practiced medicine in Illinois for nearly twenty years, beginning in 1848. He did become an active member of the Illinois Natural History Society, enabling him to cultivate his interest. In 1872, he was appointed botanist in charge of the United States National Herbarium following the ill-fated tenure of Charles Parry.

Vasey had already made field trips as an amateur to Colorado in 1867 and 1868, and the interest he had taken in grasses made him well suited to meet the expectations of the USDA. He would serve as curator of the National Herbarium for twenty-one years. His earliest efforts led to the establishment of experiment stations in the prairie states for the testing of grasses for forage, while his organization of the expedition to Idaho came nearly at the end of his regime.[4] Midway, he published a plant list of grasses, providing plant descriptions and locations, following the order of Bentham and Hooker.[5]

Vasey published a good many familiar Rocky Mountain grasses during his years at the National Herbarium, where he had access to the plants of various collectors, not just his own:

Agrostis humilis Vasey (1883), subalpine-alpine
Agrostis rossae Vasey (1892), Yellowstone hot springs

Agropyron scribneri Vasey (1883), subalpine-alpine→*Elymus scribneri* (Vasey)
  Jones (1912)
Danthonia intermedia Vasey (1883), prairie-alpine
Calamagrostis koelerioides Vasey (1891), slopes-meadows
Panicum wilcoxianum Vasey (1889), montane
Stipa lettermanii Vasey (1886), montane-subalpine
Stipa scribneri Vasey (1884), mesas, dry slopes
Trisetum wolfii Vasey (1874), montane-subalpine
Poa arida Vasey (1893), sagebrush deserts–alpine
Poa grayana Vasey (1893), alpine-circumboreal, named for Grays Peak→*Poa*
  arctica R. Br. var. *grayana* (Vasey) Dorn
Poa nervosa (Hook.) Vasey (1893) var. *wheeleri* (Vasey 1874) C. L. Hitchc.,
  montane-subalpine
Poa pattersonii Vasey (1893), subalpine-alpine
Poa cusickii Vasey (1893), high elevations
Poa occidentalis Vasey (1893), montane-subalpine
Poa reflexa Vasey ex Scribn. (1885), upper montane–alpine

Not every Western botanist agrees with the lumping of at least six traditional
poas, three of which were Vasey's, into *Poa secunda* by Robert J. Soreng. The type
species was of Chilean origin (*Reliquiae haenkeanae*, J. S. Presl., 1:271. 1830).
There are many habitats and many ecological forms; but the subspecies tend to
intergrade, and there is high-number polyploidy.

Poa nevadensis Vasey ex Schribn. (1883), foothills-montane→*Poa secunda* J. S.
  Presl. ssp. *juncifolia* (Scribn.) R. Soreng
Poa gracillima Vasey (1893) high montane–alpine→*Poa secunda* J. S. Presl.
  ssp. *secunda*
Poa sandbergii Vasey (1893), lower elevations→*Poa secunda* J. S. Presl. ssp.
  secunda

Vasey was honored not only with two new genera outside the Rocky Mountain
region—*Vaseyenthus* Cogn. in Cucurbitaceae (California) and *Vaseyochloa* Hitchc.
in Poaceae (Texas)—but with *Biglovia vaseyi* Gray (1876)→*Chrysothamnus vaseyi*
(Gray) Greene (1895), which Vasey had collected in Middle Park, Colorado.

He confided the expedition to Idaho in 1892 to the leadership of John Her-
man Sandberg (1848–1917). Born in Sweden, Sandberg came to the United
States at the age of twenty. Little is known of him except that he had studied
medicine before becoming a field agent for Vasey in 1892. Sandberg was assigned three knowledgeable assistants: Daniel T. MacDougal, Amos Arthur
Heller, and John B. Leiberg, all widely different in background. Leiberg
(1853–1913), also born in Sweden, had settled initially in Iowa in 1868, but
had later moved to Hope, Idaho, employed by the Northern Pacific Railroad. As

an amateur he collected plants in Kootenai County, becoming increasingly interested in forestry. After serving with the Vasey expedition in 1892, he became an employee of the U.S. Geological Survey.

Daniel Trembly MacDougal (1865–1958) of Indiana was part of the post-1890 generation that aspired to a Ph.D. He had worked for the USDA in Arizona before his appointment to the Vasey Expedition. Arthur Heller (1867–1944), a Pennsylvanian, took his master's degree at Franklin and Marshall in 1892, immediately thereafter becoming a field agent for the USDA, and remaining in government service until 1896.

In truth, the exploration of northern Idaho had been promoted somewhat earlier by the Northern Transcontinental Survey (the Canby and Tweedy connection). The Sandberg party was in the field from the beginning of April into early September of 1892. While they worked primarily in northern Idaho, they also crossed into adjacent parts of Montana and Washington. The collection came to a total of 1,035 numbers, of which 120 were grasses.

A number of specialists were recruited to determine the plants after they reached Washington, and the report was written by John M. Holzinger, a bryologist from the state college in Winona, Minnesota (1882–1922). He was on leave from 1890 to 1893 to prepare papers for the USDA and had not been on the trip.[6]

The grasses were the first collection of substantial importance from that region. L. H. Dewey, who examined them, emphasized their economic interest for a region that would depend for some time into the future on timber and pastures for both beef and mutton. "A careful and considerate use of these grazing lands will permit them to continue productive and valuable for many years; while a single season of overstocking is likely to ruin them for all time, as the more valuable varieties are always killed out first, and their places are usually taken by less valuable annual plants or by weeds that are positively injurious."[7]

Several new species were published in the report:

Cardamine leibergii Holz. 212. 1895. Packsaddle Peak, Kootenai County, Ida.→*Cardamine breweri* S. Wats. var. *leibergii* (Holz.) C. L. Hitchc.
Peucedanum salmoniflorus Coult. & Rose ex Holz. 228. 1895. Clearwater River above Lewiston→*Lomatium salmoniflorum* (Coult. & Rose ex Holz.) Mathias & Constance
Poa sandbergii Vasey ex Holz. 263. 1895. Clearwater River, Nez Perce County
The *Trifolium leibergii* Nels. & Macbr. (1918) was not collected until 1896, by Leiberg in Oregon.

Daniel MacDougal, after further study in Leipzig and Tübingen, was granted a Ph.D. by Purdue in 1897, with a specialization in plant physiology. The following year he returned to Arizona to continue the study of its flora, turning over possible new species to Arthur Heller for publication.[8] MacDougal then joined the staff of the New York Botanical Garden in 1899.

Mertensia franciscana Heller. 549. 1899. Near Flagstaff, 1898
Mertensia macdougalii Heller. 550. 1899. Mormon Lake so. of Flagstaff
Verbena macdougalii Heller. 588. 1899. Near Flagstaff
Brittonastrum pallidiflorum Heller. 621. 1899. Bill Williams Mt., w. of Flagstaff→
    Agastache pallidflora (Heller) Rydb.
Senecio hartiannus Heller. 622. 1899. Near Flagstaff

Arthur Heller, remaining in the service of the USDA, did fieldwork in New Mexico, especially near Santa Fe, and in Arizona. He married Emily Gertrude Halbach in 1896, and she became his collaborator in collecting and illustrated many of his publications. Leaving the USDA in 1896, they moved to California, founding a botanical journal, *Muhlenbergia,* in Los Gatos in 1900. The name of the journal did not imply a specialization in grasses, but simply signaled Heller's Pennsylvania origins. The Hellers moved to the University of Nevada at Reno in 1908, and he continued to edit the journal from there until 1915.

The following Heller species are listed separately to distinguish them from MacDougal's collections:

Crepis atrabarba Heller, *Bull. Torr. Bot. Club* 26:314. 1899. Nez Perce County, Ida.
Erigeron pulcherrimus Heller, Ibid. 25:200. 1895. no. of Santa Fe
Valeriana occidentalis Heller, Ibid. 25:269. 1895. Nez Perce County, Ida.
Hydrophyllum albifrans Heller, Ibid. 25:267. 1895. Nez Perce County, Ida.→
    Hydrophyllum fendleri (Gray) Heller (1897) var. *albifrans* (Heller) Macbr.
Gymnosteris parvula Heller, *Muhlenbergia* 1:3. 1900. Yellowstone Park, a Tweedy collection
Pyrrocoma insecticruris Heller, Ibid. 1:7. 1900. Camas County, Ida.
Astragalus arthuri M. E. Jones (1898) was collected by Heller & Heller in Nez Perce County, Ida., in 1896.

Louis Forniquet Henderson (1853–1942) was in Idaho as a plant scientist within a year of the Vasey expedition, but he had no association with that party. Born in Massachusetts, he received his training in the natural sciences at Cornell, graduating in 1874. He went to Idaho in 1893 to join the Agricultural Experiment Station of the University of Idaho, where he would remain until 1909. His botanical pioneering occurred during his survey of the Snake River country for the USDA in 1895. While his original collection of plants was destroyed in a university fire, he had fortunately distributed duplicate sets to the Gray Herbarium and to several Western university herbaria. In his later years, he moved to the University of Oregon to become curator of its herbarium.[9] A number of Henderson's Idaho species still stand:

Angelica roseana Henderson, *Contr. U.S. Nat. Herb.* 5:201. 1899. Near Salmon
Sisymbrium perplexum Henderson, *Bull. Torr. Bot. Club* 27:342. 1900. Salmon
    River→*Halimolabos perplexa* (Henderson) Rollins (1943)

Microseris nigrescens Henderson, Ibid. 27:348. 1900. Near Warren→*Nothocalais
nigrescens* (Henderson) Heller (1900)
Nemophila kirtheyi Henderson, Ibid. 27:350. 1900. Near Florence
Phacelia minutissima Henderson, Ibid. 27:351. 1900. Camas County
Chionophila tweedyi (Canby & Rose) Henderson, Ibid. 27:352. 1900. Idaho &
Custer Counties
Castilleja covilleana Henderson, Ibid. 27:353. 1900. Blaine County
Allium simillimum Henderson, Ibid. 27:355. 1900. Idaho County.
The species honoring him, *Angelica hendersonii* Coult. & Rose, was collected
by Henderson in Pacific County, Washington.

The reader will recall that Marcus Jones, in 1894, had accepted a commission
from Frederick V. Coville of the USDA to collect plants in the Colorado River
valley from Grand Junction, Colorado, to Eldorado Canyon in Nevada. Because
of persistent drought and dreadful weather, Jones's actual exploration had been
limited to Utah and portions of Arizona. Even though Coville was displeased by
some aspects of Jones's enterprise, he took considerable interest in Jones's remark that, as early as April in 1894, he had found the country so eaten out by
livestock that he had been forced to collect on cliffs inaccessible to the stock.[10]
Coville, a botanist himself, in subsequent years would aggressively promote research on the deterioration of Western rangelands. He and other botanists gave
numerous early warnings of a vegetal disaster in the making, and its history, far
from an uplifting story, has had no conclusion.

16

The Indomitable Alice Eastwood

Since Alice Eastwood (1859–1953) is so properly known as an important figure in the development of botany in California, one may be surprised to see her treated within the context of the Rocky Mountains. Her extraordinary career, however, depended not only on her formative years as a botanist in Colorado, but in no small measure on how she met and overcame daunting obstacles that would have thwarted most ordinary mortals, whether male or female.

She was born in 1859 on the grounds of the Toronto Asylum for the Insane, where her father was steward and her mother's cousin, a neurologist, was director. Her mother, a semi-invalid after the birth of Alice, died when Alice was six. In the aftermath, the father became unstable and unreliable, and Alice had to be housed intermittently with relatives or in convents. It would appear that a precocious love of flowers and plants provided the only centrality to her life, not to speak of her purpose in life. The attachment was evidently so strong that she would form no others in the course of a long life.

Eastwood's fortune began to change in 1873 when, at the age of fourteen, she was summoned by her father to Denver, where he had found employment. As his residence there was a cheap hotel, entirely unsuitable for a teenage girl, he placed her in the home of a prosperous cattleman as a nursemaid to two infants. Her employer was generous enough to see that she attended public school, and it seems probable that her salvation derived from the sensitive instruction she received. A teacher, recognizing her interest in plants, gave her Porter and Coulter's *Flora of Colorado* and Asa Gray's *Manual,* meaning that she would have to learn botany on her own. The books were only of limited help: the Gray was not adapted to the Rocky Mountain region, and the Porter-Coulter, a synopsis by definition, only provided descriptions for its new species.

In the casual condition of frontier life, Eastwood eventually progressed from pupil to teacher at East Denver High School. Being forced to teach others meant that she had to keep learning herself; and the summers became her opportunity for botanizing in the mountains. The appearance of Coulter's *Manual of Rocky Mountain Botany* in 1885 was a godsend.[1] During the 1880s, she botanized widely in the Front Range.

On the morning of 19 May 1887, Alfred Russel Wallace (1823–1913), on a lecture trip in the United States, arrived in Denver while on a train trip between Washington and California. Having a four-hour stopover, he went to the local high school to inquire whether there was a local botanist who might give him information about localities favorable for finding alpine plants. He was taken to Alice Eastwood's classroom, where he found her giving a lesson on ancient history. The two chatted for about an hour, during which time she showed him dried specimens she had collected on Pike's Peak; and she recommended Graymount, near Grays Peak, as a good collection spot.[2]

It was arranged that Wallace would again stop in Denver on his return trip from California in midsummer, when Eastwood would be free to be his guide for a field trip. He did return, on 18 July 1887, and they set off on the morning of the 19th up Clear Creek canyon for Georgetown. From there, it was an additional eight miles to Graymount, the settlement nearest Grays Peak, at an elevation of about 9,670 feet. From that base, there were two valleys available for collecting: Grizzly Gulch, which penetrated to the north side of Grays Peak; and a smaller, steeper valley, which led to a small group of miners' huts called Kelso's Cabin. From there, one passed through an upland valley to the foot of Grays Peak, then followed a winding mule track to the summit.

Many brilliant species were in bloom, some of them familiar to Wallace from the Alps and Britain; but others were entirely new to him. He admired in particular the alpine forget-me-not, which he identified as *Omphalodes nana* Gray var. *arctioides* Gray (as he was using Coulter's *Manual*), tufts of exquisite blue that we now call *Eritrichium nanum* (Villars) Schrad. ex Gaudin. He also found, in Grizzly Gulch, what he believed to be a species new to Colorado, *Bryanthus empetriformis*, now *Phyllodoce empetriformis* (Smith) D. Don. As it has never since been found in Colorado, it seems probable that he collected *Kalmia microphylla* (Hook.) Heller.

The field trip had obviously given Wallace great pleasure. When he left Denver for Chicago on the morning of 26 July 1887, he had been with Alice Eastwood for nearly a week. Yet, she goes unmentioned in his memoirs from the moment they set out for Georgetown; so that we are deprived of his impressions of her.[3] Subsequently, Wallace did mention his trip to Colorado in correspondence with Theodore Cockerell, after Cockerell reported that there were five species of *Aquilegia* (columbine) in Colorado. Replied Wallace, "But have they not each their stations, two seldom occurring together?"[4]

During his week in Colorado, Wallace had seen only two species of columbine, *coerulea* and *brevistyla* (*saximontana*), each in its own area. He told Cockerell that he had been struck in particular by what appeared to be a real scarcity of Monocotyledons in the Rocky Mountains, notably bulbous Liliaceae, Amaryllids, and Orcheses. He welcomed more information on the matter, as well as bulbs or tubers to plant in his garden.

By the time of that exchange (1890), Cockerell had already met Alice Eastwood, presumably in Denver, after which she visited him in West Cliff (now Westcliff). They had botanized together in the Wet Mountain Valley, where he was living temporarily. When the moment came for him to return to England, May of 1889, Eastwood wrote to him on the assumption that she might not see him again. She wanted him to know that "I have learned much from you, in some respects more than from anyone else. I do not hope to be able to return the obligation to you, but perhaps I can, to my fellow men."[5]

By that time, Eastwood was preparing a popular flora of the Denver area. It was meant to help high school students learn the names of plants growing around the city and was primarily a plant list. For analytical keys and descriptions of genera and higher orders, the student was referred to Coulter's manual; for nomenclature and pronunciation, she followed Gray's manual. She acknowledged the assistance of Charles S. Crandall of the agricultural college in Fort Collins, who had begun collecting plants in Larimer County in 1890, and who verified the names of Eastwood's grasses.

In her brief preface, she made the additional observation that identifying a plant was merely the first step toward knowing it. "There should follow observations of its habit and environment; the noting of the insect visitors, their actions and results; comparison with other plants of the same species and those of allied species to discover variation and detect relationships that may be unsuspected." Those remarks reflected the instruction she had received from Cockerell during his sojourn in Westcliff, about which more below. One entry in her flora, selected at random, will illustrate the character of the book: "No. 396 *Iris missouriensis* Nutt. may be found near Baker's Pond near the Larimer Street viaduct. Spring."[6]

Beginning in June of 1890, Eastwood had the resources to venture far beyond the Denver area. Initially, in southwestern Colorado, Durango was her base. Later in the year, she moved on to San Diego, which opened up a new botanical world to her. She wandered northward through what seemed to be a botanical wonderland, notably the region of Santa Cruz and the Monterey Peninsula, finally descending on the California Academy of Sciences in San Francisco, May of 1891, where she met the Brandegees.

Almost immediately she returned to Colorado to botanize during that summer. Her collection sites indicate that she was around Gunnison, the Flattop Mountains, and Steamboat Springs from May into June; then in the Arkansas valley above Canon City in July before returning to Denver. There she received an offer of a salary from Katharine Brandegee if she would return to San Francisco to help organize the academy's herbarium. Eastwood accepted, although without any intent at that moment to leave the Colorado scene permanently.

Indeed, she did return to the Rocky Mountains by summer, 1892, collecting in Mesa Verde and the Mancos and San Juan valleys in May and June, around Moab, Utah, and Mesa County, Colorado, and again on the upper Arkansas in August. But during that summer, a second offer came from Katharine Brandegee that was too tempting to refuse—a full position at the California Academy of Sciences. From then on, Alice Eastwood would be identified with the academy. She would make occasional trips to Colorado (there are records from 1897, 1910, 1918, and 1938), and she would edit another textbook for Rocky Mountain high school students in 1900; but she had become primarily a California botanist.[7]

This later textbook was a more extensive and sophisticated introductory text than the earlier one prepared for Denver; it was meant for the entire Rocky Mountain region. The book was designed to give students practical experience in *classifying* plants and in understanding the characteristics of the larger plant groups. Eastwood acknowledged her reliance on the Coulter *Manual*. The keys, if very simplified, were based on the same divisions we would use today: Gymnosperms, Angiosperms, Monocotyledons, and Dicotyledons; ovary position and petal structure. As Eastwood had been a high school teacher, her book reveals to us what was expected of high school students a century ago, and what technical competence would have been expected of a teacher in order to use the text.[8]

It does not appear that Eastwood, when accepting a permanent position at the academy, had any inkling that she was entering a war zone. She soon met E. L. Greene, by then at the University of California. A warm friendship developed between the two, based on their common love for the flora of the Rocky Mountains. What is more, she came to agree with him in his nomenclatural departures from Asa Gray, defending him openly despite Katharine Brandegee's fierce loyalty to the Asa Gray tradition. We are reminded that Greene did have loyal supporters in California, among them his graduate student William L. Jepson. This may have contributed to the decision of the Brandegees, despite their alliance with Marcus Jones, to cut themselves off from the academy in 1893. They moved their private library and herbarium to San Diego; and, the following year, Eastwood was appointed curator of herbarium of the California Academy of Sciences.[9]

Some of Eastwood's species known in the Rocky Mountains were not collected in that region; these include *Hackelia micrantha* (Eastw.) J. Gentry and *Cryptantha celosioides* (Eastw.) Payson. Below are a few new species that she definitely collected in our region:

Aquilegia coerulea James var. *daileyae* Eastw., *Proc. Calif. Acad. Sci.* ser. 3, 1:76. 1897. North-central Colo., 1891

Oreocarpa elata Eastw., *Bull. Torr. Bot. Club* 30:241. 1903. Grand Junction, 1892→*Cryptantha elata* (Eastw.) Payson

Oreocarpa aperta Eastw., Ibid. 30:241. 1903. Grand Junction, 1892→*Cryptan-tha aperta* (Eastw.) Payson. Apparently endemic to Mesa County

Oreocarpa wetherillia Eastw., Ibid. 30:242. 1903. Moab, Utah, 1892→*Cryptantha wetherillia* (Eastw.) Payson. May be endemic to eastern Utah west of the Colorado River

Oreocarpa tenuis Eastw., Ibid. 30:244. 1903. Moab, Utah, 1892→*Cryptantha tenuis* (Eastw.) Payson. Possibly endemic to e. and s.e. Utah

Oreocarpa capitata Eastw., *Leafl. W. Bot.* 2:9. 1937. Hermit Trail, Grand Canyon, Ariz.→*Cryptantha capitata* (Eastw.) I. M. Johnston

All of Eastwood's collections made before 1906 were destroyed in the San Francisco fire that April, except for a few specimens she managed to save or that were on loan. Some duplicates had fortunately been distributed, and a collection of her Colorado plants had been given to the herbarium in Boulder. As for the total loss of the Academy's herbarium, she wrote: "I do not feel the loss to be mine, but it is a great loss to the scientific world and an irreparable loss to California. My own destroyed work I do not lament, for it was a joy while I did it, and I can still have the same joy in starting it again." Any new beginning had to face at the outset the destruction of the entire herbarium library. There were no references left, a grievous loss.[10]

At her own request, Eastwood retired on her ninetieth birthday, receiving the title curator-emeritus, gratefully and lovingly honored by her scientific associates. She remarked on the occasion, "I count my age by friends, not years, and I am rich in friends!"[11]

In assessing Eastwood's record of exploration in the Rocky Mountains, one must acknowledge that in 1890, when she explored around Durango, Mancos, the La Plata Mountains, and up the Animas River to Silverton, she was in a region previously explored by T. S. Brandegee. But by crossing Red Mountain Pass into Ouray County, she went into a country quite botanically unknown. That was also true in 1891 when she ventured into the Gunnison region and into the Flattop Mountains, areas mainly west of Coulter's route in 1873. Although Marcus Jones preceded her in Mesa County, she had been ahead of him around Moab in 1892, intruding unwittingly on his territoriality. She would much later make an attempt to acquire the Jones herbarium for the California Academy of Sciences, but in vain. Even after taking up residence in California, Eastwood made occasional sentimental journeys into the Colorado Rockies, for that is where she had prepared herself to become the curator of the herbarium at the California Academy of Sciences, which post she held from 1893 to 1949. She surpassed by seven years the record for the longest stay as head of an herbarium, set by the comte de Buffon at the Jardin du Roi; and Eastwood's record is likely to stand. She retired beloved by her colleagues, quite unlike Buffon.

Within the Rocky Mountain area, Eastwood's eponomy includes *Arenaria eastwoodiae* Rydb., found from northwest Colorado into Utah and New Mexico, and *Salix eastwoodiae* Cockerell ex Heller, a subalpine willow from north and central Wyoming into southern Montana. *Eastwoodia* Brandegee is a monotypic California genus in the Compositae.

17

Three Notable Collectors

PURPUS, COCKERELL, AND OSTERHOUT

*C*arl Albert Purpus (1851–1941) is virtually unknown to Rocky Mountain botanists today, but he is a curious example of a commercial collector of plants and seeds, who seems to have roamed widely. He gathered plant material initially for the Darmstadt Botanical Garden in Germany. Ultimately he was a freelancer trying to support himself from the sale of plant collections. His older brother, Joseph Anton, was the head gardener in Darmstadt for many years; and while it has been said that Carl Albert had studied for a medical degree, it is probable that his degree had been in pharmacy.

His itineraries have been difficult to ascertain. Apparently he did not number his specimens at the time of collection, only numbering them when preparing sets for distribution. He first appeared in Colorado in 1892, his collection sites being in Gunnison, Delta, and Hinsdale Counties. There is no indication he knew that Alice Eastwood had recently preceded him in that region, or that she knew about him at that time.

Around 1894, Purpus settled in San Diego, and he botanized in California for the next four years. He became a friend of Townshend and Katharine Brandegee, and Townshend undertook the determination of many of the species that Purpus collected. His letters to the Brandegees, when he was in the field, expressed his growing anger over the devastation to mountain pastures caused by flocks of grazing sheep. He would have killed them all had he not been opposed to killing animals (except rattlesnakes). His wrath was vented equally on the woodchoppers he witnessed in the Sequoia region. He yearned to pass amongst them with a club to knock them flat.

In the spring of 1899, he took the train to Utah to spend the summer collecting in the La Sal Mountains. At least three new taxa, based on Purpus's collections in the La Sal Mountains, still stand:

Potentilla pancijuga Rydb.→*Potentilla pensylvania* L. var. *paucijuga* (Rydb.) Welsh & Johnston
Saxifraga caespitosa L. ssp. *exaratoides* (Simm.) Engl. & Irmsch.
Gilia sedifolia A. Brand.

In subsequent years, Purpus collected primarily in Mexico, where he died in 1941. While a substantial collection of his plants is held in the Field Museum in Chicago, he sent much material to Germany, where it was published, frequently in seed catalogues. Such prominent botanists as K. M. Schumann, B. A. E. Koehne, and August Brand took an interest in his material, and their work may be consulted by anyone endeavoring to identify type species. Marcus Jones must have learned about Purpus from the Brandegees, but there is no evidence the two met in Utah.[1] *Purpusia* Brandegee, a monotypic genus in Rosacea, has not stood; but Purpus remains honored by *Delphinium purpusii* Brandegee, the Kern County larkspur.

As in the example of Purpus, it is without doubt unusual to mention Theodore Dru Alison Cockerell (1866–1948) among the explorers of the Rocky Mountain region. His name, to be sure, is attached to a number of species, not all of which have stood. But he was neither a professional botanist nor an employee of any of those governmental agencies that promoted exploration in the later nineteenth century. He was a phenomenon the likes of which may be gone forever: he was an unspecialized naturalist who belonged to the nineteenth century of his birth rather than to the twentieth century into which he lived. In prior centuries he would have been called an amateur without any of the condescension that tag implies today. If he ultimately became a professor, a rank implying professional status, he remained more entomologist than anything else—but also zoologist, botanist, ecologist, paleontologist, and evolutionist, and in a manner that illustrates why modern science can be counted among the humanities.

Born in 1866 in a London suburb to a family of some means, Cockerell attended private schools and enrolled in the Middlesex Hospital Medical School, but never completed a degree. Instead, he undertook independent research, with encouragement from within his family, and his first confirmed publication is dated 1882, when he would have been sixteen. From then on, his publications, which would reach the astounding number of about thirty-nine hundred items, would generally be short communications in the fashion of the nineteenth century. Communicating his findings to colleagues as quickly as possible would always be his motive. He lacked the monographic mentality more characteristic of the twentieth century.

In 1887, Cockerell began to suffer a pulmonary ailment that was believed to be tuberculosis, which accounts for his move to Colorado, the favored climate for a cure in that day. He settled in Westcliffe, an outpost at the base of the Sangre de Cristo Mountains southwest of Canon City. Although only twenty-one, he assumed the responsibility for bringing culture to Custer County. In short order, he had the locals recruited for a Literary and Debating Society. Broadening his scope, he established a local branch of the Colorado Biological Association, and he began to prepare a catalogue of the flora and fauna of Colorado. At the end of three years, he believed his health sufficiently restored to return to England. By the time he left, the ladies of Custer County had been given botanical instruction; and a surviving announcement of a meeting of the local Colorado Biological Association, dated 29 January 1889, promised a paper to be read by Cockerell on "The Balance of Nature, or Insects and their Parasites." (Memberships were one dollar, and nonmembers could attend for ten cents.) How much of this uplift survived his departure offers the opportunity for an instructive inquiry beyond the scope of this chapter.[2]

During 1890, Cockerell found valuable employment at the British Museum helping to prepare Alfred Russel Wallace's *Island Life* (1880) for a second edition. The association with Wallace likely accounts for Cockerell becoming a convinced evolutionist, but of the Wallace persuasion. That is, he claimed that man had not, like the other animals, been produced by the unaided operation of natural selection, but that other forces had been in operation. The position at the British Museum also put Cockerell in line to become curator, in 1891, of the Public Museum in Kingston, Jamaica. The climate proved to be unfavorable. Cockerell's pulmonary symptoms reappeared after little more than a year, indicating he should return to the American West. It seems remarkable that he was able to arrange an exchange of positions with C. H. T. Townsend of the New Mexico Agricultural College in Las Cruces in 1893. He would remain in New Mexico for a decade, although he moved to New Mexico Normal University in Las Vegas in 1900.[3]

New taxa from Cockerell's Westcliffe and New Mexico years:

Calochortus gunnisonii S. Wats. var. *perpulcher* Cockl., *West Amer. Scientist* 4 (41): 17. 1888. Mora and San Miguel Counties, N.M.

Castilleja haydenii (Gray) Cockl., *Bull. Torr. Bot. Club* 17:34–37. 1890. Colo. and N.M.

Castilleja integra Gray var. *gloriosa* (Britt.) Cockl., Ibid. 17:34–37. 1890. Colo. and N.M.

Allium cernuum Roth. f. *obtusum* Cockl., Ibid. 18:173. 1891. Custer County, Colo.→*Allium cernuum* Roth. var. *obtusum* Cockl. ex J. F. Macbr.

Sophia halictorum Cockl., Ibid. 25:460. 1898. Colo. and N.M.→*Descurainia pinnata* (Walt.) Britt. ssp. *halictorum* (Cockl.) Detling

Aquilegia desertorum (M. E. Jones) Cockl. in Cooper, *Southwest* 2:89. 1900. Flagstaff, Ariz., a Jones collection, 1884

Primula ellisiae Pollard & Cockl., *Proc. Biol. Soc. Wash.* 15:177–179. 1902. Las
  Vegas Range, N.M.
Achillea laxiflora Pollard & Cockl., Ibid. 15:177–179. 1902. Las Vegas Range,
  N.M.
Delphinium sapellonia Cockl., *Bot. Gaz.* 34:453–454. 1902. Endemic to N.M.
Mertensia caelestina A. Nels. & Cockl., *Proc. Biol. Soc. Wash.* 16:45–46. 1903.
  N.M.→*Mertensia viridis* A. Nels. var. *caelestina* (A. Nels. & Cockl.) L. O.
  Williams

Beginning in 1903, Cockerell was a resident of Colorado. He spent one academic year at Colorado College, during which time he began to study what
he called the Colorado rubber plant, *Picradenia floribunda* (A. Gray) Greene.
The genus was Hooker's, and Cockerell came to believe it to be a synonym of
Cassini's *Hymenoxys*. That led to a new group of transfers in 1904, plus one
new species.

Hymenoxys lemmonii (Greene) Cockl., *Bull. Torr. Bot. Club* 31:479. 1904. Utah
  to Calif.
Hymenoxys subintegra Cockl., Ibid. 31:480. 1904. Kaibab Plateau
Hymenoxys helenioides (Rydb.) Cockl., Ibid. 31:481. 1904. Utah Plateau to La
  Sal Mountains
Hymenoxys richardsonii (Hook.) Cockl., Ibid. 31:492. 1904. S. Canada to Ariz.
Hymenoxys cooperi (A. Gray) Cockl., Ibid. 31:496. 1904. Utah to Idaho

As Colorado College did not have the financial resources to retain Cockerell
as a faculty member, he moved to Boulder in 1904 to seek employment. By the
beginning of that year, he had published 1,677 papers. No professorship was
available at that moment at the University of Colorado, so he remained a lec-
turer in entomology for two years until a professorship became his in 1906. He
then began the study of fossils at Florissant. Obviously he had no yen to become
a specialist, and there would be no place for him today in a university. The only
rationale for the way Cockerell conducted his professional life emerges not from
what he said, but from what he did.

For instance, during the years that Cockerell was in New Mexico, he had
found the bee fauna to be rich and varied, many of the species associated with
particular plants. He came to suspect that there are instances when botanists see
only one species in a given plant population; but where the selectivity of bees
indicates that, in fact, two or more closely related species are actually present.
In such cases, a closer study of the plants would reveal grounds for segregation.[4]

Cockerell was not always specific about insect association in his descriptions of
a new plant species, even though it was of concern to him. But when publishing
Sophia halictorum Cockl.—a plant abundant in Mesilla Park, New Mexico—as a

new species, he noted that "it is freely visited by bees of the genus *Halictus,* whence the specific name." Examination had led him to segregate the plant from *Sisymbrium canescens* Nutt. (now *Descurainia pinnata* [Walt.] Britt. ssp. *pinnata*), which he had known from his prior sojourn in Westcliffe. It is still good today as *Descurainia pinnata* (Walt.) Britt. ssp. *halictorum* (Cockl.) Detling.[5]

The selectivity of bees had been known before Cockerell brought the phenomenon to bear on the segregation of species, and it had implications for successful agriculture as well. Darwin recognized that bees form a large and natural family comprising many genera and species, and that bees are specialized in correspondence with the flowers from which they draw the bulk of their food. The European honeybee, *Apis mellifera,* can easily suck nectar from *Trifolium incarnatrum* L., but not from *Trifolium pratense* L., for which it would have to have a longer or differently constructed proboscis. Darwin added that bumblebees alone visited *Trifolium pratense* L., the common red clover.[6]

The first colony of hive bees were brought into Colorado in 1862 by Isaac McBroom, who settled on Bear Creek near the foothills west of Denver. The native bloom was abundant, but not enough honey was produced to enable the bees to survive the winter. Another colony, established in 1866, met the same fate. Commercial production of honey only became possible by 1870 through the introduction of those European legumes compatible with the honeybees. *Trifolium repens* L. (Dutch white clover) was preeminent; but also introduced were *Trifolium hybridum* L. (alsike), *Onobrychis viciifolia* Scop. (sainfoin), *Melilotus officinalis* (L.) Pallas (sweet clover), and *Medicago sativa* L. (alfalfa), although honeybees are poor pollinators of alfalfa. All of these plants are now naturalized in the Rocky Mountains.[7] John M. Coulter, in his Rocky Mountain manual of 1885, noted these recent introductions in his footnotes, indicating that alfalfa (first sown in Denver in 1863 and promoted by the Union Colonists of Greeley in 1872) had spread to Wyoming and Utah. The east European leafcutter bee, *Megachile rotundata,* is now the major pollinator of alfalfa. Its original distribution, like that of alfalfa, was in Eastern Europe and southwest-central Asia. The coevolution of flowering plants and bees is an example of a general phenomenon, and Cockerell believed it could be useful information in the determination of plant species.[8]

It is evident from Cockerell's list of publications that, from 1906 until his retirement in 1934, his attention to plants diminished as he became increasingly focused on entomology, paleontology, and the affairs of the communities in which he lived. His new taxa from that period includes only five items that stand:

Salix cascadensis Cockl., *Muhlenbergia* 3:9. 1907. Alpine, Colo., Utah, Wyo., Mont.
Salix arctophilia Cockl. ex Heller, *Cat. N. Am. Pl.* 3:89. 1910. Greenland, no. Canada, n.e. Alaska

Salix eastwoodiae Cockl. ex Heller, Ibid. 3:89. 1910. Sierra Nevada, Mont., Wyo.
Cirsium scopulorum (Greene) Cockl. in Daniels, *Missouri Univ. Studies* 2 (2):
253. 1911. Colo. alpine
Mertensia lanceolata (Pursh) DC. var. *secundorum* Cockl., *Torreya* 18:180.
1918. Cen. Colo.

It would be difficult today to measure Cockerell's influence, as William A.
Weber emphasized. He explored broadly and communicated much in professional publication. He also corresponded frequently with his Western colleagues
and could put more on a postal card in his miniscule script than most of us confine to an entire page, exchanging opinions on collections and research, especially with those he considered his closest neighbors—Eastwood, Osterhout,
and Nelson. His numerous articles in the popular press revealed the importance
he gave to communicating the work of scientists to the general public, to promoting higher standards in public instruction, and to criticizing university administrators for their inability to understand that research on campus was necessary to invigorate classroom instruction.

Cockerell believed that administrators valued scientific research to the extent that it attracted outside money; but he doubted that they, as a group,
would much extend themselves to raise money for such purposes. While his
criticisms were directed specifically at the University of Colorado, they were
applicable to most of the Western public universities. That assertion seems
confirmed by the sources of the two honorary degrees of Sc.D. he received—
Colorado College, in 1913, and the University of Denver, in 1942, both private
institutions.[9] Cockerell was also honored with a new species collected in the
mountains of New Mexico by Elmer O. Wooton in 1893: *Sedum cockerelii* Britt.,
Bull. N.Y. Bot. Gard. 3:41. 1903.

Cockerell's career serves to remind that the naturalists of the nineteenth century were often described as knowing a great deal about a great many things,
Darwin being the supreme example; setting them apart from the specialists of
today, who likely regard those naturalists as too superficial to be taken seriously.
Since both types are needed, the loss of the nineteenth-century type ought to be
regretted.[10] Who will there be to defend the specialists against the antiscientism
of the multitude?

The life and times of George E. Osterhout (1858–1937) offers a partial answer to the cultural dilemma the question above implies. His example does not
argue against the need for specialization, but rather for the opportunities and
choices that a liberal undergraduate education provides before eventual specialization. It has been the traditional remedy against the onset of terminal tunnel
vision, not only for professionals, but for the general public.

Osterhout was born in Pennsylvania and did his undergraduate work at
Lafayette College. Thomas Conrad Porter was his instructor in the natural sci-

ences. Porter, who had been ordained, may have encouraged Osterhout's study of religion. Thereafter, Osterhout studied law and was admitted to the Pennsylvania bar. There is no evidence that he ever practiced law. Judging more by what he did than anything he said, he had become obsessed with the idea of botanizing in Colorado while under Porter's influence. In 1885, he moved to Colorado and established a lumber business in Windsor. During leisure hours, he began the study of the local flora. The prosperity of his business soon enabled him to make annual field trips dedicated to building a personal herbarium; and he purchased a substantial library in both the natural sciences and theology, remaining a devout Baptist. As he married late, in 1894 at the age of thirty-six, his wife knew well in advance that she would share the house with dried specimens.

Neither Osterhout's collection books nor his correspondence remains; but his herbarium, roughly twenty thousand sheets, was legated to the Rocky Mountain Herbarium in Laramie. Records in both New York and Laramie prove that Osterhout had had frequent correspondence with both P. A. Rydberg and Aven Nelson. Between 1897 and 1934, Osterhout published forty-four papers, making his name known to professional botanists. Probably no other amateur contributed more to our knowledge of Rocky Mountain botany. His personal collection came to 8,330 numbers, testimony to leisure time arduously spent.

Osterhout rarely numbered his specimens in the order of collection, but grouped them for convenient study, then numbered and mounted them. But he was scrupulous about recording collection dates and sites. Consequently, the Osterhout taxa that stand are listed below by date, giving a rough idea of his itineraries. Locations are in Colorado unless otherwise indicated.[11]

Rumex densiflorus Osterh. Larimer County. 1898

Potentilla rupicola Osterh. Larimer County. 1899

Mentzelia speciosa Osterh. Larimer County. 1901

Agroseris agrestis Osterh. Larimer County→*Argoseris glauca* (Pursh) Raf. var. *agrestis* (Osterh.) Q. Jones ex Cronq. 1901

Cryptantha gracilis Osterh. Garfield County. 1903

Aulospermum planosum Osterh. Eagle County→*Cymopteris planosum* (Osterh.) Mathias. 1903

Touterea multicaulis Osterh. Eagle County→*Mentzelia multicaulis* (Osterh.) A. Nels. ex J. Darl. 1903

Astragalus puniceus Osterh. Las Animas County. 1906

Carduus laterifolius Osterh. Larimer County→*Cirsium laterifolium* (Osterh.) Petrak. 1906

Townsendia leptotes (A. Gray) Osterh. n. comb. 1908

Artemisia spiciformis Osterh. var. *longiloba* Osterh. Grand County→*Artemisia arbuscula* Nutt. ssp. *longiloba* (Osterh.) L. Shultz. 1908

Carduus crassus Osterh. Grand County→*Cirsium* x *crassum* (Osterh.) Petrak. 1910

Carduus canalensis Osterh. Larimer County→*Cirsium* x *canalense* (Osterh.) Petrak. 1910

Carduus vernalis Osterh. Mesa County→*Cirsium vernale* (Osterh.) Cockl. 1911

Cogswellia concinna Osterh. Delta County→*Lomatium concinnum* (Osterh.) Mathias. 1912

Carduus modestus Osterh. Larimer County→*Cirsium modestum* (Osterh.) Cockl. 1913

Phacelia denticulata Osterh. Larimer County. 1916

Hymenopappus polycephalus Osterh. Larimer County→*Hymnenopappus filifolius* Hook. var. *polycephalus* (Osterh.) B. L. Turner. 1918

Phacelia formosula Osterh. Jackson County. 1918

Oreocarya stricta Osterh. Moffat County→*Cryptantha stricta* (Osterh.) Payson. 1923

Oreocarya breviflora Osterh. Uinta County, Utah→*Cryptantha breviflora* (Osterh.) Payson. 1926

Astragalus linifolius Osterh. Mesa County. 1928

Eponomy from Osterhout collections:

Astragalus osterhoutii M. E. Jones. Grand County. 1905
Penstemon osterhoutii Pennell. Garfield County. 1911
Cryptantha osterhoutii (Payson) Payson. Mesa County. 1921

A number of Osterhout labels in the Rocky Mountain Herbarium bear the following description: "Mountains of Southern Wyoming along a branch of Encampment Creek, Fino Creek." They refer to Damfino Creek, a place name unacceptable to a confirmed Baptist.

18

Per Axel Rydberg

THE GENTLE BOTANIST

*C*onsidering Per Axel Rydberg's importance in the history of American botany, and the fact that he survived well into the twentieth century, one is struck by how little biographical detail remains available about him. That he was a man of great reserve and very kind, one who avoided thrusting himself into the intellectual and political controversies of his day, accounts in part for his obscurity, no matter that his professional practice aroused considerable controversy. But the destruction of his personal papers by his family, after his death—an incomprehensible action, as there can have been nothing in his quiet life to provoke a need for concealment—has ruled out anything but a limited intellectual biography.

Rydberg was born into a farming family in Sweden in 1860 and reared in the Swedish Lutheran faith, a faith he would never abandon and which, in later years, meant he refused to botanize on Sundays. He was trained to become a mining engineer in the Royal Gymnasium at Skara; but even in that context, his interest in plants was awakened, and he began to build a personal herbarium. He graduated in 1881 and emigrated to the United States the following year, expecting to work as an engineer in the iron mines of Michigan. In 1884, he suffered a fall, injuring a leg; this left him permanently lame and forced him to seek a more sedentary life.

Rydberg's liberal education enabled him to find other work, and, in 1884, he was engaged as a teacher of general science at Luther Academy in Wahoo, Nebraska, with which he would remain affiliated until 1893. His education had also made him competent in Greek and Latin. During 1890, Rydberg took the first steps towards a botanical career. That summer, he ventured for a month into western Nebraska to study the flora, and he found that his lame leg was not an insuperable handicap. He also began work toward a bachelor's of science degree at the nearby University of Nebraska. The following summer, 1891, he enlisted as a plant collector in western Nebraska for the United States Department of Agriculture; and, in the summer of 1892, he extended his range into the Black Hills. For eleven summers thereafter, he would collect for both the USDA and the New York Botanical Garden.[1]

Rydberg resigned from Luther Academy in 1893 to begin work on a master's degree at Nebraska under Charles E. Bessey, a taxonomist just then becoming renowned for his development of an innovative phylogenetic system of plant classification. Finishing the degree in 1895, Rydberg accepted a professorship in general science at Upsala Institute in Brooklyn (later Upsala College in Kenilworth, New Jersey). The move enabled him to begin work toward a Ph.D. under Nathaniel Lord Britton at Columbia, and he completed the degree in 1898.[2]

As a doctoral student, Rydberg concentrated in particular on the Rose family; and his doctoral dissertation was a monograph on the genus *Potentilla* L., a genus whose validity he quite accepted. But his treatment presaged what would be his lifelong career as a major splitter; for he also recognized *Argentina* Hill, *Drymocallis* Four., and *Dasiphora* Raf. as legitimate segregations from *Potentilla*.

A judgment about such matters must acknowledge that, in Rydberg's day, taxonomists did not yet have the taxonomic tools of the later twentieth century, which can be brought to bear to justify either splitting or lumping. Instead, he was heavily dependent on morphology, and he would have been aware, coming in the aftermath of Darwin, that some variability was of ecological origin. Rydberg, moreover, as in the case of E. L. Greene, seems not to have liked the idea of varieties. In his opinion, small, consistent differences within a given genus merited specific rank, not varietal. Rydberg's reputed "eagle eye" in spotting subtle differences may have reflected only a predisposition to see differences rather than similarities, an aspect of personality acquired long before any acquaintance with technical botany.

Because that predisposition is usually not taken into account, lumpers may suspect that splitters have no concept of genus or species; and splitters may have similar suspicions about lumpers. Such charges are generally unfair. Marcus Jones made such a charge against Rydberg, more than once publishing the claim that Rydberg practiced "bughole botany," counting the number of bug holes in a leaf to justify segregation.

In Rydberg's case, one matter seems never to have been pursued. To what degree had he been influenced by Charles Bessey's view that species have no actual existence in nature, but are mental concepts and nothing more? In other words, do we invent species in order to refer to great numbers of individuals collectively?[3] Such a nominalism was virtually Buffonian; or, to cite its inspiration, John Lockean. Such a nominalism might give a believer free rein to apply specific names fairly casually; but there is nothing in Rydberg's career to lead us to believe that he was anything but a highly principled, scrupulous practitioner.

The segregations he recognized from *Potentilla* are a case in point and also indicate the development of a species concept:

Argentina anserine (L.) Rydb. *A Monograph of the North American Potentilleae.* *Mem. Dept. Bot. Columbia Coll.* 2:159. 1898. Rydberg recognized that the twenty to twenty-five stamens, in three series, were inserted exactly as in *Potentilla,* perigynous-superior; but he elected to recognize the segregation of *Argentina* because of its slender, prostrate stolons.

Drymocallis arguta (Pursh) Rydb. Ibid. 2:192. 1898. As the basis for segregation in this case, he noted that the style was nearly basal, that is, attached near the base of the ovary. In *Potentilla,* the style is attached near the apex of the ovary.

Dasiphora fructicosa (L.) Rydb. Ibid. 2:188. 1898. In this instance, he observed that not only were the styles inserted near the middle of the ovaries, but that the stigmas were large and evidently four-lobed. The monotypic genus was also distinctive in being shrubby. In recent years, the need for a transfer has been widely recognized, but to the genus *Pentaphylloides* Duhamel for its evident priority.

Rydberg's completion of his Ph.D. in 1898 under Britton's direction led to an assistant curatorship in 1899 at the New York Botanical Garden, where Britton was the director. Rydberg would remain at the garden until his death in 1931; and among the eminent botanical explorers of the Rocky Mountain region, he was the first to achieve a high position in botany based on professional university training. Thanks to the summers he had spent doing fieldwork, beginning in 1890, Rydberg had published considerably before his appointment in New York. In 1892, he was the first to make an extensive botanical survey of the Black Hills. They had remained botanically obscure in part because they lay between the two major river routes, the Missouri and the North Platte, and partly because they had remained a well-defended stronghold for plains Indians. Given the isolation of the Black Hills, their inclusion in the Rocky Mountains might be questioned. But the Black Hills are recognized by geologists as an isolated uplift of the Rocky Mountains.[4]

Small collections of plants had been made on the periphery of the Black Hills as early as 1855 by F. V. Hayden and 1859 by Captain William F. Raynolds; collections were also made by N. H. Winchell and A. B. Donaldson on the Custer expedition of 1874. But such men were topographical engineers whose principal interest was geological. Rydberg not only made a substantial collection of plants from the interior; he saw, and reported, the extensive damage already done by local timber and mining industries.[5]

During his next eleven summers in the field, sponsored by both the USDA and the New York Botanical Garden, Rydberg botanized widely in Montana,

Yellowstone Park, Colorado, and Utah, with briefer visits to eastern Idaho and southern Wyoming. He had the company of various assistants, whom he gratefully acknowledged. In 1895, a fellow Swede from Luther Academy, Julius H. Flodman, was with him in Montana. The submontane thistle *Cirsium flodmanii* (Rydb.) Arthur honors him. Cornelius L. Shear, who would become an eminent phytopathologist and agronomist, was with Rydberg in Montana in 1895 and in Colorado in 1896. Ernest A. Bessey, son of Charles E. Bessey, was with Rydberg in Montana in 1897. As a mycologist, he would serve for many years at Michigan State Agricultural College. The genus *Besseya* Rydb. honors the father, not the son.

In 1900, Frederick K. Vreeland, recently a student at Columbia College, collected with Rydberg in Colorado. Although he would became a physicist, Vreeland would continue collecting as an amateur, making his collections available to Rydberg. *Quercus vreelandii* Rydb. was meant to honor him, but did not stand. Albert O. Garrett, a high school teacher in Salt Lake City, became an experienced plant collector. In 1905, he accompanied Rydberg for botanizing in the La Sal Mountains. Garrett's field experience made him a respected correspondent. The species *Atriplex garrettii* Rydb. and *Penstemon scariosus* Pennell var. *garrettii* A. Nels. testify to the desire to honor him.[6]

In 1900, Rydberg published his *Catalogue of the Flora of Montana and Yellowstone National Park* as a memoir of the New York Botanical Garden, then turned his concentration to a flora of Colorado.[7] Even though Rydberg by temperament was loath to engage in controversies, as a student and employee of Nathaniel Lord Britton, he had been of necessity an adherent to the nomenclatural principles known as the American Code. The arguments over the relative merits of splitting and lumping did, indeed, concern the botanists of the Rocky Mountain West; but these were issues about an acceptable taxonomy, disputes involving differing concepts of species and how they should be classified.

The nomenclatural issues, strictly speaking, were distinct from taxonomic disputes. A basic nomenclatural order had been established by Linnaeus in 1753 through the creation of a standardized binomial plant description; and he had given arbitrarily a binomial name to all plants known to science at that time. In the next century and a half, vast numbers of new plants had been discovered and named by botanists of many nationalities. As there was no standard list of all plant species to serve as a convenient reference, it was inevitable that any plant might have been discovered more than once, the given names being different. Nor were there yet any universal rules as to how to cope with such refinements as varieties.

By the later nineteenth century, as a consequence, regional differences in nomenclatural practices had developed. One might find that a plant name had inadvertently been bestowed on more than one species; or a given species might be recognized under different names depending on region. Part of the confusion was addressed by the founding of the *Index Kewensis,* as earlier noted, an index to *all* plants.

Attempts to standardize nomenclatural *procedures* were made in both Europe and America, from which attempts emerged both an International Code and an American Code, the latter widely held to be a renegade code. In fact, the competing codes were similar in most respects. Of the unresolved disagreements, two were critical: the international rules required the use of botanical Latin for the diagnoses accompanying the names of new taxa. The American rules did not require the use of Latin. The international position rested on the assumption that a universal science required a universal language for precise communication. The Americans were fearful that the decline of classical studies in the United States would eventually place its botanists in a highly inconvenient situation.

Secondly, the internationalists wanted to establish a list of generic names to be conserved because of their wide use (*nomina generica conservanda*), thus invalidating lesser-known names even if they antedated the more widely used names. By no means were American botanists of one mind on these issues. Those who reflected the lingering influence of Asa Gray advocated adherence to the international principles. Those who followed the leadership of N. L. Britton insisted on absolute priority *in usage* for the recognition of legitimate generic names and refused to accept adoption of an arbitrary *nomina generica conservanda.*

As for the botanists of the Rocky Mountain region, at this late date one can only speculate about their motives for taking one side or the other. But none could have been indifferent to the outcome. It was possible to see the internationalists, in their insistence on a practical solution in establishing a *nomina generica conservanda,* as repeating the arbitrary action taken by Linnaeus over a century before, in *Genera Plantarum* and *Species Plantarum.* Each action, however practical, could be seen as indifference to tradition, to history. One should recognize at once that E. L. Greene would insist on absolute priority rather than a *practical* solution.

Neither Greene nor Rydberg could have been troubled by the internationalists' insistence on diagnoses in Latin, given their competence in languages; but they both had a vested interest in the survival of a considerable number of new generic and specific plant names. Given his inclination to split somewhat radically, Rydberg cannot have been eager to submit his names for reconsideration by a conservative committee of botanists charged with maintaining the correctness of the *nomina generica conservanda.* Rydberg's adherence to the American Code was made clear in his *Flora of Colorado* in 1906.

The flora was based on work originated, but not completed, by Charles S. Crandall (1852–1929), an active collector at Colorado Agricultural College between 1889 and 1899. While Rydberg's goal was a flora of Colorado, it appears that he gradually became demoralized by the persistent rejection of his new species when he submitted them for verification to Robinson and Fernald, the successors to Gray and Watson at the Gray Herbarium. His species were rejected even though Crandall adhered to a conservative taxonomic and nomenclatural treatment consistent with the school of Asa Gray. At the time he abandoned the flora—when he departed for a post at the University of Illinois—his manuscript contained about fourteen hundred species. *Penstemon crandallii* A. Nels., a Crandall collection in Park County, Colorado, was named for him by his sympathetic neighbor, who knew firsthand the perils of dependence on the Gray Herbarium. *Arabis crandallii* B. L. Robins., from western Colorado, was named by an author with probably little awareness of the irony.

Rydberg's final treatment included 2,923 species, more than double Crandall's number, indicating a dependence on other collections, including his own from several summers in Colorado. He acknowledged in particular the importance of collections by Charles F. Baker (1873–1927), an ethnologist-botanist at the Colorado Agricultural College from 1892 to 1897, later a commercial collector of plants throughout the West. He had generally sent his plants to E. L. Greene for determination, but nearly complete sets of his plants had been purchased by the New York Botanical Garden. Plants of special interest had been collected along the Colorado–New Mexico border in 1899 by Charles Baker, assisted by Franklin S. Earle and Samuel M. Tracy.[8]

That trip had begun in Hermosa, Colorado, in March of 1899, and the group had spent the summer camping in the San Juan River country on both sides of the state border. At the beginning of June, around Arboles, Colorado, Baker noted that "numerous flocks of sheep were rapidly devastating the narrow bottoms. The destruction could scarcely have been more complete had the work been done by fire." In July, near Pagosa Springs, Baker was struck by the magnificent forest of *Pinus ponderosa,* but added: "The end of these forests is in sight, their destruction being actively underway now. The desolation caused by the lumberman, and the fires that follow in his wake, is an evidence of an appalling lack of foresight, not possible in the more scientifically enlightened countries." The trip ended on Cumbres Pass above Chama, New Mexico, where "the sheep had been there first."[9] *Poa tracyi* Vasey and *Juncus tracyi* Rydb. commemorated assiduous exploration.

In a departure from Crandall, Rydberg adopted the sequence of plant families recommended by Engler and Prantl of Berlin for his Colorado flora. What was more startling, and perplexing, to many of the Westerners was the frequent appearance of unfamiliar genera. Most stunning of all was Rydberg's removal of seventeen genera from *Astragalus* as segregates. In all fairness, it must be noted that some of them had been published earlier by others; but nine of them were his own taxa. The segregations were based nearly exclusively on perceived differences in the structure or character of the pods. Baffled by such extreme splitting, the Rocky Mountain botanists questioned the usefulness of such a flora. In fact, none of those seventeen genera has stood the test of time.[10]

Rydberg was always careful, when splitting a familiar genus or species, to provide a synonymy, so that his readers were not left adrift when confronting his unfamiliar taxa. That care was carried over into his *Flora of the Rocky Mountains and Adjacent Plains,* finally completed late in 1917, a second edition in 1922. The book was the culmination of an immense amount of fieldwork and preliminary publication, the product of twenty-five years of study. It has been calculated that Rydberg, in the course of his career, described over one hundred genera and seventeen hundred species as new.[11] The new flora itself was immense. The text ran to 1,121 pages, and 5,897 species were treated within 1,038 genera. It was obviously no field manual. While its magnitude was in part a result of Rydberg's radical splitting, the volume also testified to Rydberg's mastery of a huge flora. Not surprisingly, his sharpest critic proved to be Marcus Jones, who revived his crack about the practice of "bughole botany."

It serves as a corrective to note that Rydberg said quite plainly that he did not expect all recent segregates, whether his or others', to survive. They should be regarded as tentative proposals, as contributions to additional biosystematic research. By pointing out plant characters, Rydberg hoped to be of help to later students of ecology and evolution. Later research might well lead to the elimination of some of his taxa. Others would attribute Rydberg's species-making industry to vanity, a desire to see his name attached to as many plants as possible. They may have been wrong, but no consensus about his motives has ever been reached. Yet, his volume remains even today, once one has learned to cope with the segregations, an indispensable reference to the plants of the Rocky Mountains published before 1918.[12]

Rydberg's predisposition to split cost him the sympathy of many Western botanists in his day. If one looks only at his potentillas as examples of his work (given below by year of publication), one sees that some of his proposals did not stand; but many did. What is most striking is how many of his species have found validity as varieties or subspecies, suggesting at once his command of the miniscule:

Potentilla subjuga Rydb. Colorado. 1896

Potentilla bicrenata Rydb.→*Potentilla concinna* Richards. var. *bicrenata* (Rydb.)
   Welsh & Johnston. New Mexico. 1896

Potentilla convallaria Rydb.→*Potentilla arguta* Pursh ssp. *convallaria* (Rydb.)
   Keck. Montana. 1897

Potentilla macounii Rydb. Alberta. 1898

Potentilla atrovirens Rydb.→*Potentilla pensylvanica* L. var. *atrovirens* (Rydb.)
   T. Wolf. Wyoming. 1898

Drymocallis glabrata Rydb.→*Potentilla glandulosa* Lindl. ssp. *glabrata* (Rydb.)
   Keck. Washington. 1898

Drymocallis pseudorupestris Rydb. var. *intermedia* Rydb.→*Potentilla glandulosa*
   Lindl. var. *intermedia* (Rydb.) C. L. Hitchc. Montana. 1900

Drymocallis pseudorupestris Rydb.→Potentilla glandulosa Lindl. ssp. pseudorupestris (Rydb.) Keck. Montana. 1900

Potentilla brunnescens Rydb.→Potentilla gracilis Dougl. ex Hook. var. brunnescens
(Rydb.) C. L. Hitchc. Wyoming. 1901

Potentilla permollis Rydb.→Potentilla gracilis Dougl. ex Hook. var. permollis
(Rydb.) C. L. Hitchc. Washington. 1901

Potentilla paucijuga Rydb.→Potentilla pensylvanica L. var. paucijuga (Rydb.)
Welsh & Johnston. Utah. 1908

Potentilla perdissecta Rydb.→Potentilla diversifolia Lehm. var. perdissecta
(Rydb.) C. L. Hitchc. Montana. 1908

Potentilla argyrea Rydb.→Potentilla hippiana Lehm. var. argyrea (Rydb.)
Boivin. Saskatchewan. 1908

These few examples of Rydberg's new taxa barely suggest the magnitude of
his proposals, a total list of which may be found in Tiehm and Stafleu's *Per Axel
Rydberg*, but without their ultimate dispositions. It was, in fact, a feat to assem-
ble the total list. Rydberg continued to publish into the year of his death, 1931;
and he died still steadfast in the faith of his Swedish Lutheran Church, to the
end a kindly, gentle man.[13]

Many species and several genera were named to honor Rydberg, not surprising
given his many years of collecting and extensive publication. Many of them did
not stand, which is not unusual, but a good number of them are still recognized
in the Rocky Mountain region:

Arnica rydbergii Greene (1899), Montana-Colorado

Cirsium rydbergii Petrak (1917), San Juan Basin, Utah

Erigeron rydbergii Cronq. (1947), Montana-Wyoming

Haplopappus rydbergii S. F. Blake (1925)→Ericameria obovata (Rydb.) Nesom
(1990), Utah

Helianthus rydbergii Britton (1901)→Helianthus nuttallii T. & G. ssp. rydbergii
(Britt.) R. W. Long, Nebraska

Penstemon rydbergii A. Nels (1898), Colorado-Wyoming westward

Rhus rydbergii Small ex Rydb. (1900)→Toxicodendron rydbergii (Small ex Rydb.)
Greene (1905), western poison ivy

Rydbergia Greene (1898), So. Colorado–New Mexico–No. Arizona. A segregate
from Hymenoxys Cass.

19

Aven Nelson

THE GREAT TEACHER

*A*ven Nelson (1859–1952), the last of our botanical explorers of the Rocky Mountains, and almost an exact contemporary of Rydberg, was a major beneficiary of Rydberg's guidance. For Rydberg, though heavily preoccupied with hard work, was a kindly man who gave attention to the botanical needs of others, especially in promoting their publication. His eagle eye was no sign of a predatory temperament.

Nelson's dilemma was rooted in the fact that he had been hired as one of the first faculty at the University of Wyoming in 1887, expecting to teach English. He had to be converted into a biologist when the trustees belatedly realized they had failed to hire one. As a consequence, he became one of the last self-trained botanists to achieve professional eminence, perhaps in the tradition of Nuttall, Torrey, Gray, and Greene, but without the Ph.D. that would become the license to practice in the twentieth century. His initial taxonomic library comprised two books: Coulter's *Manual of the Botany of the Rocky Mountain Region* and Asa Gray's *Manual of Botany*. During his service at Drury College in Springfield, Missouri—his first position as an English teacher—Nelson had been an assistant in biology; but he cannot have had anything but the most elementary preparation for the unexpected assignment.

Conditions in the tiny university were further exposed when, in 1891, the directorship of horticulture was added to Nelson's obligations. He took the new duty seriously until relieved of it many years later. He had been reared on an Iowa farm, the son of Norwegian immigrants, and was familiar with the husbandry necessary to make farming viable. He soon began writing periodic bulletins issued by the Wyoming Extension Station for the instruction of the rural population, an undertaking that won him encouragement from Charles Bessey of Nebraska, who advocated strongly the application of botanical knowledge to agricultural development.[1]

Nelson had come to Wyoming sharing most outsiders' assumption that the region, as part of the Great American Desert depicted by Major Long and Edwin James, could support little else than the range-cattle industry. Slowly this view eroded. Nelson began to collect and preserve plants for exchange, in order to build a herbarium, and for sale, to acquire money to build a botanical library. In 1894, and continuing into 1895, he undertook a systematic survey of the state, submitting his plants for verification or determination to both E. L. Greene and B. L. Robinson. In the course of this botanical exploration, he was surprised to discover that first-rate fruits and vegetables were already being grown in the state.

He also saw that the cattle rancher's practice of irrigating hay fields by flooding them for most of the growing season not only was wasteful of water, but produced a growth of sedges and rushes at the expense of the more nutritious native grasses. In an arid state with a finite water supply, he soon became controversial for his advocacy of a more economic use of water. He argued that a greater proportion of the water should be allocated to agriculture, at the expense of the cattle industry, but that the crops should be more carefully selected as suitable to the climate and soils of Wyoming than had frequently been the practice on the drier lands. The practice of grazing livestock in the forests during the summer he condemned as defeating the primary purpose of the national forest lands. That the issues he raised are still unresolved a century later indicate a failure to hitch botanical knowledge to economic development; and until the cowboy mentality becomes attenuated, no resolution ought to be expected.

Based on the responses of Greene and Robinson to the specimens Nelson sent them, it is evident that he had made considerable improvement in his ability to identify plants by 1895. In the process, he became aware of the taxonomic conservatism at Harvard and grew increasingly sympathetic to Greene's opinion that western plants frequently diverged sufficiently from their eastern relatives to merit specific rank. That observation would lead him to become something of a splitter and goad him to consider publishing his own new species. At the same time, he became increasingly offended by Greene's deepening egotism and eccentricity, doubting whether he could rely much longer on Greene, despite having just been honored with *Delphinium nelsonii* Greene (1896). Nelson collected the specimen (now *Delphinium nuttallianum* Pritz. ex Walpers, 1843) in Telephone Canyon east of Laramie.

He secured his independence from both Harvard and Greene as the result of three opportunities: Nelson's "First Report on the Flora of Wyoming," published in Laramie (1896), contained a proposed new potentilla that caught Rydberg's eye—*Potentilla pinnatisecta* (Wats.) A. Nels. As that name was already taken, Rydberg republished the species as *Potentilla nelsoniana* Rydb. (*Potentilla ovina* Macoun var. *decurrens* [S. Wats.] Welsh & Johnston). The upshot was that the pages of the *Bulletin of the Torrey Botanical Club* were opened to Nelson's new species; but only after they had been reviewed by Rydberg, who was eager to get an early glimpse of anything new coming out of the Rocky Mountains. Some of the best known of Nelson's new species appeared in that journal in 1898:

Angelica ampla A. Nels., Albany County, Wyo.

Oreocarya flava A. Nels.→*Cryptantha flava* (A. Nels.) Payson, Sweetwater County, Wyo.

Gentiana elegans A. Nels.→*Gentianopsis detonsa* (Rottb.) Ma var. *elegans* (A. Nels.) Holmgren, Medicine Bow Mts., Wyo.

Penstemon arenicola A. Nels., Sweetwater County, Wyo.

Penstemon radicosus A. Nels., Uinta County, Wyo.

Penstemon rydbergii A. Nels., Laramie Mts., Albany County, Wyo.

Phlox multiflora A. Nels., Laramie Mts., Albany County, Wyo.

In the second place, Nelson had the good fortune to have two short pieces accepted for publication in the *Botanical Gazette* by John M. Coulter, in the second of which he published *Thermopsis divaricarpa* A. Nels. It stood until reduced to a variety of *Thermopsis rhombifolia* in 1978, only to be recognized again as a good species by several Rocky Mountain botanists in recent years. Of greater importance was the association with Coulter, who would provide cordial, valuable encouragement.

The third opportunity grew from Nelson's awareness that the United States Department of Agriculture had been sponsoring considerable fieldwork on the western lands. After his proposal to undertake a revision of the genus *Paronychia*—a small genus and largely western—had been shot down by B. L. Robinson with the statement that original work could not be done in the West, Nelson wrote a proposal to explore the Red Desert of southern Wyoming. That region had never been completely studied. Frank Lamson-Scribner of the USDA, who had collected grasses in the Northern Transcontinental Survey, was enthusiastic about the Red Desert project and provided a contract for the summer of 1897. Nelson was expected to provide not only dried specimens and seeds of grasses and forage plants, but the general flora as well.

The exploration was carried out in three stages (spring, summer, and fall) to accommodate the study of the flora, topography, geology, climate, soils, and water supply. Nelson's instructions required him to assess how the region should be used to preserve vegetal integrity. He found the quality of the grasses and forage plants (the greasewoods and sagebrushes) to be remarkably high, excellent for winter grazing. He recommended that livestock be removed from the Red Desert by June to allow forage plants to recover during the growing season, noting that ranchers could improve their ranges by seeding the ground with native grasses and saltbushes (*Atriplex*).

In this instance, Nelson's recommendations were heeded and followed by the Wyoming wool growers. A review of vegetal conditions twenty-five years later confirmed that the Red Desert had been holding its own despite intensive winter grazing. But by then, Nelson had become painfully aware that the removal of live-stock for summer grazing into the neighboring mountains, during the growing season, was quite contrary to good forest management.[2]

It is probable that any botanical explorer is a splitter by instinct. In the search for the new, humans are apt to find novelties. Unlike Nelson's prior collecting trips, his experience in the Red Desert provided him with the opportunity to examine plants within a well-defined terrain over three different periods of the growing season. It was also the first time that soils had been collected in the West for analysis by a competent chemist. Nelson emerged from that examination with a heightened awareness of the importance of soil conditions in affecting changes in plants. Nelson's slow drift toward a more moderate species concept can be dated from that summer in 1897.

That summer was doubly beneficial in that Nelson's collections and reports were very favorably reviewed by the botanists in the USDA and by the consultants they asked to examine certain groups. His credentials, as a result, were at last established. Furthermore, the success encouraged Nelson to undertake a more distant exploration: Yellowstone in the summer of 1899. That area had already been botanized by Coulter, Parry, Tweedy, and Rydberg, so that, except for in the southeast quadrant of the park, the discovery of new species was not likely.

Nelson's primary objective, in fact, was to secure as inclusive a collection as possible for his young herbarium in Laramie, and to collect abundantly so that Yellowstone sets could be made up for sale in Europe and America. Lacking financial support from his university, he saw no other source of funds for the development of his program. Not only was the mission of the trip reasonably fulfilled, but it provided valuable field experience for two of Nelson's students, Leslie M. Goodding and Elias E. Nelson.

When Rydberg's new *Catalogue of the Flora of Montana and Yellowstone National Park* appeared in 1900, Nelson volunteered to review it for Coulter's *Botanical Gazette* if Rydberg approved. While his appraisal of Rydberg's work was both favorable and friendly, he used the review to express uneasiness about the American Code then sponsored by the New York group. Its use had resulted in the displacement of many familiar plant names. Even if he agreed that the principle of priority should prevail, was it not regrettable that so many changes would have to be made!

The review laid bare the dilemma confronting most Rocky Mountain botanists by the turn of the century. They had become uneasy about evidence of extreme splitting, at the same time recognizing the distinctiveness of the Western flora, which required new names. In a reference to Nuttall in the review, Nelson returned to the origin of the dilemma and to the legitimacy of Western claims:

Keen in observation, discriminating in description, Nuttall stands without a peer as regards the field in question. For sixty years following his time, some of the regions that he visited have not been entered by other botanists. On account of the inadequate specimens that he made, and their inaccessibility to the majority of workers, many of his species were for years rather discredited, or at least misunderstood. With the renewed interest that has sprung up during the last decade, Nuttallian species are again at par. From a long period of conservatism, during which the plants of the interior West were often disposed of as mere forms of species of widely different geographical range, we have now come to look upon this flora as quite as sharply defined as that of any other area of equal size.[3]

Such observations indicate that Nelson was moving toward a more moderate, if not entirely conservative, position; and that stance proved to be timely. By 1900, Coulter knew that a new edition of his regional flora was overdue. He also recognized that his decision to accept the duties of academic administration had indefinitely postponed serious scholarship. He had published a number of Nelson's articles in the *Botanical Gazette* and was reaching the conclusion that Nelson was more familiar with the Rocky Mountain field than any other botanist acceptable to him, or available. Rydberg was already embarked on his own regional flora that gave promise of featuring extreme splitting; Greene had already retreated to Washington to be a world unto himself; and Jones was beyond Coulter's toleration.

Thus was born the *New Manual of Botany of the Central Rocky Mountains* by Coulter and Nelson, which would not appear until the end of 1909, entirely rewritten by Nelson alone, and following Engler's sequence of plant families and the format of Gray's *Manual*. It would serve the Rocky Mountain region as its primary flora for thirty-five years despite becoming outmoded, and despite the publication of Rydberg's *Flora of the Rocky Mountains and Adjacent Plains* in 1917—a book criticized in the West for excessive splitting and as much too bulky to be used in the field.

During the ensuing years, Nelson became greatly respected in both East and West. In 1934, when he was seventy-five, he was elected to the presidency of the Botanical Society of America, the first Rocky Mountain botanist so honored. The following year, he was chosen to be the first president of the Society of Plant Taxonomists, serving during its organizational year, 1936. The creation of the society reflected the maturation of taxonomy as a scientific discipline.

It would be the opinion of some botanists today that, while Nelson did retreat from extreme splitting following lengthy association with Rydberg and Greene, his ongoing sympathy for certain generic segregations did not reflect true conservatism. If he continued to recognize the validity of *Machaeranthera* Nees, for example, he also recognized the segregation of *Xyloriza* Nutt. from *Machaeranthera*. What is more, the genus *Haplopappus* Cass. had no place in his flora. His acceptance of *Macronema* Nutt., *Oonopsis* Greene, *Pyrrocomo* Hook., and *Stenotus* Nutt.—not to speak of his creation of *Tonestus* A. Nels.—suggests his kinship with those Westerners prone to seeing the distinction of the Rocky Mountain flora. Some examples:

> *Macronema aberrans* A. Nels. (1912)→*Tonestus aberrans* (A. Nels.) Nesom & Morgan. Elmore County, Ida.
>
> *Oonopsis foliosa* (Gray) Greene var. *monocephala* (A. Nels.) (1901) Kartesz & Gandhi. Las Animas County, Colo.
>
> *Stenotus latifolius* A. Nels. (1904)→*Stenotus acaulis* Nutt. Provo, Utah
>
> *Tonestus lyallii* (Gray) A. Nels. Colo., Ida., Mont., alpine
>
> *Tonestus pygmaeus* (Torr. & Gray) A. Nels. A James collection in Colo., Wyo.-N.M., subalpine-alpine
>
> *Tonestus eximius* (Hall) Nels. & Macbr. (1918), El Dorado & Inyo Counties, Calif., alpine
>
> *Xylorhiza glabrieuscula* Nutt. var. *villosa* (Nutt.) A. Nels. (1909), south-central Wyo.

A number of Nelson's generic proposals did not stand. Aside from *Tonestus* (1904), which has been recognized only in the past several decades, there is the monotypic genus *Idahoa* A. Nels. & J. F. Macbr. (1913), *Idahoa scapigera* (Hook.) A. Nels. & J. F. Macbr., transferred from *Platyspermum* Hook. in the Cruciferae and found in Montana and Idaho. The genus *Enceliopsis* A. Nels. (1909), segregated from *Helianthella* Torr. & Gray, belongs primarily to the Great Basin. But *Enceliopsis nutans* (Eastw.) A. Nels. was based on an Alice Eastwood collection in Mesa County, Colorado. The generic name recognized the close affinity to *Encelia* Adans.

The careers of E. L. Greene and Aven Nelson marked the end of the century of Rocky Mountain botanical exploration; but the men were also transitional figures in that both held university positions that entailed teaching. Henceforth, botanical research in the Rocky Mountains would largely be the work of college or university professors, or scholars working for academies or museums. Willis L. Jepson, a student under Greene at Berkeley, remained devoted to him. The Danish botanist Theodor Holm, already experienced in arctic flora in Europe and Colorado, took his doctoral degree under Greene at the Catholic University of America. Father Julius Nieuwland also worked with Greene at Catholic University and, in later years, helped to relocate Greene to the University of Notre Dame for a sheltered retirement.

Nelson's students at the University of Wyoming, rural or small-town in origin, enjoyed the blessing of falling into the hands of an inspiring teacher. Even though they necessarily went elsewhere for postgraduate training, most retained a lifelong attachment to the Rocky Mountain region. Among the better known: Leslie N. Goodding and his daughter, Charlotte Goodding Reeder; Elias E. Nelson; Edwin B. Payson; J. Francis MacBride; Louis O. Williams; George J. Goodman; C. William T. Penland; Reed C. Rollins; and Marion Ownbey.

A number of taxa dedicated to Nelson, including those by Greene and Rydberg, did not stand; but the following are still recognized as valid:

Anelsonia MacBride & Payson (1917), Custer County, Idaho. Type: *Anelsonia eurycarpa* (Gray) Macbr. & Pays., transferred from *Draba eurycarpa* Gray. A monotypic genus.

Astragalus nelsonianus Barneby (1964), Bitter Creek, Sweetwater County, Wyo.

Carex nelsonii Mack. in Rydb. (1917), La Plata Mines, Albany County, Wyo.

Descurainia pinnata (Walt.) Britt. var. *nelsonii* (Rydb.) Peck (1907), Yellowstone National Park

Phacelia anelsonii J. F. Macbr. (1917), Meadow Valley Wash, Nev. A Goodding collection.

Stipa nelsonii Scribn. (1898), Woods Landing, Albany County, Wyo.

On E. L. Greene's seventieth birthday, 2 December 1913, the Botanical Society of Washington, of which he was the president, hosted a dinner in his honor. As the principal speaker for the occasion, Aven Nelson found the right formula for bringing the quarrelsome taxonomists of the terminal years of Rocky Mountain exploration under a common roof:

> That other eyes fail to see the things that [Greene] sees; that even from similar observations different judgments are formed and different conclusions drawn are not to him of such serious moment that each may not go on with friendship for the other, each cultivating his own wee bit of the ever-widening field. To live honestly with nature, to deal justly with your fellow worker, to love mercy is a creed to which we can all subscribe. . . . Differ as we may as to what constitutes a species, the object of us all is to know plants and help others know them. To know and to use plants that they may contribute to our wealth is well; to know them that they may contribute to the health and pleasure of body and mind is better; to know them that we may read a few of God's thoughts after Him and thus enrich our souls is best.[4]

Epilogue

*ewis H. Pammel (1863–1931), originally from Wisconsin, joined the faculty of Iowa State College in 1889. An assiduous plant collector, he usually spent his summers in the field and accumulated a large collection for his college herbarium. Between the years 1900 and 1908 (by which time he had completed his doctorate at Washington University in Saint Louis), he concentrated his summer work on the Uinta Mountains, his departure point generally being Park City, Utah, or Evanston, Wyoming.

Clarence King, the geologist, had earlier described the unique characters of the Uintas: with an immense, single mountain block; a great lofty plateau; a type of mountain architecture only paralleled by the uplands of the Caucasus, and essentially dry after the disappearance of the winter snow. Given the Uintas' xerophytic vegetation, Pammel had good reason to expect a distinct plant population. But his first published report,[1] while describing the species he had found at different elevations, claimed no new species found. His second report was similarly descriptive: it contained a long list of grasses by genus and their locations, but, once again, nothing new.[2] (The *Melica* named for him by Scribner, now a synonym, had been collected by Pammel during the summer of 1897, evidently in Teton County, Wyoming.) The Uinta region had already been visited by Charles Parry, Marcus Jones, Sereno Watson, and Aven Nelson.

The outcome of Pammel's fieldwork serves as one illustration that the era of *extensive exploration* in the expectation of discovering numerous novelties had reached its end. Asa Gray's earlier conviction that the knowledge of the Rocky Mountain flora was virtually complete had proved to be premature. But soon after the turn of the twentieth century, fieldwork would become the province of the university laboratory. That is, *intensive* research into more limited groups would be the focus of taxonomic fieldwork. In time, new taxonomic tools would be brought to bear on the definition of species.

An assumption that the flora of the Rocky Mountains was at last completely known soon became widespread. Marcus Jones's earlier warning to John Coulter to stay out of his terrain, meaning the entire Rocky Mountains, was matched in arrogance by his later expression of regret that future botanists would have nothing to do, as he had already named all the Western taxa. Even the occasional publication of a new species did not seem to shake the general assumption that nothing remained to be found, until late in the twentieth century. In 1987, reliable figures *from California alone* revealed that, in the two decades from 1969 to 1986, 219 new vascular plants had been described.[3]

A more extensive survey, published in 1998, showed that, for the two decades from 1975 through 1994, a total of 1,197 vascular plant taxa in North America had been described as novelties.[4] The great majority were from the western and southeastern United States. Five of the ten states recording the most new holotypes were within the Rocky Mountain region: Utah (183), Arizona (57), New Mexico (41), Idaho (33), and Wyoming (32). It is understood, of course, that not all new taxa will be recognized in the future as valid; but the authors calculated about 90 percent validity to be a reasonable conjecture.

As might be expected, a majority of recent discoveries were made in remote sites. But a notable number have come from significant population centers, even from places where there has been a long tradition of botanical exploration and with substantial herbaria. Reasonable extrapolations from the above two studies would indicate that at least eighteen hundred more novelties (vascular plants) may be expected from North America.

Floristic research has been valuable, beyond the discovery of new taxa, in providing data about the distribution of known plants—that is, data about where species are, and what their habitat requirements are. On occasion, species thought to be extinct may be rediscovered; or a species, deliberately exterminated because of its supposed toxicity, may reoccur from seeds dormant for decades. In the Rocky Mountain region there remains a particular interest in studying the large number of Asian–Rocky Mountain disjunctions, such as J. D. Hooker observed in 1877. Which species are introductions? Which are natives? Another more publicized concern is the discovery of an increasing number of invasive nonnatives that may contribute to the decline of native species.

Fresh plant material brought into herbaria for the necessary comparative study may not only reveal taxa previously unknown, but may shed light on older materials that were inadequately studied at the time of their collection. In short, not all the novelties cited in the figures provided by Hartman and Nelson reflect fresh collections; 60 percent of the novelties had type specimens that were over ten years old.

One example, cited by Ertter, ought to serve as a rein on anyone inclined to believe that the work of taxonomists is finished. Within Reed Rollins's recent (1993) and massive study, *The Cruciferae of Continental North America,* he treated eighty-three species of *Lesquerella,* nearly half of which were either authored or coauthored by him in the course of his career. That number goes substantially above the sixty-nine species of *Lesquerella* in a monograph he published in 1973. The cautionary implication of such an example is clear: until our major genera are all monographed with a similar degree of taxonomic sophistication, the true extent of our flora will remain incompletely known.[5]

The foregoing chapters in this book have given the reader a history of the botanical exploration of the Rocky Mountains, recalling the dedication and exploits of remarkable individuals in the nineteenth century. They were an extension of the ethos of exploration and discovery that has characterized our civilization since the end of the fifteenth century. Considering this fact, the usual omission of their scientific and cultural contributions from histories of the American West might well be perceived as a virtual indifference to matters cultural, of which the sciences are surely a part.

As a consequence, it is permissible to speculate about to what degree the creation and the dogged survival of well-known myths about our Western history have been inadvertently fostered by an inattention to the reports and warnings written by botanical explorers, especially in the latter half of the nineteenth century, which were markedly free of romantic illusions about land and water use. There is a tenable analogy in European history that is both sobering and, possibly, in the long run, encouraging.

From the medieval period on, woodlands were cleared to provide agricultural land for an increasing population. In time, learned observers began to worry about a future timber famine. By the eighteenth century, deforestation was extending into the higher mountains in France, augmenting flooding and erosion. Both natural scientists and agronomists published warnings about the peril along with admonitions that the state must interfere to promote conservation. The arresting parallel derives from the ensuing dispute between central government, endeavoring to promote reform, and local landowners, peasants, and communities, defending local practices in defiance of the general public interest. It is depressing to note that scientific knowledge did not effectively prevail over calculated ignorance until after 1860, the beginning of systematic reforesting and regrassing of the mountains in France. There has been no turning back, despite the equally dismaying survival of a conviction that the claims of deforestation were a myth propagated to justify governmental suppression of local liberties.

Like their French counterparts, the botanical explorers of the Rocky Mountains in the nineteenth century were the first to call the government's attention to the abuses of rapacious timbering and grazing. Some of them even made proposals for sane agricultural development. The prejudice in this book is that they deserve exposure in the teaching of Western history at least equal to that accorded to mountain men and cowboys, and that Alice Eastwood merits equal space on the coinage as Heroic Woman.

Notes

അ≉ჯჯ≉ඉ

Introduction

1. Torrey 1826–1827.
2. McKelvey 1955, xxi–xxii.
3. Nuttall 1818, vi–vii.
4. Rodgers 1942, 80–82.

Chapter 1

1. The introduction of Bernard DeVoto, editor, to *The Journals of Lewis and Clark* remains balanced and insightful.
2. DeVoto 1953, 483–486.
3. Moulton 1999.
4. Ronda 1984, 46–47.
5. Metcalf 1998, 485.
6. Cutright 1976, 166, 207.
7. Cutright 1976, 197, 220; Ronda 1984, 256.
8. Ronda 1984, 114–115.
9. DeVoto 1953, 77.
10. Heiser 1976, 176–177.
11. DeVoto 1953, 155–158.
12. DeVoto 1953, 162.
13. DeVoto 1953, 166.
14. For a recipe, see Harrington 1967, 229.
15. DeVoto 1953, 198.
16. Haines 1998, 524, 1044.
17. DeVoto 1953, 206.
18. Haines 1998, 1044.
19. DeVoto 1953, 240–241.
20. DeVoto 1953, 315–316.
21. DeVoto 1953, 371.
22. Cutright 1969, 413.
23. DeVoto 1953, 389.

24. DeVoto 1953, 397.
25. DeVoto 1953, 400–401.
26. DeVoto 1953, 403–410.
27. Moulton 1983.
28. Moulton 1999, n.p.
29. Moulton 1983, map 61.
30. DeVoto 1953, 423.
31. Cutright 1969, vii–viii.
32. Humphrey 1961, 202–203.
33. Cutright 1969, 357–360.
34. Jackson 1962, 354–356.
35. Jackson 1962, 389–390, 398.
36. Jackson 1962, 398.
37. Cutright 1969, 373–374; Baron 1987, 127–136.
38. Jackson 1962, 485.
39. Jackson 1962, 462–463.
40. Pursh 1814, 1:x–xi.
41. Cutright 1969, 360–364.
42. Burroughs 1966, 58–59.
43. McKelvey 1955, 72–75.
44. Cutright 1969, appendix A, 399–423.

Chapter 2

1. Goodman and Lawson 1995, xiii–xiv; Evans 1997, 18–19, 21.
2. McKelvey 1955, 104; Goodman and Lawson 1955, xii; Evans 1997, 20–22.
3. Evans 1997, 10–11.
4. Fowler 1998, 151.
5. Benson 1988, vii–viii, 8. This is an abridged edition of Edwin James's *Account* published in 1823. Material omitted is clearly indicated as to subject.
6. Benson 1988, 193, 196.
7. Goodman and Lawson 1995, 278.
8. Torrey 1827, 2:202.
9. Benson 1988, 199–201.
10. Osterhout 1923, 81–84.
11. Benson 1988, 205–209.
12. Benson 1988, 211–213.
13. Goodman and Lawson 1995, 213.
14. Benson 1988, 222–223.
15. Osterhout 1920, 557.
16. Benson 1988, 227.
17. Evans 1997, 149.
18. Benson 1988, 233.
19. McKelvey 1955, 226–227.
20. Benson 1988, 274–282.
21. Benson 1988, 326–334.
22. James 1823.
23. James 1825, 172–190.
24. Torrey 1824b, 30–36.

25. Goodman and Lawson 1995, 308.
26. Torrey 1826, 161–164; 1827, 165–254.
27. Benson 1988, xiv–xv.
28. For an introduction to these issues, begin with Billington 1949, especially the bibliography provided by Benson 1988.
29. Evans 1997, 232.

Chapter 3

1. Sargent 1889, 2:321–328.
2. Drummond 1830, 190–202.

Chapter 4

1. McKelvey 1955, xxi.
2. Dupree 1988, 98.
3. Graustein 1967, 39–40.
4. Graustein 1967, 67.
5. McKelvey 1955, 103, 111, 131.
6. Graustein 1967, 56, 70–76.
7. Pennell 1936, 17–22.
8. Graustein 1967, 79–89.
9. McKelvey 1955, 103, 146–147.
10. Dupree 1959, 104–105.
11. Graustein 1967, 277–284.
12. Nuttall 1834, 5–60.
13. Graustein 1967, 327.
14. Graustein 1967, 292.
15. Townsend 1839, 74, 74n. In the recent edition, Corvallis, Oregon: Oregon State University Press, 1999, the pagination is different from the original.
16. Townsend 1839, 63.
17. Townsend 1839, 64.
18. Townsend 1999, 51.
19. Townsend 1999, 52–54.
20. McKelvey 1955, 595–598.
21. Graustein 1967, 297–303.
22. Townsend 1839, 126.
23. Townsend 1839, 163.
24. Townsend 1999, 183–188.
25. McKelvey 1955, 625, 630–632.
26. Hooker and Walker-Arnott 1830–1841, 315–409.
27. Torrey 1836, 239–451.
28. Dupree 1959, 302; Graustein 1967, 324–327.
29. Dupree 1959, 94–96.
30. Graustein 1967, 327–329.
31. Graustein 1967, 337–338, 351.
32. Graustein 1967, 352; Nuttall 1840–1841, 283–453.
33. Dupree 1959, 98–99.
34. Dupree 1959, 99, 300.
35. Graustein 1967, 360.

36. Graustein 1967, 365–367.
37. Nuttall 1848, 149–189.
38. Evans 1933, 91–94.
39. Graustein 1967, 342–343, 346–350, 370–372, 389–390.
40. Candolle 1880, 437.
41. Graustein 1967, 223.

Chapter 5

1. Sargent 1969, 2:439; Lurie 1988, 179.
2. Sargent 1889, 2:440.
3. Sargent 1889, 2:440–442.
4. Anderson 1942, 100–110.
5. Rodgers 1944, 208–209.
6. The story was repeated to me by the late Louis O. Williams, but has since been confirmed in Lenz 1986, 43.
7. Sargent 1889, 2:444.
8. Trelease and Gray 1887, 284.
9. Dupree 1988, 394–395.
10. Trelease and Gray 1887; also note Engelmann 1880a, 161–189.
11. Humphrey 1961, 81–82; de Virville et al. 1954, 277.
12. Trelease and Gray 1887, 533.
13. Sargent 1889, 2:446.

Chapter 6

1. Welsh 1998, 1–15.
2. Frémont 1988.
3. Preuss 1958, xxi–xxiv. The reader should be aware that the Guddles' geographical references are not always reliable.
4. Welsh 1998, 12, 19.
5. Preuss 1958, 8.
6. Preuss 1958, 35.
7. Frémont 1845, 32–35.
8. McKelvey 1955, 766–767; Welsh 1998, 29.
9. Frémont 1845, 61–65.
10. Frémont 1845, 70.
11. Frémont 1845, 121–122.
12. Frémont 1845, 280–287.
13. Frémont 1845, 311; Preuss 1958, 139; McKelvey 1955, 880; Welsh 1998, 104.
14. Welsh 1998, 185–186.
15. Welsh 1998, 412.

Chapter 7

1. McKelvey 1955, 770–777.
2. Geyer 1845, 4:656; 1846, 5.
3. Dupree 1959, 159–160.
4. Geyer 1845, 4:482.
5. Geyer 1845, 4:482–292, 653–662; 1846, 5:22–41, 198–208, 285–310, 509–524.
6. Greene 1894, 2:183, 189.

7. Ewan and Ewan 1981, 32.
8. McKelvey 1955, 792–798, 815.

Chapter 8

1. Wislizenus 1912.
2. McKelvey 1955, 941.
3. Wislizenus 1848, 26:1–86.
4. Trelease and Gray 1887, 39–58.
5. Wislizenus 1848, 26:95–96.
6. McKelvey 1955, 948, 960.
7. Sargent 1889, 2:465.
8. McKelvey 1955, 1023–1024; Dupree 1988, 162–163.
9. Gray 1849, 1–116.
10. McKelvey 1955, 1029.
11. Gray 1849, 4:87.
12. Sargent 1889, 2:466–467.
13. McKelvey 1955, 1077–1078.
14. Stansbury 1988, appendix D by John Torrey, 383–397. This is a reprint of his original report published in 1852 under a somewhat different title: *Exploration and Survey of the Great Salt Lake of Utah, Including a Reconnaissance of a New Route Through the Rocky Mountains.*
15. Stansbury 1852, 105.

Chapter 9

1. Weber 1997, 13–45.
2. Parry 1997, appendix B, 156–157.
3. Dupree 1959, 325.
4. Parry 1862, 231.
5. Rodgers 1942, 278–279; Weber 1997, 53–54.
6. Parry 1862, 33:234–235.
7. Engelmann 1868, 126–133.
8. Reproduced in Weber 1997, 74–80.
9. Weber 1997, 68–73; Rodgers 1942, 279–280.
10. Gray 1863, 55–80.
11. Parry 1997, 25.
12. Parry 1997, 110, 117–123.
13. Rodgers 1942, 279.
14. Parry 1867, 272–286.
15. Parry 1997, 129–131.
16. Parry 1997, 131–132; see Knight 1994, 201–204.
17. Nuttall 1840, 7:347–348.
18. See Nelson 1909; Rydberg 1917; and Weber 1987.
19. Lurie 1988, 94–97.
20. Darwin 1860, 318–319.
21. Darwin 1860, 321.
22. Hooker 1861, 251–348.
23. Sargent 1889, 1:123.
24. Sargent 1889, 1:126.

25. Rodgers 1942, 282.
26. Weber 1997, 159–165.
27. Henry to Gray, 23 October 1871, Joseph Henry's Letterpress Books.
28. Henry to Gray, 17 November 1871, Joseph Henry's Letterpress Books.
29. Rodgers 1942, 281–282.
30. Weber 1997, 135–139.
31. Rodgers 1944a, 49–53.
32. Evans 1993, 71.

Chapter 10

1. Graham 1999, 302.
2. Sargent 1969, 1:37–39.
3. Gray 1859, 377–452.
4. Dupree 1988, 209, 249–250.
5. Rodgers 1944a, 93.
6. Darwin 1860, 347.
7. Huxley 1918, 2:205–212.
8. Rodgers 1944a, 97.
9. Huxley 1918, 2:208–211.
10. Hooker 1877, 539–540.
11. Hooker 1878, 14.
12. Gray and Hooker 1880, 6:1–9.
13. Gray and Hooker 1880, 6:19.
14. Gray and Hooker 1880, 6:60.
15. Gray and Hooker 1880, 6:61–62.
16. Hultén 1968, 60–61.
17. Graham 1999, 191–193, 202–220.
18. Huxley 1918, 2:218–220.

Chapter 11

1. Bartlett 1962, 149–150.
2. King 1871, 5:1–426.
3. Sargent 1889, 1:185. The familiar Rocky Mountain fern, *Woodsia scopulina* D.C. Eat., did not derive from the fortieth parallel, but was based on a collection of Charles Parry in Colorado, no. 690.
4. Dupree 1988, 352.
5. Lenz 1986, 203–204.
6. Sargent 1889, 1:183.

Chapter 12

1. Foster 1994; Cassidy 2000.
2. Ewan and Ewan 1981, 1, 4.
3. Cassidy 2000, 139–152.
4. Bartlett 1962, 13–15.
5. Britton 1901, 369.
6. Cassidy 2000, 144.
7. Foster 1994, 181–182.
8. Rodgers 1944a, 26.

9. Bartlett 1962, 25–31.

10. Foster 1994, 162–163, 177–178; Cassidy 2000, 165, 180. The Great Lignite was renamed the Laramie Formation in 1877. Wyoming coal is found in rocks of both Cretaceous and early Tertiary age.

11. Porter 1872, 477–498.

12. Bartlett 1962, 59–60.

13. Trelease 1930, 99–101.

14. Coulter 1873, 748–750.

15. Coulter 1873, 750–752; Rodgers 1944a, 40–41.

16. Cassidy 2000, 287.

17. Bartlett 1962, 72.

18. Willey 1873.

19. Rodgers 1944a, 41.

20. Porter and Coulter 1874.

21. Setchell 1926, 157–161.

22. Brandegee 1876, 227–232.

23. Brandegee 1878, 32–33, 146, 166.

24. Rothrock, et al. 1878.

25. Ewan and Ewan 1981, 188, 242.

26. Rothrock, et al. 1878, 301–351.

27. Rothrock, et al. 1878, 41–52.

28. Steinel 1926, 195–196.

29. Rodgers 1944a, 199.

30. Coulter and Rose 1888, initially mistaken for *Ligusticum apiifolium* Benth. & Hook.

31. Coulter 1885.

32. Coulter 1885, 119, 179.

33. Trelease 1930, 105–109.

34. Williams 1984, 107, 293.

Chapter 13

1. McIntosh 1983, 1:18–45.

2. Lincoln 1842.

3. Alphonso Wood was a schoolteacher in New Hampshire who wrote a textbook covering the plant families of North America, an earnest attempt to provide what was lacking despite his want of scientific preparation. Asa Gray, remarking that "no idea is more fallacious, than that those who know little of a science may yet be qualified to write elementary books for those who know nothing," was goaded into preparing the first edition of his *Manual of the Botany of the Northern United States* (1848). Dupree 1959, 169–173; McIntosh 1983, 1:19–21.

4. McIntosh 1983, 1:19–21.

5. McIntosh 1983, 1:23–25.

6. McIntosh 1983, 1:26–27.

7. Greene 1872, 734–736.

8. Greene 1874, 31.

9. McIntosh 1983, 1:26–28.

10. Dupree 1988, 396–398.

11. McIntosh 1983, 1:30–32.

12. Rodgers 1944a, 206.

13. McIntosh 1983, 1:33–34.
14. Dupree 1988, 400.
15. Brandegee 1893, 63–103; Ertter 2000, 82; Dupree 1988.
16. McIntosh 1983, 1:39.
17. McVaugh 1983, 1:58–61.
18. Greene 1910, 189–194.
19. Williams 1994, 144.
20. McVaugh 1983, 79–80.
21. Greene 1907.
22. Greene 1907, 241–271.
23. McVaugh 1983, 81.
24. Williams 2001, 27–28.

Chapter 14

1. Lenz 1986, 24–26.
2. Lenz 1986, 37–43.
3. Rodgers 1944a, 203–204.
4. Lenz 1986, 52–56.
5. Lenz 1986, 65–67, 100, 123–128.
6. Lenz 1986, 161.
7. Lenz 1986, 182–184.
8. Cronquist 1987, 141–142.
9. Lenz 1986, 167–175.
10. Lenz 1986, 239.
11. Lenz 1986, 200–202.
12. Lenz 1986, 197–199.
13. Broaddus 1935, 152–157.
14. Barneby 1989.

Chapter 15

1. Ewan and Ewan 1981, 35–36.
2. Tweedy 1886.
3. Ewan and Ewan 1981, 224.
4. Ewan and Ewan 1981, 227.
5. Vasey 1883.
6. Holzinger 1895, 205–287.
7. Holzinger 1895, 259.
8. Heller 1899, 547–552, 588–593.
9. Ewan and Ewan 1981, 100–101.
10. Lenz 1986, 100–105.

Chapter 16

1. Wilson 1955, 4–17.
2. Wallace 1905, 2:155.
3. Wallace 1905, 2:180–184.
4. Weber 1976, 168–169.

5. Weber 1976, 212.
6. Eastwood 1893.
7. Wilson 1955, 29, 34–38, 46–50; Wilson 1953: 65–68.
8. Eastwood 1900.
9. Wilson 1955, 57.
10. Wilson 1955, 96–97.
11. Wilson 1955, 208–211.

Chapter 17

1. Ertter 1989, 304–307; Ewan and Ewan 1981, 179.
2. Weber 1976, 172.
3. Weber 1965, 10–11.
4. Ewan 1950, 97.
5. *Sophia halictorum* Cockl., *Bull. Torr. Bot. Club* 25:460. 1898.
6. Darwin 1860, 71, 89.
7. Steinel 1926, 411–415, 462–463.
8. O'Toole and Raw 1999, 32–33, 140–141.
9. Weber 1965, 5–11.
10. Ewan 1950, 98.
11. Williams 1987, 149–156.

Chapter 18

1. Rydberg 1907, 42.
2. Tiehm and Stafleu 1990, 307.
3. Bessey 1908, 220.
4. Dorn and Dorn 1977, 325–328.
5. Rydberg 1896, 463–536.
6. Rydberg 1969, v–vi.
7. The supplement of Rydberg's *Flora of Montana,* published by Joseph W. Blankinship in 1905, added very little of permanent value, as Blankinship's new species rarely survived. He had been well trained, with a doctorate from Harvard, but it appears that his talent lay in plant pathology.
8. Rydberg 1969, v.
9. Greene 1901, 2:iv–vi.
10. Tiehm and Stafleu 1990, 10.
11. Lawrence 1955, 113.
12. Tiehm and Stafleu 1990, 10–15.
13. Tiehm and Stafleu 1990, 16–18.

Chapter 19

1. Material in this chapter is drawn from my biography of Nelson: R. L. Williams, *Aven Nelson of Wyoming* (Boulder: Colorado Associated University Press, 1984).
2. Nelson 1898.
3. Nelson 1900, 61–64.
4. Nelson 1914, 109–111.

Epilogue

1. Pammel 1903, 57–68.
2. Pammel 1913, 133–149.
3. Ertter 2000, 82–83.
4. Hartman and Nelson 1998, 1–59.
5. Ertter 2000, 84–90.

Bibliography

Albright, George L. 1921. *Official Explorations for Pacific Railroads, 1853–1855*. Berkeley: University of California Press.

Anderson, Edgar. 1942. "Formative Days of Mr. Shaw's Garden." *Bulletin of the Missouri Botanical Garden* 30:100–110.

Barneby, Rupert C. 1989. Dedication to *Intermountain Flora 3*, part B, by Arthur Cronquist et al. Bronx: New York Botanical Garden.

Barnhart, J. H. 1931. "Per Axel Rydberg." *Journal of the New York Botanical Garden* 32:229–233.

Baron, Robert C., ed., 1987. *The Garden and Farm Books of Thomas Jefferson*. Golden, Colo.: Fulcrum.

Bartlett, H. H. 1916. "The Botanical Work of Edward Lee Greene." *Torreya* 16:151–175.

Bartlett, R. A. 1962. *Great Surveys of the American West*. Norman: University of Oklahoma Press.

Benson, Maxine F., ed., 1988. *From Pittsburgh to the Rocky Mountains: Major Stephen Long's Expedition, 1819–1820*. Golden, Colo.: Fulcrum.

Bessey, Charles E. 1908. "The Taxonomic Aspect of the Species Question." *American Naturalist* 42:220.

Billington, Ray Allen. 1949. *Westward Expansion*. New York: Macmillan.

Blankinship, Joseph William. 1905. "Supplement to the Flora of Montana." *Montana Agricultural College Science Studies* 1 (2): 33–109.

Brandegee, Katharine. 1893. "The Botanical Writings of Edward L. Greene." *Zoe* 4:63–103.

Brandegee, Townsend Stith. 1876. "The Flora of Southwestern Colorado." In *Bulletin of the Geological and Geographical Survey of the Territories*, by F. V. Hayden. Washington, D.C.: Government Printing Office, 2 (3): 227–248.

———. 1878. "The Conifers of the Crestones." *Botanical Gazette* 3:32–33, 146, 166.

Britton, Nathaniel Lord. 1901. "Thomas Conrad Porter." *Bulletin of the Torrey Botanical Club* 28:369–373.

Broaddus, Mabel Jones. 1935. "Marcus E. Jones, A. M., Biographical Sketch." *Contributions to Western Botany* 18:152–157.

Burroughs, Raymond Darwin. 1961. *The Natural History of the Lewis and Clark Expedition.* East Lansing: Michigan State University Press.

———. 1966. "The Lewis and Clark Expedition's Botanical Discoveries." *Natural History* 75 (1): 56–62.

Candolle, Alphonse de. 1880. *Le phytographie ou l'art de décrire les végétaux.* Paris: G. Masson.

Candolle, Augustin Pyramus de, and Kurt Sprengel. 1978. *Elements of the Philosophy of Plants.* New York: Arno.

Cassidy, James G. 2000. *Ferdinand V. Hayden: Entrepreneur of Science.* Lincoln: University of Nebraska Press.

Cockerill, T. D. A. 1891. "Notes on the Flora of High Altitudes in Custer County, Colorado." *Bulletin of the Torrey Botanical Club* 18:167–174.

———. 1900a. "Notes on some Southwestern Plants." *Bulletin of the Torrey Botanical Club* 27:87–89.

———. 1900b. "Some Plants of New Mexico." *Botanical Gazette* 29:280–281.

———. 1913a. "Some Plants from New Mexico." *Proceedings of the Biological Society of Washington* 26:203–204.

———. 1913b. "Some Plants from the Vicinity of Longs Peak Inn, Colorado." *Torreya* 13:265–273.

Coulter, John Merle. 1873. "Special Report on Botany." In *Sixth Annual Report of the United States Geological Survey of the Territories, Embracing Portions of Montana, Idaho, Wyoming, and Utah: Being a Report of Progress of Explorations for the Year 1872,* by F. V. Hayden. Washington, D.C.: Government Printing Office, 747–792.

———. 1885. *Manual of the Botany (Phaenogamia and Pteridophyta) of the Rocky Mountain Region, from New Mexico to the British Boundary.* New York: Ivison, Blakeman, Taylor.

Coulter, John Merle, and Aven Nelson. 1909. *New Manual of Rocky Mountain Botany.* New York: American Book.

Coulter, John Merle, and Joseph Nelson Rose. 1888. *Revision of North American Umbelliferae.* Crawfordsville, Ind.: Herbarium of Wabash College.

Cronk, Quentin C. B., and Janice L. Fuller. 1995. *Plant Invaders: The Threat to Natural Ecosystems.* London: Chapman & Hall.

Cronquist, Arthur, et al. 1986. *Vascular Plants of the Intermountain West.* Vol. 1. Bronx: New York Botanical Garden.

———. 1987. "Marcus E. Jones." *Brittonia* 39 (1): 141–142.

Cutright, Paul Russell. 1969. *Lewis and Clark: Pioneering Naturalists.* Urbana: University of Illinois Press.

———. 1976. *A History of the Lewis and Clark Journals.* Norman: University of Oklahoma Press.

Dakin, Susanne Bryant. 1954. *The Perennial Adventure: A Tribune to Alice Eastwood, 1859–1953.* San Francisco: California Academy of Sciences.

Darwin, Charles. 1860. *On the Origin of Species by Means of Natural Selection, or the Preservation of Favoured Races in the Struggle for Life.* New York: D. Appleton.

DeVoto, Bernard, ed. 1953. *The Journals of Lewis and Clark.* Boston: Houghton Mifflin.

Dorn, Robert D., and Jane L. Dorn. 1977. *Flora of the Black Hills.* Cheyenne: self-published.

Drummond, Thomas. 1830. "Sketch of a Journey to the Rocky Mountains and to the Columbia River in North America." *Botanical Miscellany* (Hooker) 1:178–219.

Dupree, A. Hunter. 1959. "Thomas Nuttall's Controversy with Asa Gray." *Rhodora* 54:293–303.

———. 1988. *Asa Gray*. Cambridge, Mass.: Belknap, 1959. Reprint, Baltimore: Johns Hopkins University Press.

Eastwood, Alice. 1943. *A Popular Flora of Denver, Colorado. 1893*. Reprint, San Francisco: Zoe Publishing.

———. 1900. *Bergen's Elements of Botany, Key and Flora*. Rocky Mountain ed. Boston: Ginn & Co.

———. 1903. "New Species of Oreocarya." *Bulletin of the Torrey Botanical Club* 30:238–246.

Engelmann, George. 1868. "Altitude of Pike's Peak and Other Points in Colorado Territory." *Transactions of the Academy of Science, St. Louis* 2:126–133.

———. 1877. "Geographical Distribution of the North American Flora." In *The Botanical Works of the Late George Engelmann*, edited by William Trelease and Asa Gray. Cambridge, Mass.: J. Wilson & Son, 532–533.

———. 1880a. "Revision of the Genus *Pinus*," *Transactions of the Academy of Science, St. Louis* 4:161–189.

———. 1880b. *Revision of the Genus Pinus, and Description of Pinus Elliottii*. St. Louis: R. P. Studley.

Engelmann, George, and Asa Gray. 1887. "The Gymnospermy of Coniferae." In *The Botanical Works of the Late George Engelmann*, edited by William Trelease and Asa Gray. Cambridge, Mass.: J. Wilson & Son, 384–358.

Ertter, Barbara. 1989. "C. A. Purpus: His Collecting Trips in the Sierra Nevada and Owens Valley, California, 1895–1898." In *Plant Biology of Eastern California*, edited by C. A. Hall and V. Doyle-Jones. Los Angeles: White Mountain Research Station.

———. 2000. "Floristic Surprises in North America North of Mexico." *Annals of the Missouri Botanical Garden* 87:81–109.

Evans, Howard Ensign. 1993. *Pioneer Naturalists: The Discovery and Naming of North American Plants and Animals*. New York: Henry Holt.

———. 1997. *The Natural History of the Long Expedition to the Rocky Mountains, 1819–1820*. New York: Oxford University Press.

Ewan, Joseph A. 1950. *Rocky Mountain Naturalists*. Denver: University of Denver Press.

———. 1979. Introduction to *Flora Americae Septentrionalis*, by Frederick Pursh. Vaduz, Lichtenstein: J. Cramer.

Ewan, Joseph A., and Nesta D. Ewan. 1981. *Biographical Dictionary of Rocky Mountain Naturalists, 1682–1932*. Utrecht: Bohn, Scheltema, & Holkema.

Forwood, W. H. 1882. "List of Plants Collected." In *Report of an Exploration of Wyoming, Idaho, and Montana in August and September, 1882*, by Lt. Gen. Philip H. Sheridan. Washington, D.C.: Government Printing Office, 56–69.

Foster, Mike. 1994. *Strange Genius: The Life of Ferdinand Vandeveer Hayden*. Boulder, Colo.: Roberts Rinehart.

Fowler, Wilton B. 1998. "Calhoun, John C." In *The New Encyclopedia of the American West*, edited by Howard R. Lamar. New Haven, Conn.: Yale University Press, 1998.

Frémont, Brevet Captain John Charles. 1988. *Report of the Exploring Expedition to the Rocky Mountains in the Year 1842 and to Oregon and North California in the Years 1843–'44*. Washington, D.C.: Blair & Rives, 1845. Reprint, Washington, D.C.: Smithsonian Institution Press.

Geyer, Karl Andreas. 1845–1846. "Notes on the Vegetation and General Character of the Missouri and Oregon Territories, Made during a Botanical Journey from the State of Missouri, across the South-pass of the Rocky Mountains, to the Pacific, during the Years 1843–1844." *London Journal of Botany* 4:479–492, 653–662; 5:22–41, 198–208, 285–310, 509–524.

Goodman, George J., and Cheryl A. Lawson. 1995. *Retracing Major Stephen H. Long's Expedition: The Itinerary and Botany.* Norman: University of Oklahoma Press.

Graham, Alan. 1999. *Late Cretaceous and Cenozoic History of North American Vegetation North of Mexico.* New York: Oxford University Press.

Graustein, Jeanette E. 1967. *Thomas Nuttall, Naturalist: Explorations in America, 1808–1841.* Cambridge, Mass.: Harvard University Press

Gray, Asa. 1849. "*Plantae Fendlerianae Novi-Mexicanae:* An Account of a Collection of Plants Made Chiefly in the Vicinity of Santa Fé, New Mexico, by Augustus Fendler; with Descriptions of the New Species, Critical Remarks, and Characters of Other Undescribed or Little Known Plants from Surrounding Regions." *Memoirs of the American Academy of Arts and Sciences,* n.s., 4:1–116.

———. 1859. "Diagnostic Characters of New Species of Phaenogamous Plants, Collected in Japan by Charles Wright, Botanist of the North Pacific Exploring Expedition." *Memoirs of the American Academy of Arts and Sciences,* n.s., 6.

———. 1863. "Enumeration of the Species of *Plants* Collected by Dr. C. C. Parry, and Messrs. Elihu Hall and J. P. Harbour, during the Summer and Autumn of 1862, on and Near the Rocky Mountains, in Colorado Territory, Lat. 39°–41°." *Proceedings of the Academy of Natural Sciences, Philadelphia* 15:55–80.

Gray, Asa, and Joseph Dalton Hooker. 1880. "The Vegetation of the Rocky Mountain Region and a Comparison with That of Other Parts of the World." *United States Geological and Geographical Survey of the Territories Bulletin* 6:1–77.

———. *Scientific Papers.* See Sargent 1969.

———. *Bibliography.* See Dupree 1988.

Greene, Edward Lee. 1872. "Alpine Flora of Colorado." *American Naturalist* 6:734–738.

———. 1874. "Rambles of a Botanist in Wyoming Territory." *American Naturalist* 8:31–34.

———. 1887–1905. *Pittonia.* 5 vols.

———. 1894. *Erythea.*

———. 1901. *Plantae Bakerianae.* 3 vols. Washington: n.p.

———. 1903–1912. *Leaflets of botanical observation and criticism.* 2 vols.

———. 1907. "Linnaean Memorial Address." *Proceedings of the Washington Academy of Sciences* 9:241–271.

———. 1910. "Rocky Mountain Botany, A General Review." *American Midlands Naturalist* 1:189–194.

———. 1983. *Landmarks of Botanical History.* 2 vols, edited by Frank N. Egerton. Stanford, Calif.: Stanford University Press.

Haines, Francis. 1998. "Shoshone Indians." In *The New Encyclopedia of the American West,* edited by Howard R. Lamar. New Haven, Conn.: Yale University Press.

Harrington, H. D. 1967. *Edible Native Plants of the Rocky Mountains.* Albuquerque: University of New Mexico Press.

Hartman, Ronald L., and Burrell E. Nelson. 1998. "*Taxonomic* Novelties from North America North of Mexico: A 20-Year Vascular Plant Diversity Baseline." *Monographs in Systematic Botany, Missouri Botanical Garden* 67 (1998): 1–59.

Heiser, Charles B., Jr. 1976. *The Sunflower.* Norman: University of Oklahoma Press.

Heller, Amos Arthur. 1899. "New and Interesting Plants from Western North America–VI, VII." *Bulletin of the Torrey Botanical Club* 26 (10–11): 547–552, 588–593.

Henderson, Louis Forniquet. 1899. "Two New Species of Plants from the Northwestern United States." *Contributions, U.S. National Herbarium* 5:202.

———. 1900. "New Plants from Idaho and from other Localities in the Northwest." *Bulletin of the Torrey Botanical Club* 27:342–359.

Henry, Joseph. Letterpress Books. Record unit 7001. Smithsonian Institution Archives.

Holzinger, John M. 1895. "Report on a Collection of Plants made by J. H. Sandberg and Assistants in Northern Idaho, in the Year 1892." *Contributions from the United States National Herbarium* 3 (4):205–287.

Hooker, Sir Joseph Dalton. 1861. "Outlines of the Distribution of Arctic Plants." *Transactions of the Linnean Society* (London) 23.

———. 1877. "Notes on the Botany of the Rocky Mountains." *Nature* 16 (25 October): 539–540. Extract in *Botanical Gazette*. 1878. 3, no. 2 (February): 14.

———. 1878. *Journal of a Tour of Marocco and the Great Atlas.* London: Macmillan.

Hooker, Sir William J. [1829], 1833–1840. *Flora Boreali-Americana.* 2 vols. London: Treuttel & Würtz.

———. 1847. "Catalogue of Mr. Geyer's Collection of Plants Gathered in the Upper Missouri, the Oregon Territory, and the Intervening Portion of the Rocky Mountains." *London Journal of Botany* 6:65–79.

Hooker, Sir William J., and G. A. Walker-Arnott. 1830–1841. *Botany of Captain Beechey's Voyage.* London: Journal of Botany.

Hultén, Eric. 1968. *Flora of Alaska and Neighboring Territories: A Manual of the Vascular Plants.* Stanford, Calif.: Stanford University Press.

Humphrey, H. B. 1961. *Makers of North American Botany.* New York: Ronald Press.

Huxley, Leonard. 1918. *Life and Letters of J. D. Hooker.* 2 vols. London: John Murray.

Jackson, Donald Dean, ed., 1962. *Letters of the Lewis and Clark Expedition with Related Documents, 1783–1854.* Urbana: University of Illinois Press.

James, Edwin. 1823. *Account of an Expedition from Pittsburgh to the Rocky Mountains, Performed in the Years 1819 and '20.* Philadelphia: Corey & Lea.

———. 1825. "Catalogue of Plants Collected during a Journey to and from the Rocky Mountains, during the Summer of 1820. By E. P. James, Attached to the Expedition Commanded by Major S. H. Long, of the United States Engineers. And by the Major Communicated to the Society, with the Permission of the Hon. J. C. Calhoun, Secretary of War." *Transactions of the American Philosophical Society,* n.s., 2:172–190.

Jepson, Willis L. 1918. "Edward Lee Greene: The Man and the Botanist." *Newman Hall Review* 1:24–29.

Jones, Marcus E. Bibliography. See Lenz 1986.

King, Clarence. 1871. *United States Geological Exploration of the Fortieth Parallel.* Washington, D.C.: Government Printing Office.

Knight, Dennis H. 1994. *Mountains and Plains, the Ecology of Wyoming Landscapes.* New Haven, Conn.: Yale University Press.

Lamar, Howard R. 1998. *The New Encyclopedia of the American West.* New Haven, Conn.: Yale University Press.

Lawrence, George H. M. 1955. *An Introduction to Plant Taxonomy.* New York: Macmillan.

Lenz, Lee W. 1986. *Marcus E. Jones: Western Geologist, Mining Engineer, and Botanist.* Claremont, Calif.: Rancho Santa Ana Botanic Garden.

Lincoln, Elmira Hart. 1842. *Familiar Lectures on Botany, Practical, Elementary, and Physiological.* 2nd ed. New York: Huntington.

Lindley, John. 1831. *An Introduction to the Natural System of Botany.* New York: G. & C. & H. Carvill.

Lurie, Edward. 1988. *Louis Agassiz, a Life in Science.* Baltimore: Johns Hopkins University Press, 1960. Reprint, Chicago: University of Chicago Press.

MacDougal, Daniel Trembly. 1898. *Plants of Arizona. Collected by Dr. D. T. MacDougal, 1898.* Lancaster, Pa.: A. A. Heller.

McIntosh, Robert P. 1983. "Edward Lee Greene: The Man." In *E. L. Greene.* Landmarks of Botanical History, 2 vols. Stanford, Calif.: Stanford University Press.

McKelvey, Susan Delano. 1955. *Botanical Exploration of the Trans-Mississippi West, 1790–1850.* Jamaica Plain, Mass.: Arnold Arboretum.

McMahon, Bernard. 1997. *The American Gardener's Calendar.* Philadelphia: B. Graves, 1806. Reprint, Charlottesville, Va.: Thomas Jefferson Memorial Foundation.

McVaugh, Rogers. 1983. "Edward Lee Greene: An Appraisal of His Contribution to Botany." In *E. L. Greene.* Landmarks of Botanical History, 2 vols. Stanford, Calif.: Stanford University Press.

Metcalf, P. Richard. 1998. "Hidatsa Indians." In *The New Encyclopedia of the American West,* edited by Howard R. Lamar. New Haven, Conn.: Yale University Press.

Moulton, Gary E., ed. 1983. *Atlas of the Lewis and Clark Expedition.* Lincoln: University of Nebraska Press.

———. 1983. *The Journals of the Lewis & Clark Expedition.* Vol. 12. Lincoln: University of Nebraska Press.

———. 1999. *Herbarium of the Lewis & Clark Expedition.* Lincoln: University of Nebraska Press.

Nelson, Aven. 1898. *The Red Desert of Wyoming and Its Forage Resources.* Washington, D.C.: Government Printing Office.

———. 1900. "The Flora of Montana." *Botanical Gazette* 30, no. 1 (July): 61–64.

———. 1909. *New Manual of Botany of the Central Rocky Mountains.* New York: American Book Co.

———. 1914. "Rocky Mountain Flora." *Science,* n.s., no. 994 (16 January): 109–111.

———. Bibliography. See Williams 1984.

Nuttall, Thomas. 1818. *Genera of North American Plants with a Catalogue of the Species through 1817,* 2 vols. in 1. Philadelphia: Heartt.

———. 1834. "Catalogue of a Collection of Plants Made Chiefly in the Valleys of the Rocky Mountains." *Journal of the Academy of Natural Sciences, Philadelphia* 7:5–60. The Nathaniel Wyeth collection.

———. 1835–1836. "Collection toward a Flora of the Territory of Arkansas." *Transactions of the American Philosophical Society,* n.s., 5:139–203.

———. 1840–1841. "Description of New Species and Genera of Plants in the Natural Order of the Compositae, Collected in a Tour across the Continent to the Pacific, a Residence in Oregon, and a Visit to the Sandwich Islands and Upper California, during Years 1834 and 1835 [sic]." *Transactions of the American Philosophical Society,* n.s., 7:283–453.

———. 1848. "Description of Plants Collected by Mr. William Gambel in the Rocky Mountains and Upper California." *Journal of the Academy of Natural Sciences, Philadelphia,* ser. 2, 1 (2): 149–189.

Osterhout, George E. 1920. "Rocky Mountain Botany and the Long Expedition of 1820." *Bulletin of the Torrey Botanical Club* 47:555–562.

———. 1923. "What Is *Geranium caespitosum* James?" *Bulletin of the Torrey Botanical Club* 50:81–84.

O'Toole, Christopher, and Anthony Raw. 1999. *Bees of the World.* London: Bradford.

Pammel, Louis Hermann. 1903. "Some Ecological Notes on the Vegetation of the Uintah Mountains." *Proceedings of the Iowa Academy of Sciences* 10:57–68.

———. 1907–1908. "Dr. Edwin James." *Annals of Iowa,* ser. 3, 8:161–185, 277–295.

———. 1913. "The Grasses of the Uintah Mountains and Adjacent Regions." *Proceedings of the Iowa Academy of Sciences* 20:133–149.

Parry, Charles Christopher. 1862. "Physiographical Sketch of That Portion of the Rocky Mountain Range, at the Head Waters of South Clear Creek, and East of Middle Park: With an Enumeration of the Plants Collected in this District, in the Summer Months of 1861." *American Journal of Science and Arts,* 2nd ser., 33 (May): 231–237.

———. 1867. "Notice of Some Additional Observations on the Physiography of the Rocky Mountains Made during the Summer of 1864." *Transactions of the Academy of Science, St. Louis* 2.

———. 1874. "Botanical Report." In *Report upon the Reconnaissance of Northwestern Wyoming,* edited by William A. Jones. Washington, D.C.: Government Printing Office.

———. 1997. Bibliography. See Weber 1997.

Pennell, Francis W. 1936. "Nuttall and his Travels." *Bartonia* 18:1–51.

Porter, Thomas Conrad. 1872. "Catalogue of Plants." In *Preliminary Report of the United States Geological Survey of Montana and Portions of Adjacent Territories: Being a Fifth Annual Report of Progress,* by F. V. Hayden. Washington, D.C.: Government Printing Office, 477–498.

Porter, Thomas Conrad, and John Merle Coulter. 1874. *Synopsis of the Flora of Colorado.* Washington, D.C.: Government Printing Office.

Preuss, Charles. 1958. *Exploring with Frémont: The Private Diaries of Charles Preuss, Cartographer for John C. Frémont on His First, Second and Fourth Expeditions to the Far West.* Edited by Erwin G. Guddle and Elizabeth K. Guddle. Norman: University of Oklahoma Press.

Pursh, Frederick. 1814. *Flora Americae Septentrionalis.* 2 vols. London: White, Cochrane & Co.

Rodgers, Andrew Denny, III. 1942. *John Torrey: A Story of North American Botany.* Princeton, N.J.: Princeton University Press.

———. 1944a. *American Botany, 1873–1892: Decades of Transition.* Princeton, N.J.: Princeton University Press.

———. 1944b. *John Merle Coulter.* Princeton, N.J.: Princeton University Press.

Ronda, James P. 1984. *Lewis and Clark among the Indians.* Lincoln: University of Nebraska Press.

Rothrock, Joseph Trimble, et al. 1878. *Botany.* Report upon United States Geographical Surveys West of the One Hundredth Meridian, vol. 6. Washington, D.C.: Government Printing Office.

Rydberg, Per Axel. 1896. "Flora of the Black Hills of South Dakota." *Contributions from the U.S. National Herbarium* 3.

———. 1907. "Scandinavians Who Have Contributed to the Knowledge of the Flora of North America." *Augustana Library Publications* 6:1–49.

———. 1917. *Flora of the Rocky Mountains and Adjacent Plains.* New York: the author.

———. 1969. *Flora of the Rocky Mountains and Adjacent Plains: Colorado, Utah, Wyoming, Idaho, Montana, Saskatchewan, Alberta, and Neighboring Parts of Nebraska, South Dakota, North Dakota, and British Columbia.* 2nd ed. New York: self-published, 1922. Reprint, New York: Hafner Publishing.

———. Bibliography. See Tiehm and Stafleu, 1990.

Sargent, Charles Sprague, ed. 1969. *Scientific Papers of Asa Gray,* 2 vols. Boston: Houghton Mifflin, 1889. Reprint, New York: Kraus.

Savage, Henry, Jr. 1979. *Discovering America, 1700–1875.* New York: Harper & Row.

Setchell, William Albert. 1926. "Townsend Stith Brandegee and Mary Katharine (Layne) (Curran) Brandegee." *University of California Publications, Botany* 13:155–178.

Smith, C. E., Jr. 1954–1956. "A Century of Botany in America." *Bartonia* 28:1–32.

Stansbury, Howard. 1988. *Exploration of the Valley of the Great Salt Lake.* Washington, D.C.: Smithsonian Institution Press. Originally published as *Exploration and Survey of the Great Salt Lake of Utah, Including a Reconnaissance of a New Route through the Rocky Mountains* 1852, Philadelphia: Lippincott, Gramb.

Steinel, Alvin T. 1926. *History of Agriculture in Colorado, 1858–1926.* Fort Collins, Colo.: State Agricultural College.

Tiehm, Arnold, and Frans A. Stafleu. 1990. *Per Axel Rydberg: A Biography, Bibliography, and List of His Taxa.* Bronx: New York Botanical Garden.

Torrey, John. 1824a. "Description of Some New Grasses Collected by Dr. E. James in the Expedition of Major Long to the Rocky Mountains, in 1819–1820." *Annals of the Lyceum of Natural History* 1:148–156.

———. 1824b. "Descriptions of Some New or Rare Plants from the Rocky Mountains, Collected in July, 1820, by Dr. Edwin James." *Annals of the Lyceum of Natural History* 1:30–36.

———. 1826–1827. "Some Account of a Collection of Plants Made during a Journey to and from the Rocky Mountains in the Summer of 1820, by Dr. Edwin P [sic] James, M.D., Assistant Surgeon U.S. Army." *Annals of the Lyceum of Natural History* 2 (1826): 161–164; (1827): 165–254.

———. 1836. "Monograph of North American Cyperaceae." *Annals of the Lyceum of Natural History* 3.

———. 1988a. "Catalogue of Plants Collected by Lieut. Frémont, in his Expedition to the Rocky Mountains." In *Report of the Exploring Expedition to the Rocky Mountains in the Year 1842 and to Oregon and North California in the Years 1843–'44,* by Brevet Captain John Charles Frémont. Washington, D.C.: Blair & Rives, 1845. Reprint, Washington, D.C.: Smithsonian Institution Press.

———. 1988b. "Catalogue and Description of Plants Collected." Appendix D in *Exploration of the Valley of the Great Salt Lake,* by Howard Stansbury. Reprint, 1852. Washington, D.C.: Smithsonian Institution Press.

Torrey, John, and Asa Gray. 1838–1840. *Flora of North America.* 2 vols. New York: Wiley & Putnam.

Townsend, John Kirk. 1999. *Narrative of a Journey across the Rocky Mountains to the Columbia River and a Visit to the Sandwich Islands, Chile, etc., with a Scientific Appendix.* Philadelphia: Henry Perkins, 1839. Reprint, Corvallis: Oregon State University Press.

Trelease, William. 1930. "A Biographical Memoire of John Merle Coulter, 1851–1928." *National Academy of Sciences Biographical Memoires* 14:97–123.

Trelease, William, and Asa Gray, eds. 1887. *The Botanical Works of the Late George Engelmann.* Cambridge, Mass.: J. Wilson & Son.

Tweedy, Frank. 1886. *Flora of Yellowstone National Park.* Washington, D.C.: Government Printing Office.

Vasey, George. 1883. *The Grasses of the United States.* Washington, D.C.: Government Printing Office.

Virville, Ad. Davy de, et al. 1954. *Histoire de la Botanique en France.* Paris: Société d'Edition d'Enseignement Supérieur.

Wallace, Alfred Russel. 1905. *My Life: A Record of Events and Opinions.* 2 vols. London: Chapman & Hall.

Watson, Sereno, Daniel E. Eaton, et al. 1871. *Botany.* United States Geological Exploration of the Fortieth Parallel, vol. 5. Washington, D.C.: Government Printing Office.

Weber, William A. 1965. *Theodore Dru Alison Cockerell, 1866–1948.* Boulder: University of Colorado Press.

———. 1976. *Theodore D. A. Cockerell: Letters from West Cliff, Colorado, 1887–1889.* Boulder: Colorado Associated University Press.

———. 1987. *Colorado Flora: Western Slope.* Boulder, Colo.: Colorado Associated University Press.

———. 1997. *King of Colorado Botany: Charles Christopher Parry, 1823–1890.* Niwot: University Press of Colorado.

———, ed. 2000. *America's Cockerell, the Life of a Naturalist.* Boulder: University Press of Colorado.

Welsh, Stanley L. 1998. *John Charles Frémont, Botanical Explorer.* St. Louis: Missouri Botanical Garden Press.

Willey, Henry. 1873. *Lichens Collected by J. M. Coulter in the Yellowstone Region in 1872.* Washington, D.C.: Government Printing Office.

Williams, Roger L. 1984. *Aven Nelson of Wyoming.* Boulder: Colorado Associated University Press.

———. 1987. "On the Mountain Top with Mr. Osterhout." *Brittonia* 39 (2): 149–158.

———. 2001. *Botanophilia in Eighteenth-Century France: The Spirit of the Enlightenment.* Dordrecht: Kluwer Academic.

Wilson, Carol Green. 1953. "A Partial Gazetteer and Chronology of Alice Eastwood's Botanical Explorations." *Leaflets of Western Botany* 7:65–68.

———. 1955. *Alice Eastwood's Wonderland, the Adventures of a Botanist.* San Francisco: California Academy of Sciences.

Wislizenus, Frederick Adolph. 1848. "Memoir of a Tour to Northern Mexico, Connected with Col. Doniphan's Expedition, in 1846 and 1847," 30th Cong., 1st sess., S. Doc. 26, 1–86.

———. 1912. *A Journey to the Rocky Mountains in the Year 1839.* St. Louis: Missouri Historical Society.

Index